MAIN LIBRARY
QUEEN MARY, UNIVERSITY OF LONDON
Mile End Road, London E1 4NS

DATE DUE FOR RETURN.

WINSTON CHURCHILL
and the British Constitution

Kevin Theakston

POLITICO'S

First published in Great Britain 2004 by
Politico's Publishing, an imprint of
Methuen Publishing Limited
215 Vauxhall Bridge Road
London SW1V 1EJ

1 3 5 7 9 10 8 6 4 2

A CIP catalogue record for this book is available from the British Library

ISBN 1 84275 075 5

Printed and bound in Great Britain by
Mackays of Chatham Ltd, Chatham, Kent

CONTENTS

To Breda

ACKNOWLEDGEMENTS

This book examines Winston Churchill's thinking about and impact on the British constitution. In the course of one of the longest and most remarkable political careers in twentieth-century British politics, he both took the constitution very seriously and was active on a wide range of constitutional issues. These included House of Lords reform, Home Rule for Ireland and devolution within the United Kingdom, votes for women, and electoral reform. The book also looks at his views and opinions about the House of Commons, the Cabinet and the premiership, the civil service, and the British system of constitutional monarchy. I hope to show the range and depth of Churchill's thinking on issues still debated to this day.

I would like to acknowledge the support of the British Academy, under its Small Research Grants scheme, for my project 'Inside View: British politicians and the political system', this book representing the first stage of that project.

I am grateful for the assistance and advice of the staff at the Churchill Archives Centre at Churchill College, Cambridge.

At the University of Leeds, Dr Owen Hartley very kindly read and commented on most of the book in draft, and Professor Geoffrey Fry, Dr David Seawright and Ed Gouge also helped on particular points. But I alone, of course, am responsible for the contents of the book.

My biggest debt is to my family, and particularly Breda Theakston. It is to her that the book is dedicated.

Kevin Theakston

ONE

Churchill, Democracy and the Constitution

Winston Churchill took the British constitution, democracy and the institutions of parliamentary government immensely seriously. He was born in 1874, just a few years after the franchise reforms of 1867, which had doubled the size of the electorate to about two and a half million male voters – a move that some politicians feared as a 'leap in the dark' into a democratic age. It was certainly the thin end of a slow-moving wedge. By the time Churchill entered politics in 1900, about 60 per cent of men had the vote (the electorate being 6.7 million strong). By the end of Churchill's life (1965), 36 million men and women had the vote. Mass universal suffrage democracy arrived during Churchill's political lifetime. Yet far from it sweeping away, undermining or destabilizing the traditional institutions of the British state – which the pessimists had feared in the nineteenth century, and which Churchill himself was concerned about in the 1930s – mass democracy was accommodated and incorporated into the constitutional system of Parliament and monarchy he had long celebrated.

Extracts from three speeches sum up Churchill's attitude towards and views about democratic government in Britain. He was a democrat – but there are some revealing paradoxes, doubts, qualifications and reservations. He was, he declared in 1923, 'in favour of government by talking' as opposed to 'government by terror or government by corruption – or government by bayonet, or government by superstition – or government by claptrap'. (Having devoured the works of Macaulay, Churchill undoubtedly knew of the great historian's remark that 'parliamentary government is government by speaking'.) Government by talking was, for Churchill, 'talking by the responsible representatives of great constituencies who meet each other face to face' and who debate issues in a serious manner far from 'the raucous caucus clamour of popular elections'. He always emphasized that British government was based on representative democracy. Parliament, rather than elections, had the primary place in Churchill's democratic order (elections exist for the sake of the House of Commons and not the other way round, he once said [see chapter 4]). In this system MPs were representatives not delegates, and there was no place for referendums. People voted for MPs to debate and decide on the great issues of state, rather than deciding them directly themselves.[1]

'I was brought up in my father's house to believe in democracy,' Churchill said, in a speech to the US Congress in 1941. '"Trust the people" – that was his message . . . Therefore I have been in full harmony all my life with the tides which have flowed on both sides of the Atlantic against privilege and monopoly, and I have steered confidently towards the Gettysburg ideal of "government of the people by the people for the people".' In the same speech he described himself as a 'child of the House of Commons' and a 'servant' of the House of Commons – not, note, a servant of the people. In fact, Churchill's views about 'the people' were at times highly ambivalent, as his attitude towards and actions on the women's suffrage question before the First World War and again in the 1920s show; also his support for 'plural voting' (extra votes for better-educated citizens or those with a stake in the community) in the 1930s (see chapter 4). In practice it must be said that he did not always appear to be 'in full harmony' with the democratic ideal, and in the 1930s in particular 'argued for checks and balances to counteract universal suffrage'.[2]

Finally, it is worth quoting from his speech to the Commons in May 1945, following victory over Germany in the Second World War, eulogizing as it does Britain's constitutional system in characteristic Churchillian terms. 'If it be true, as has been said, that every country gets the form of government it deserves, we may certainly flatter ourselves,' he told MPs. 'The wisdom of our ancestors has led us to an envied and enviable situation. We have the strongest Parliament in the world. We have the oldest, the most famous, the most honoured, the most secure and the most serviceable monarchy in the world. King and Parliament both rest safely and solidly upon the will of the people expressed by free and fair election on the basis of universal suffrage.'

2

It was a system, he said, that 'has long worked harmoniously both in peace and war'. In regarding the British political system as 'envied and enviable', as uniquely stable, as successfully blending traditional institutions and modern democracy, and as the product of a propitious historical process, Churchill was a representative figure at that time. Self-congratulation was perhaps understandable in 1945. But it is remarkable that, on the level of practical institutional arrangements, Churchill was, throughout his career, often far from being an unthinking and complacent defender of the constitutional status quo, but was actively interested in reform – whether of the electoral system, the House of Lords, the governing arrangements for the different parts of the UK (Ireland, Scotland, Wales and the English regions), or the ministerial set-up in Whitehall (see chapter 7 for his 'Overlords' scheme for co-ordinating ministers). As Paul Addison says, 'Churchill enjoyed constitution-making.' But while ingenious, his ideas often ran into the sands or had only a limited impact on the actual reforms that occurred, as this book shows.[3]

Churchill and Democracy

In a parliamentary debate about the India Bill in February 1935, Churchill recalled 'the lady who wrote a metaphysical treatise' beginning with the words 'I accept the Universe.' 'Gad, she'd better,' was Thomas Carlyle's famous response. 'That is rather like my feeling about democracy,' Churchill continued. 'I accept it.' But he expressed doubts about 'whether democracy believes in Parliamentary institutions', arguing that across Europe at that time democracy was tending to be 'injurious' to parliamentary systems and to personal liberties.[4]

In what he called 'these anxious and dubious times' in the 1930s, Churchill looked back nostalgically to the apparently settled society and political order of the late Victorian era. He was sure that the British system in those days was democratic – referring (in 1909-10) to 'the democratic franchise of 1885' and the 'broadening of the Constitution on democratic foundations' in the nineteenth century. In his (1908) book *My African Journey* he described Britain as having 'a Parliament elected on a democratic franchise'. (In his *History of the English-Speaking Peoples* he later wrote of

3

the 'democratic electorate' of the 1870s – when only about a third of men had the vote.) There was, he admitted, a 'gulf which in those days separated the rulers and the ruled'. English society still existed in its old form, with a closely interconnected and interrelated aristocratic ruling class (in which 'every one knew every one else'), a glittering social scene straight out of the novels of Disraeli, and a tight social circle 'in close relation to the business of Parliament, the hierarchies of the Army and Navy, and the policy of the State'. It was, as he wrote in 1930, a 'vanished world' – within a generation there had been a profound revolution 'almost entirely' depriving that traditional 'governing class' of its political power (and to a large extent its estates and property too, he believed).[5]

The historical governing competence of the aristocracy ('the few hundred great families who had governed England for so many generations') was something that impressed Churchill. In the 1930s, writing about his great ancestor the Duke of Marlborough, he argued that that 'small but serious ruling class', based on rank, wealth and landed property, had produced for many generations 'a succession of greater captains and abler statesmen than all our widely extended education, competitive examinations, and democratic system have put forth'. But, as Kirk Emmert has put it, Churchill 'knew that conventional aristocracies could no longer be sustained as a ruling class in modern civilized nations: some form of popular government had become the only viable and defensible regime'. The opening up of political life in the nineteenth century had strengthened the country, Churchill saw, by allowing the discovery of 'fresh reserves of leadership in the men of the new middle classes', created by the expansion of enterprise, industry and wealth (his examples included Peel, Gladstone, Disraeli, the Chamberlains, Asquith, Bonar Law, Baldwin, and F. E. Smith). And he was to claim (in 1910) that Lloyd George's career illustrated the 'democratic freedom of the British Constitution', which enabled 'a man of merit and parts to rise from a village school to a position of the highest consequence under the Crown'.[6]

Churchill did not, however, claim that democracy was 'perfect or all-wise'. He liked to quote the saying that 'Democracy is the worst form of government except all those other forms that have been tried from time to time'. He did not think that it was a universal panacea. In 1897 he had

4

argued that 'East of Suez democratic reins are impossible. India must be governed on old principles'. He more or less stuck to this view throughout his career. It lay behind his opposition to the British government's policy towards India in the 1930s – he believed that India was not ready for or suited to western-style democracy. And later, in 1954, Churchill was doubtful about the scope or prospects for democracy in the colonies of the remaining British Empire, telling US President Eisenhower: 'I am a bit sceptical about universal suffrage for the Hottentots even if refined by proportional representation. The British and American Democracies were slowly and painfully forged and even they are not perfect yet.'[7]

In many ways, Churchill had an aristocratic view of democracy, politics and society. To be sure, John Colville, his Number 10 private secretary, testified (in 1941) to 'the P.M.'s genuine love of democracy'. Churchill's long-time friend Violet Bonham Carter also described him as 'a democrat to the bone, imbued with a deep reverence for Parliament and a strong sense of human rights'. But she commented that whereas Lloyd George was 'saturated with class-consciousness', Churchill 'accepted class distinction without thought'. To Churchill '"the masses" were a political abstraction'; he had no first-hand experience or knowledge of their conditions. '"I am all for the social order,"' Lucy Masterman quoted Churchill as declaring in 1909, when he was a radical social-reforming Liberal minister, and later she wrote of him 'praising government by aristocracy and revealing the aboriginal and unchangeable Tory in him'. 'Democracy properly understood means the association of all through the leadership of the best,' was Churchill's definition in 1909 – that he saw himself as one of those fitted to lead went without saying.[8]

The ideas of 'Tory Democracy' as articulated by Lord Randolph Churchill greatly influenced and shaped Winston Churchill's own outlook. Lord Randolph 'saw no reason why the old glories of Church and State, of King and Country, should not be reconciled with modern democracy; or why the masses of working people should not become the chief defenders of those ancient institutions by which their liberties and progress had been achieved'. The biography Winston wrote of his father is replete with quotations from Lord Randolph's speeches in the 1880s about democracy and the constitution, which Winston himself was to echo many times during his own career. Thus, the British system, said Lord Randolph, was 'democratic, aris-tocratic, Parliamentary, [and] monarchical'; the institutions of Queen, Lords and Commons were 'not so much the work of the genius of man, but rather the inspired offspring of Time'; they were 'the tried guarantees of individual liberty [and] popular government'; they 'possess[ed] the virtue of stability' and represented the 'harmonious fusion of classes and interests'; 'by them has our Empire been founded and extended in the past, and . . . by them alone can it prosper and be maintained in the future'. 'Trust the people, and they will trust you – and they will follow you and join you in the defence of [the] Constitution,' proclaimed Lord Randolph. 'I have no fear of democracy . . . Give me a fair arrangement of the constituencies and one part of England will correct and balance the other.' In speeches, articles, cabinet memoranda and private remarks over many years these were Winston Churchill's themes too.[9]

'Reform at home' and 'Imperialism abroad' is how Churchill summarized 'Tory Democracy' in 1897. He stood, he said, for a universal male franchise, 'wide measures of local self-government', the payment of MPs (so that lack of wealth was not a bar to election to the House of Commons), 'the present constitution of Queen – Lords – Commons' and 'the legislative union' (i.e., opposition to Irish Home Rule). A key aspect of 'Tory Democracy', he wrote in 1906, was the conviction that 'the British Constitution, so far from being incompatible with the social progress of the great mass of the people, was in itself a flexible instrument by which that progress might be guided and secured'. It was a paternalistic view of politics and social reform: 'conde-scension from above', says Maurice Cowling, 'designed to prove that the working classes could be given enough to keep them satisfied with the existing order of society'. The new working-class electorate could be brought to support the Conservative Party, the political elite and the British Constitution in a democratic system that was marked by both hierarchy and deference.[10]

Democratic leaders and governments should not be slaves to public opinion, Churchill believed. It was sometimes necessary for them to stand firm against public outcries and passions. 'People who are not prepared to do unpopular things and to defy clamour are not fit to be Ministers in times of stress,' he wrote, in his Second World War memoirs. The statesman should 'have his eyes on the stars rather than his ears on the ground', he once said. He was clear-sighted and tough-minded about upholding the authority of Parliament and the state – whether against militant suffragettes, striking workers, or rebellious Irishmen and Ulstermen. He was 'never quite a Liberal', thought Violet Bonham Carter, because 'he never shared the reluctance which inhibits Liberals from invoking force to solve a problem'.[11]

All the same, Churchill was very clearly and strongly committed to individual liberty and the protection of individual rights against the state. He liked to say that the nations of the world could be divided into two groups: those in which the government owned the people, and those in which the people owned the government. Posing the question, does a government exist for the individual or do individuals exist for the government, he insisted that he ranked 'the citizen higher than the State, and regard[ed] the State as useful only in so far as it preserves his inherent rights'. He had a set of 'simple tests', he said: 'What is the degree of freedom possessed by the citizen or subject? Can he think, speak and act freely under well-established, well-known laws? Can he criticize the executive government? Can he sue the State if it has infringed his rights? Are there also great processes for changing the law to meet new conditions?' 'To abuse the Government', he once declared (1926), was 'an inalienable right of every British subject.' Britain had no constitutionally enacted formal bill of rights but Churchill spoke confidently of 'the great fabric of British liberties', which had been 'built up by so many exertions'. 'All English [*sic*] men and women are equal before the law, with the same rights in the Constitution, the same political liberties,' he explained. In the 1920s he frequently depicted the Labour Party as threatening 'those inherent fundamental rights and liberties which have made our civilization what it is'.[12]

For Churchill the American enactment of Prohibition raised fundamental issues about rights. Did an electoral majority have 'a right to do anything which it can get voted by the legislature', he asked, or did its powers when extended beyond a certain point 'degenerate into tyranny'? It was wrong and dangerous to 'invade the inward and fundamental rights of individuals', he argued. 'Governments do not exist for the purpose of invading those rights, but to enable individuals to exercise their rights so long as they do not trench upon the interests or the rights of others.' In the 'sphere of manners and morals', he believed, 'the law must carry with it the real consent of the governed'. A law that did not carry with it public opinion might endure but could not succeed, and by failing and/or being evaded breed 'many curious and dangerous evils'.[13]

The independence of the courts and the judiciary was a vital guarantee of freedom, the rule of law, and of the rights and liberties of the citizen, Churchill knew. But the ultimate defender of the individual and of democratic rights and freedoms was Parliament. The idea that the law lords might start acting like the US Supreme Court and be able to strike down an Act of Parliament, declaring it invalid, illegal or unconstitutional, he found unimaginable. When he wrote that 'we simply cannot conceive' the courts questioning or challenging the authority of Parliament, it was plain that he did not believe that that was desirable. He stood for the traditional doctrine of parliamentary sovereignty: Parliament made the law, and judges and the courts were bound by it. This meant that the ultimate 'constitutional remedy' for a disgruntled minority lay through parliamentary and electoral politics: 'They should obey the law. If they dislike the law . . . let them agitate for a majority when an election comes, and then, if they choose, they can amend or . . . repeal a law against which the country would then have pronounced.' This was the only course legitimately open to the Ulster Protestants opposed to Irish Home Rule in 1914, Churchill insisted – which was a perfectly correct view of their constitutional position, but which ignored the issue of the rights of a minority in the face of what it sees and experiences as a parliamentary majority steam-rollering over it. Years later, in 1948, Churchill – then in opposition – talked of 'our duty to submit ourselves with all the grace we can to whatever may be the will of the people from time to time, subject to the procedure of Parliament and to the inalienable rights of the minority'. But he did not pose the uncircumscribed nature of parliamentary sovereignty under the British constitution as a potential problem for rights and for minorities in the way that a later generation did (as with talk in the 1970s and after of 'elective dictatorship').[14]

Churchill's longtime involvement with the murky world of the security and intelligence services provides some fascinating illustrations of how he weighed the balance between state power and individual liberties. He was a strong and enthusiastic supporter of the secret services as a tool of statecraft throughout his career, encouraging and backing the 'cloak and dagger' aspects of government: codebreaking, spying, intelligence, subversion and so on. Before 1914, as home secretary and first lord of the Admiralty, and caught up in the growing anti-German-spy mania, he helped to extend and strengthen the powers of the 'secret state': authorizing an extension of clandestine interception of the mails and backing the illiberal and draconian Official Secrets Act of 1911, rushed through Parliament in an afternoon. In 1940, as prime minister, he ordered a massive round-up of aliens and suspected fifth-columnists. Most of those locked up were harmless, it was soon realized, and within a short time he was having doubts about the 'witch-finding' activities of MI5. Although in 1920 he had favoured the creation of a single intelligence service, he now rejected this idea, believing that the increased powers of the spy chiefs might be a threat to ministerial control and to parliamentary democracy. 'Look what has happened to the liberties of this country during the war,' he complained in 1943. 'Men of position are seized and kept in prison for years without trial and no "have your carcase" [Habeas Corpus] rights . . . a frightful thing to anyone concerned about British liberties.' The power of arbitrary detention set out in Regulation 18B was, he said, 'in the highest degree odious'. After 1951 he was determined to ensure that there was nothing like a McCarthyite witch-hunt in Britain and that the purges of Communists in the civil service were limited and low-key. Overall, it is a mixed story. Churchill helped to build up the power of the security and intelligence services. But in the face of the potential threat this posed to civil liberties, he provided, as David Stafford says, 'his own best antidote'. It cannot be claimed that he was successful, however, in bringing the secret service properly to heel or in resolving the issue of its democratic accountability – problems that in one guise or another were to face his successors in the following decades.[15]

Churchill had distinctly ambivalent feelings about the organization of democratic politics through political parties and groups. Party conflict and party government, he sometimes acknowledged, were two of the vital 'conditions of a free Parliamentary democracy' and helped ensure 'the stability of democratic institutions'. But although a naturally combative and partisan political figure himself, he was never really an orthodox or a good party man, buckling under to the calls of party tribalism, unity, loyalty and discipline. Twice he was a political turncoat, and he had a lifelong enthusiasm for coalition politics and regroupings and realignments – a middle-ground national politics 'above party'. He had, says Robert Leach, 'no feel for the dynamics of party, no understanding of party organization, and little contact with the grassroots'. In some ways he would have been at home with the great eighteenth-century aristocratic parliamentary politicians and statesmen, before the emergence of mass parties and their machines.[16]

One of the arguments he had used against tariff reform before the First World War was that the organization of industrial and commercial interests into trusts, to lobby MPs and Parliament and to press for protection, would open the door to secret and corrupt influences, and lead to the 'tieing [*sic*] up of democracy'. MPs would be forced to advocate the special interests of their local industries rather than the national or general interest; government would be besieged for special favours and advantages. 'Government of the people by the people for the people will have become a nineteenth-century daydream.'[17]

Churchill recognized trade unions to be a long-established and necessary part of Britain's national and economic life. Strong unions could be a stabilizing force, helping to maintain social order and industrial peace. And the right to strike was an essential democratic liberty, he believed – but not for political purposes. Parliament was the only body that could legitimately 'judge of the correlation of all the interests in the country' and it had to resist 'sectional aggression'. If unions challenged the authority of the state – as they did during the 1926 general strike – then firm action to uphold the constitution and restore order was needed. In 1911 he had argued that it was 'quite impossible to prevent trade unions from entering the political field. The sphere of industrial and political activity is often indistinguishable [and] always overlaps'. But after the general strike he wanted the unions to 'mind their own business': they should stick to industrial matters, while politics, elections and government were for Parliament and the parties, and it was vital 'to keep these things separate'. However, as prime minister in the 1940s and 1950s he helped to make the unions into an estate of the realm, expanding consultation between government and unions. He believed that the working classes should be 'within the pale of the constitution' (in

Gladstone's famous phrase), and in the 1920s backed state funding for elections so that all classes could exercise their constitutional rights to the full and seek representation in Parliament. (His views on the trade unions' 'political levy' changed with his changing party allegiance: he defended 'contracting out' in 1911, but as a Conservative favoured 'contracting in'.)[18]

It was as a democratic champion and reformer that Churchill often attracted attention before 1914. He was prominent in the Liberal government's constitutional battle with the House of Lords, for instance, arguing that 'the democratic character of the British Constitution' was at stake in the struggle over the 'People's Budget' and the curbing of the peers' powers (see chapter 2).[19] Abandoning his earlier opposition to the idea, he also came to take a similar high-profile stand on democratic self-government, or Home Rule, for Ireland and supported the wider devolution of power to the different nations and regions of the UK (see chapter 3). But he favoured only a gradual 'levelling up' approach to franchise reform, and while he claimed that he supported the principle of female suffrage, he opposed practical measures to give votes to women (see chapter 4). The First World War showed, he believed, the superiority of democratic, liberal, parliamentary and constitutional states over autocracies and dictatorships.

In the interwar period, Churchill came to be widely regarded as a reactionary figure and was critical of many aspects of parliamentary democracy. He campaigned stridently against the 'red peril' and the 'foul baboonery' of Bolshevism, though by 1926 he had announced that he did not fear a 'Bolshevist revolution' in Britain, with its 'educated democracy'. But his admiration for the Italian Fascist dictator Mussolini raised suspicions about the direction in which his fierce anti-Communism might take him. Churchill's talk of Britain having perhaps gone 'too far' and 'too fast' down the democratic road and of the need to 'retrace our steps' seemed a long way from the views of the Tory Democrat and the erstwhile radical Liberal. However, there are good grounds for arguing that Churchill's underlying political opinions and commitment to democracy remained basically the same, but that what changed was the wider political context (domestic and international) in which he and other politicians had to function. Democracy was precarious, Churchill suggested, and its preservation and operation posed difficult problems of statesmanship, but he did not question its worth or value.[20]

Across the political spectrum – on the left, centre and right – there were concerns about the sort of politics produced by the new mass electorate after 1918, worries about the future of democracy, and dissatisfaction with the traditional institutions and processes of representative government. Conservatives like Stanley Baldwin were anxious that the new and fragile, immature, volatile and politically uneducated democracy could lead to bitter class conflict and a 'crash'. A Liberal writer like Ramsay Muir could complain about the waning prestige of Parliament and confidence in 'the system' being undermined, with leaders less capable than in the past. 'Look at the faces of any crowd pouring out of a morning train on the way to work – some stupid, some harassed, some predatory, some vacuous, some trivial – and reflect that with them rests the determination of our destiny.' 'However ardent a democrat you may be, you will have some moments of misgiving,' he wrote. Moderate Labour leaders like Ramsay MacDonald were as concerned as any Conservative about the dangers of politically motivated industrial 'direct action' by militant workers and trade unions. And the fear that the enlarged working-class electorate might be politically unstable and produce 'a sort of flood or spate politics' was voiced on the Labour side too. Churchill was by no means an isolated figure in voicing uncertainties and doubts about the nature and the health of representative democracy in the 1920s and 1930s.[21]

To some extent, he was worried that the press was not properly performing its democratic duty of educating and informing the mass electorate. An 'unfettered and independent Press' was an essential feature of a democratic polity, Churchill recognized. But he denounced the British press in 1931 as 'a spectacle of immense democratic irresponsibility'. 'No one can pretend that reasoned discussion or careful study of the facts play any appreciable part of the decision of [the] modern mass electorate,' he argued in 1934. The speeches of leading politicians and statesmen used to be fully reported verbatim in all the newspapers, and closely studied by a 'limited but instructed' political public. But now the press had 'entirely changed its character', he complained, and 'caters for the millions with headlines, snappy paragraphs, and inexhaustible sensationalism'. We now had a 'stunt Press'. The press was no longer 'as it used to be', the 'forum of continuous political discussion'. There was no longer 'any real forum for the severe thrashing out of national affairs', and little opportunity to present serious issues to the judgement of the public. The mass public was instead fed a diet of 'the latest sensational murder . . . sporting events . . . the crossword puzzle . . . [and] comic pictures'. The depoliticized popular press emphasized entertainment. What limited coverage there was of 'the political theme' was unsatisfactory and could even be dangerous. The public could be 'misled' by the puffing up of new political figures, suddenly lifted to prominence by the press, he suggested. The newspapers, he claimed, flooded ordinary people with a mass of 'news and sensation', doing 'an immense amount of thinking for the average man and woman'. It was a 'tremendous educating process', but 'an education which passes in one ear and out the other'. The press manufactured a 'superficial' and 'standardized' public opinion – 'It produces enormous numbers of standardized citizens, all equipped with regulation opinions, prejudices and sentiments, according to their class or party.'[22]

Back in 1900, as Churchill described it, 'we had a real political democracy led by a hierarchy of statesmen, and not a fluid mass distracted by newspapers'. That was 'before the liquefaction of the British political system set in', he wrote. In 1901 he had declared that he was 'not afraid of the British public getting panic stricken . . . John Bull is a very stolid person'. But by the 1920s he was warning that 'There is no country so devoid of any form of constitutional safeguard as ours, nor is there any in which the influence of a passing mood upon the electorate is so direct and decisive'. Britain's political system and its national wealth and power rested upon the 'vast, uncertain and swaying basis' of a 'largely unorganized mass vote'. Other countries had 'rigid, fixed Constitutions or fundamental laws', strong second chambers, counter-checks, different electoral systems, federal systems and strong local bodies, 'and all kinds of other devices to prevent an unthinking mass vote from sweeping away the whole slowly erected structure of society'. In the absence of such barriers, Britain's position was precarious. Now that it was based upon universal suffrage, the parliamentary system seemed to have lost much of its reputation and authority, Churchill complained. 'Democracy seems inclined to mock and disdain the institutions to which its rights and liberties are due.'[23]

He was willing to admit, in 1931, that the British people 'are at their best on great occasions' and 'rise to emergencies when there are real emergencies to face'. The overwhelming victory of the Conservative-dominated 'National' government in the October 1931 election vindicated, he said, 'every claim which Disraeli ever made on behalf of working class psychology' and showed that 'enfranchised working people seek stability and order first of all'. But in the early 1930s he generally expressed more critical views. The electorate, he maintained, had been 'expanded till it has far exceeded the bounds of the politically interested classes'. The results were 'vague mass-driftings interrupted from time to time by spasmodic mob-votes' and 'a timid Caesarism refreshing itself by occasional plebiscites'. 'A sort of universal mush and sloppiness has descended upon us,' he claimed. 'Democratic governments drift along the line of least resistance,' he argued, 'taking short views, paying their way with sops and doles and smoothing the path with pleasant-sounding platitudes.' Instead of the eminent political leaders of the past, there was now an 'array of blameless mediocrities' and 'pygmies'. 'Mass effects', 'enormous processes of collectivization', and the growing power of organizations and of 'the machine' were grinding down the scope for individual influence. There was a danger of 'constitutional decay'. 'All experience goes to show that once the vote has been extended to everyone, and what is called full democracy has been achieved,' he declared, 'the whole system is very speedily broken up and swept away.' It was for these reasons that he called for 'more bone and structure in our parliamentary system', backing electoral reform, proportional representation and 'plural votes' for the more responsible citizens (see chapter 4), a strengthened second chamber (see chapter 2), and an 'Economic sub-Parliament' insulated from public opinion to decide on economic and industrial questions (see chapter 5).[24]

Faced by the growing Nazi threat in the late 1930s, Churchill was more concerned to emphasize the strengths and virtues of democratic government. The ideology or creed of 'freedom . . . a liberal constitution . . . democratic and Parliamentary government . . . Magna Carta and the Petition of Right' had to be defended and championed. He did not want to 'dwell upon the well-known weaknesses of Democracy', he stated in 1938, or to 'deride free institutions'. 'The British democracy . . . does not require to be taught a lesson in self-government by foreigners who have until the 19th century been serfs, and have recently done their best to make themselves serfs again.' Parliamentary institutions he now saw as 'the best defence for the ordinary citizens and the best hope for social stability and economic well-being'. He noted the 'difficulties and risks' of a 'broad franchise' and suggested that it would be possible to 'improve the system of electing the House of Commons', but argued that the flexible British constitution allowed 'necessary adjustments' to be made and that 'there is no need to alter our system of government'. He was 'full of confidence in the inherent health and vitality of our ancient institutions' and predicted a 'great revival' for them – unless they were 'shattered by outside violence'. With 'adequate leadership', democracies could defend themselves without sacrificing their 'fundamental values', he said in January 1939, providing a more efficient form of government than Fascism and being stronger in a long war.[25]

The outcome of the Second World War proved him right in that assessment and transformed him into a sort of legendary democratic hero and icon. But it is noticeable that even after 1945 he still expressed some reservations about democracy. The people should rule and public opinion 'shape, guide, and control the actions of Ministers who are their servants and not their masters', he said in November 1947. But 'the broad principles and truths of wise and sane political action do not necessarily alter with the changing moods of a democratic electorate', he warned in December 1947. Parliamentary democracies suffered from 'the weakness of chopping and changing', of 'not being able to pursue a steady policy for a long time', he argued in May 1949. He tried to depict the Attlee Labour government as a form of 'caucus' rule, 'obtaining a fixed term of office by promises, and then doing what it likes with the people'. Democracy did not mean: 'We have got our majority . . . what are you going to do about it?' he asserted. The division of power and constitutional checks and balances against an over-mighty government were vital. Democracy, he used to muse while prime minister after 1951, was 'an appalling muddle, riddled with faults, dangers, unfairness and contradictions'. It was 'a perpetual popularity contest' (the Chartists had been wrong to argue for frequent – annual – elections, he insisted). But in the end Churchill always knew that the alternatives were indeed worse.[26]

'Tradition not Logic': Churchill on the Constitution

Churchill's view of the development of the British constitution was coloured by his romantic understanding of British history in general, which

15

profoundly influenced his whole political outlook and thinking. Like others of his class and generation, he saw British (or, more properly, English) history in Whiggish terms, marked by the slow but sure development of liberty and freedom, parliamentary government, constitutional monarchy, the rule of law, and the eventual growth of democracy. The story was one of prosperity, progress and English political genius at home, under the leadership of a small but able aristocratic ruling class, and of the defeat of foreign rivals and tyrants beyond these shores and the growth of Empire. Churchill's pride in the British constitution is rooted in this sense of Britain as a great power and British history as a providential saga. The national myth of Whig history was also linked to the family myth of the Churchills, as Paul Addison notes, with the careers of the first Duke of Marlborough (John Churchill) and Lord Randolph Churchill (Winston Churchill writing biographies of both) encompassing such key events as the Glorious Revolution and the rise of Britain as a great power, and the emergence of mass parliamentary democracy in the late nineteenth century, respectively.[27]

A *History of the English-Speaking Peoples*, published in the late 1950s (although a first version had been written by 1939), is a key narrative text here, but Churchill had been rehearsing the story in journalism, talks and speeches in the 1930s and even earlier. It was a story told by Churchill in terms of the special character of the British people and various 'milestones of history'. The 'chief characteristic of the British Islander', he argued, was 'a natural instinctive hatred of tyranny in any form – aristocratic, theocratic, plutocratic, bureaucratic, democratic, all forms are equally odious'. The 'English people loathed and abominated one-man rule and tyrannies of every kind', and constituted 'a vigorous, active, law-making citizenship expressing itself through Parliament and especially through the House of Commons'.

> A high degree of personal freedom and a sense of lawful independence has certainly been the main characteristic not only of the British people but of the English-speaking races, now spread so widely through the world [he wrote in 1934]. Freedom of religion, freedom of thought, freedom of movement, freedom to choose or change employment; the inviolability even of the humblest home; the right and the power of the private citizen to appeal to impartial courts against the State and the Ministers of the day; freedom of

speech and writing; freedom of the Press; freedom of combination and agitation within the limits of long-established laws, of the right of regular opposition to the Government; the power to turn out a Government and put another set of men in their places by lawful, constitutional means; and finally the sense of association with the State and of some responsibility for its actions and conduct. All these make the greatest part of the message which the English people have given to the human race.

All this, too, had been struggled for over the centuries, with the 'rights and freedoms of citizens or subjects' asserted and arbitrary power fought and checked 'in the council chamber and on the battlefield'.[28]

Magna Carta, Habeas Corpus, the Petition of Right, trial by jury, the English Common Law, parliamentary democracy – these, for Churchill, were 'the milestones and monuments that mark the path along which the British race has marched to leadership and freedom'. He wrote a newspaper article about Magna Carta in 1934, headed 'The Greatest Half-Hour in Our History'. 'The rights and liberties of Englishmen are older and more sacred than Parliament itself,' he declared, Magna Carta coming fifty years before the first beginnings of the English Parliament and nearly six hundred years before the French Revolution 'opened the road to modern democracy'. 'The Great Charter . . . laid the foundations of English freedom' and showed that 'in the last resort every Englishman possesses a freedom which the authority of Government itself must respect'. What was important for Churchill, it could be argued, was the 'myth' of Magna Carta rather than the reality, the potential of the events of 1215, and the traditions that the 'Great Charter' could be said to embody and develop (it is important for these reasons also for a later prime minister, Margaret Thatcher, who has written about the events at Runnymede). In his *History of the English-Speaking Peoples* he made great play of the development of jury trial and the 'immemorial slow-growing custom' of the Common Law, securing English liberties, freedoms and rights without the sort of codified enactments, formal constitutional guarantees or written declarations of rights found in other countries. Magna Carta, he admitted here, was not 'a statement of the principles of democratic government or the rights of man', but was concerned with the redress of specific feudal grievances extorted from an unwilling king by discontented

17

barons concerned with their own privileges and interests. But he argued that it was of great symbolic importance because from it could be traced principles of prime importance in the future development of English society and institutions: that government means more than the arbitrary rule of any man, that the law is above the king, and that the power of the Crown and the state was not absolute. These ideas were then further developed and strengthened through the centuries.[29]

At times Churchill suggested that 'Almighty God' was behind the growth of Britain's power and its institutions. Britain was certainly a beacon of, and set a defining standard for, democratic governance. 'We have given free institutions to the whole world . . .' he declared in 1910. 'This land taught the nations how to use free institutions. We have maintained our position on a democratic basis without interruption or catastrophe for a longer period than can be shown in the history of any other country.' Similarly in 1918 he asserted that 'Wherever men seek to frame politics or constitutions which safeguard the citizen, be he rich or poor, on the one hand from the shame of despotism, on the other hand from the miseries of anarchy, which combine personal freedom with respect for law and love of country, it is to the inspiration which originally sprang from the English soil and from the Anglo–Saxon mind that they will inevitably recur'. Thirty years later – after Europe's experience of revolutions, the collapse of democracies, the rise of dictatorships, and war – he again boasted that Britain provided a model to be copied. 'The whole history of this country shows a British instinct – and, I think I may say, a genius – for the division of power,' he said, in 1947. There must always be, he said, 'proper executive power' in any system, 'but our British, our English idea . . . has always been a system of balanced rights and divided authority'. 'This essential British wisdom', as he called it, was 'expressed in many Constitutions which followed our Parliamentary system, outside the totalitarian zone'.[30]

In that same (1947) speech, he commented that 'The American Constitution, with its checks and counterchecks, combined with its frequent appeals to the people, embodied much of the ancient wisdom of this island'. In old age he would praise the US constitution as 'one of the finest political documents' ('no Constitution was ever written in better English,' he once quipped), but he told an American visitor in 1961 that 'our Parliamentary system of Government is a cut ahead of yours'.[31]

18

Churchill was to emphasize the connections between British and American democracy from the 1930s onwards, making great play of the United States' English legal and constitutional heritage. But even before then, in 1918, he claimed that the Declaration of Independence 'is not only an American document', ranking it with Magna Carta and the Bill of Rights as one of the 'title-deed[s] on which the liberties of the English-speaking people are founded'. Working on his *History of the English-Speaking Peoples* in 1939, he commented, 'the theme is emerging of the growth of freedom and law, of the rights of the individual, of the subordination of the State to the fundamental and moral conceptions of an ever-comprehending community'. With war looming, he argued that 'Of these ideas the English-speaking peoples were the authors, then the trustees, and must now become the armed champions'. In a (1939) radio broadcast to the USA, he stressed that 'the architects of the American Constitution' had similar aims and ideas to 'those who shaped the British Constitution'. 'Checks and counter-checks in the body politic, large devolutions of State government, instruments and processes of free debate, frequent recurrence to first principles, the right of opposition to the most powerful governments, and above all ceaseless vigilance, have preserved, and will preserve, the broad characteristics of British and American institutions.' 'Optimism has been the fatal defect of many Constitutions,' he had written in 1936. 'Anglo-Saxon political genius, on the other hand, has been distinguished by its pessimism. Distrust has been the secret of its success. Where power has been established by law or usage, checks have been placed upon its exercise.'[32]

Churchill preferred, however, the unwritten British constitution with its 'store of traditions and precedents' to the written American constitution. The American constitution, he argued, 'enshrined long-standing English ideas of justice and liberty'; it was based on 'Old English doctrine, freshly formulated to meet an urgent American need'. He was prepared to admit that a 'fixed constitution' could be a 'bulwark' rather than a 'fetter'. The 'rigidity' of the constitution of the United States, enforced by the Supreme Court, was 'the shield of the common man'. But he maintained that 'a written constitution carries with it the danger of a cramping rigidity. What body of men, however far-sighted, can lay down precepts in advance for settling the problems of future generations?' He was concerned about the constitutional deadlock that might result, such as when in the mid-1930s Supreme Court decisions paralysed Roosevelt's New Deal reforms. In the end, although rightly guarding against the dangers of a 'populist heave', the court should not stand in the way of necessary changes desired by the large majority of the American people, he thought. 'The judiciary have obligations which go beyond expounding the mere letter of the law. The Constitution must be made to work.' A 'true interpretation' of the American or the British constitution, he argued, 'is certainly not a chop-logic or pedantic interpretation'. To be workable, constitutions had to have a certain dynamic, rather than brittle, quality. In another comment on the American constitution, he argued that its 'rat-trap rigidity' had combined with 'the spasmodic workings of the electoral machine', 'the folly of intolerant idealism', and a mixture of political hysteria and hypocrisy to push through Prohibition – which he regarded as an unacceptable interference with individual liberty, as we have seen.[33]

Although in the mid-1930s Churchill argued that 'We need more structure in our system', and that 'There ought to be some very much stronger security against violent change in the fundamental laws of our state and society', he clearly envisaged specific institutional reforms (of the electoral system, Parliament, etc.) rather than the adoption of a written constitution. In an article in 1935 he pointed to 'the profound differences' between the British and American constitutions. Here, 'There is no limit to the powers of Crown and Parliament. Even the gravest changes in our Constitution can be carried out by simple majority votes in both Houses and the consequential assent of the Crown.'

The American citizens or jurists gaze with wonder at our great democracy expressing itself with plenary powers through a Government and a Parliament controlled only by the fluctuating currents of public opinion. When we point to the inconvenience of his system, the American retorts by warning us of the precarious fluidity of ours. So far, he admits, all has worked out well. The good sense of the British public, the experience and training of our political classes, the respect of our unwritten Constitution and tradition have carried us through. But the imprudence of trying to conduct the whole affairs of a mighty State and Empire without any fundamental laws, without any effective second Chamber, with a constitutional Sovereign acting upon the advice of

20

Ministers, and without the aid of any supreme court leaves him aghast. When we speak of his present plight [the constitutional deadlock referred to above] he reminds us of our ever-present insecurity.

But Churchill maintained that Britain did have 'a real stability of government' without a written constitution. Ultimately, political self-restraint and the check of public opinion helped to ensure that 'these vast flexible powers will not be abused' and that 'the spirit of our unwritten Constitution will be respected at every stage'. The main political parties had 'a jealous care for constitutional rights'. Governments had to maintain day by day the approval and support of the House of Commons. The permanent civil service helped to hold the ring. And 'popular opinion acts as a guardian of the unwritten Constitution'. 'Public chastisement,' he wrote, 'would speedily overtake any minister, however powerful, who fell below the accepted standards of fair play or who descended to trickwork or dodgery.' 'Public opinion, expressed through all its hydra-heads, is master . . . Here is our guarantee, here is our safeguard: it is all we have; but so far it has not failed.'[34]

Churchill would sometimes quote Napoleon to the effect that a constitution should be short and obscure. The British constitution was certainly flexible and, as he said in 1905, was marked by a 'generous vagueness'. In other words, it was a political constitution, shaped by political circumstances and adaptable to changing political needs. Churchill himself could exploit this make-it-up-as-you-go-along character of the constitution, as in 1940 when, without any legal backing, he called himself minister of defence (as well as becoming prime minister) in order to take on supreme authority to direct the war effort. But he was strongly conscious also that it was a historical constitution, growing out of 'the wisdom of our ancestors' and 'the practice of former times', as he put it. Human societies and institutions are not mechanical structures but organic ('plants that grow'), he believed. Systems of government express and grow out of and through a country's and a community's history, culture and traditions. Thus to say that the British constitution was 'mainly British common sense', as he did in 1908, was actually to affirm its reality and strength. A codified and fixed set of constitutional principles and rules was not for Britain, Churchill thought. Remarks he made in the late 1940s about European constitution-mongering have a wider relevance, criticizing 'laboured attempts to draw [up] rigid structures or constitutions', and deprecating involvement 'in all the tangles and intricacies of rigid constitution-making, which appeals so strongly to a certain type of mind'.[35]

Churchill's sense of the British constitution drew upon themes and ideas that can be traced back to Burke, Macaulay and Bagehot. The importance of historical continuity, inheritance, adaptation and preservation in the political system and political community was emphasized by Burke. Equally, as Michael Foley notes, 'To Macaulay, history demonstrated that the constitution could peacefully assimilate and adapt to change while preserving its forms and traditions.' The relationship between the different elements of the constitution might change over time, but the 'integrity of the structure would not be compromised'. And Bagehot understood the stabilizing and constraining functions of custom, tradition and the theatrical aspects of the constitution – all helping the British constitution to absorb change.[36]

Thus Churchill would refer to the country's 'ancient Parliamentary constitution' (1929), 'the venerable structure of the English constitution' (1925), 'the British constitution, with its ancient traditions and all its wonderful adaptability' (1919), 'the slow building of the British Constitution' (1937), and a system developed 'by trial and error, and by perseverance across the centuries' (1953). This was not just the language of his Conservative years. In 1909, for instance, he spoke of 'the tradition of hundreds of years, that usage of common sense and of respect for old forms and old customs which is such an important part of our unwritten Constitution' – traditions and conventions that he believed the House of Lords had breached in rejecting the 'People's Budget', reform of the Lords then being necessary to restore the balance of the constitutional order. 'It is the merit of British institutions that they adapt themselves to the changing needs of national life,' he said in another 1909 speech. The strength and stability of British society had grown through 'perpetually associating new forces with the system of Government' – the middle classes in the nineteenth century, then the forces of labour. The 'assimilative power of British institutions' was strong, he believed.[37]

'No one generation has the right, even if they have the power, to overturn the whole constitution and traditions of our island,' he argued in pure Burkean terms in 1934. 'No single generation is the owner of all that has been built up here during so many centuries. We are only the trustees and life-tenants, owing much to the past, and hoping . . . to do our duty by the future.'[38]

In his *History of the English-Speaking Peoples* Churchill praised King Henry II because, although leaving a deep mark on the country's laws and institutions, he 'cloaked innovation in the respected garb of conservatism', was careful to 'respect existing forms', 'shrewdly opposed custom to custom', and 'stretch[ed] old principles to take on new meanings'. Churchill can often be found praising or advocating that sort of conservative constitutional statecraft. 'I like to see modern principles clothed with the picturesque garments of the past,' he wrote, in 1897. Commenting on important legal reforms of the 1870s, he noted that he did not think that the House of Lords was suited for the role of a judicial court and welcomed the appointment of eminent lawyers as life peers and lords of appeal, and the creation of a new High Court. This provided for 'an efficient modern tribunal', he thought, but also did not 'destroy the manner and traditions which have been made precious by time'. The young army officer had a grasp of the importance of what Bagehot called the 'dignified' elements of the constitution. From the start he was a strong and fervent monarchist, championing 'the glitter of the past', 'high sounding titles' and 'the splendour of ceremonial pageant' (see chapter 8). 'Any old ceremony, rite or privilege which encourages reverence, sentiment or affection should be most carefully preserved in progressive times,' he wrote in 1897. But he also believed that 'such considerations must not be allowed to interfere with substantial material improvements'.[39]

More than forty years later, as prime minister, in an exchange with the secretary to the cabinet about a proposed review of Whitehall machinery, Churchill argued that 'it is a great pity to change things simply for the sake of changing, or out of a desire to arrive at unnatural symmetry'. Like other parts of the government system, government departments 'grow like plants', he said, 'and acquire characteristics in the passage of time'. 'It is very much better to give new meanings to old names than to give new names to old things,' he insisted. The Foreign Office might be renamed the 'Ministry of the Exterior', the Home Office the 'Ministry of the Interior', the lord chancellor become the 'Minister of Justice', or the Admiralty become the 'Navy

Office'. But it would be wrong to 'scrap the trappings and traditions of centuries'. 'It is doubtful . . . whether the wage-earning masses would eat better meals in consequence,' he asserted. 'Tradition must not be flouted on behalf of logic,' was Churchill's response when someone proposed making the titles of two ministerial posts more descriptive (it should be minister for war rather than for defence, and secretary of state for the army rather than for war, an MP had proposed).[40]

Similarly, in relation to Parliament – and Churchill venerated the House of Commons while not thinking much of the House of Lords – he was adamant that 'Logic is a poor guide compared with custom'. In 1934 he warned that it was vital that procedural changes designed to bring about 'any slight gain in efficiency' did not undermine or have too large a cost in terms of 'Parliamentary custom and tradition'. When it was destroyed by enemy bombing during the Second World War, Churchill insisted on having the House of Commons chamber rebuilt and 'restored in all essentials to its old form', arguing that its distinctive shape was a fundamental feature of the British system of party and parliamentary politics (see chapter 5). The confrontations, debates and 'drama' of the House of Commons were of vital importance to politics and the people, he maintained. The House of Commons was 'much more than a machine', he argued – it was a 'living organism', capable of adaptation to be sure, but with a strong 'code of its own which everyone knows, and . . . means of its own of enforcing those manners and habits which have grown up and have been found to be an essential part of our Parliamentary life'. The institution and the culture of Parliament, he boasted, were 'capable of digesting almost anything or almost any body of gentlemen, whatever be the views with which they arrive' – the willingness of generations of radical and socialist MPs to play the parliamentary game by the parliamentary rules testifying to the truth of this claim.[41]

This, then, is how Churchill saw the constitution and the democratic system in Britain. He was a product of the Victorian era, he admitted, and his attitudes were essentially late Victorian.[42] He favoured, and saw himself operating within, a parliamentary and representative system, with free elections, 'government by talking' and the 'leadership of the best'. He had a Whiggish view of an organic and historical constitution, maintaining its traditional strengths and flexibility while adapting through evolutionary change. He was not complacent about the difficulties and dilemmas of democratic politics, however, and neither did he take the constitution for granted. Indeed, for much of his career, as this book will show, he was deeply involved in the politics of constitutional and democratic reform in the first half of the twentieth century.

TWO

'The People's Rights' – a 'House of Swells':
Churchill and the House of Lords

The Peers versus the People

'The quarrel between a tremendous democratic electorate and a one-sided hereditary chamber of wealthy men has often been threatened, has often been averted, has been long debated, has been long delayed, but has always been inevitable, and it has come at last. (Cheers.) . . . It must now be carried to a conclusion (Cheers.)' So Churchill declared at an election meeting in Southport in December 1909 at the start of the general election campaign following the House of Lords' rejection of the Finance Bill giving effect to Lloyd George's 1909 budget. These were also the opening words of his pungent and hard-hitting book *The People's Rights*, put together from his campaign speeches and published as voting got under way in January 1910 – he described it, with relish, as 'ammunition passed along the firing line' to his supporters in the constitutional crisis then dominating British politics. Churchill was prominent, vocal and a radical force in that crisis. As Paul Addison notes, 'In the struggle between the Liberal Government and the House of Lords, he was second only to Lloyd George as the leader of popular radicalism, and much reviled by Conservatives as a traitor to his class.'[1]

It had been different when Churchill had been an aspiring Conservative politician. In 1897 he had described (in a letter to his mother) how he wanted 'to maintain the present constitution of Queen – Lords – Commons'. And in June 1899, as a Tory by-election candidate at Oldham, he had denounced the Liberals for their 'animosity' to the House of Lords, which he said was 'a bulwark of the English Constitution'. A year after he had crossed the floor to join the Liberals, however, he can be found in 1905 making the standard Liberal point that 'the check [upon governments] exercised by the House of Lords . . . if it operated at all, operated only when one political Party was in power'. The Lords, he said in October 1904, had become 'the merest utensil of the Carlton Club'. The massive Conservative predominance in the Lords from the mid-1880s onwards (as a result of the Liberals' split over Home Rule) and the Lords' destruction of Gladstone's last Home Rule measure in 1893 were clearly in his mind, but at that time neither Churchill nor the Liberal Party leadership had really given much (if any) thought to what to do in practical terms about the House of Lords.[2]

Looking back in March 1910, Churchill said that 'it might have been much better to have introduced a measure dealing with the Veto of the House of Lords in the first full flush of the victory of 1906'. But, he went on, it would not have been possible to do so: 'it was not practical politics'. The Liberals, he suggested, had not then had an explicit mandate to deal with the Lords ('at an election an instrument is created which, while the effect of the election lasts, can only be used within certain limits and for certain purposes'). Also, the Liberals did not in fact have a basic policy for dealing with the upper house until 1907. And even if they had had a definite policy, before they knew what sort of treatment they would get from the Lords, it would have been very difficult for them to rally opinion behind a sort of pre-emptive strike against them. It was the Conservative reaction to the Liberals' 1906 landslide election victory that, in the end, made the House of Lords issue a priority for the Liberals. When the Conservative leader Arthur Balfour – with 400 Liberal MPs, 30 Labour and 83 Irish Nationalists, as against 157 Conservatives – reacted to the loss of 245 seats and the end of a twenty-year period of Tory domination by saying that 'the great Unionist party should still control, whether in power or in opposition, the destinies of this great Empire', it became clear that the Lords' veto powers would be used to thwart and frustrate Liberal policies. Sure enough, over the next few years the Lords wrecked Liberal bills dealing with education, plural voting, licensing, and Scottish and Irish land measures. As Churchill mockingly put it, Balfour had only to 'write a note on a half sheet of notepaper . . . and send it 200 yards down the corridor to the House of

Lords . . . [to] mutilate or reject or pass into law any clause or any bill'. The so-called watchdog of the constitution had become Mr Balfour's 'poodle', Lloyd George famously declared. But, wary about the reactions of organized labour, the Lords let through popular welfare reforms and labour legislation (such as the Trade Disputes Act).[3]

As a pushy and ambitious junior minister, anxious to win radical plaudits, Churchill was outspoken about the House of Lords in a major speech in February 1907. 'The fortress of negation and reaction', he called it, talking of the 'plain absurdities in the composition of our hereditary chamber, where a man acquires legislative functions simply through his virtue in being born, where the great majority of the members never come near the place from year's end to year's end, where if they go mad or are convicted of a crime or become mentally incompetent to manage their estates, acquire an unwholesome acquaintance with intoxicating beverages, nevertheless they are still considered perfectly fit to exercise the highest legislative functions'. Rather than acting as an 'impartial chamber of review', the Lords were 'an irresponsible body', 'the spoke in the wheel', 'the footpad who waits for the dark night to stab his enemy', and were motivated purely by partisan purposes – they were 'the agents of one party' (the Conservatives) and 'the champions of one interest . . . the landed interest', fighting to 'protect the rights of property'. What should the Liberals do? Churchill rejected the idea of an immediate dissolution (which Campbell-Bannerman, the prime minister, had toyed with but most ministers opposed) and also what was then called 'filling the cup' (in effect, leaving the initiative with the Lords by sending up more Liberal measures for them to wreck in the hope that sooner or later public opinion would swing against the peers). 'There are more ways of killing a cat than drowning it in cream,' said Churchill. 'No doubt the end of any constitutional struggle such as this must be an appeal to the people, but there are a good many things to do first,' he insisted. The government had got to pass 'one or two good Radical Budgets first', develop a popular land policy, and then it had to 'educate the country on the constitutional issue involved in the present position of the second chamber'. The government should use to the full the weapons it had at its disposal, notably 'the power of the purse' – issues of taxation and spending belonging to the Commons alone. This had been effective against the monarchy in the past, said Churchill, and now would be effective against 'this effete oligarchy'. He also speculated about 'tacking bills to money bills', creating new peers ('perhaps even . . . temporary peers'), and possible legislation.[4]

A few months later – in May 1907 – he proposed, in an article in the *Nation*, the inclusion of privy councillors in the upper house to balance 'the frivolous, lethargic, uninstructed or disreputable elements'. This would help the cause of party balance and have a beneficial effect in terms of 'responsibility . . . more equal conflict . . . [and] fairer partisanship'. Government policy was developing along different lines, however, with arguments at cabinet level about three possible policies. A cabinet committee appointed to consider the matter proposed that differences between the two Houses be settled at joint sittings (known as the Ripon plan: a delegation of 100 peers sitting and voting with all MPs, which would have meant that only a Liberal government with a majority of about seventy or more would have been able to override the peers). The idea of submitting bills blocked by the Lords to a referendum was also discussed. Campbell-Bannerman, however, in the face of ministerial resistance, insisted on a third approach, namely the idea of a suspensory veto, restricting the peers' delaying power to two sessions (something first mooted by John Bright in 1883), and this proposal (although some ministers, such as Asquith, then chancellor of the exchequer, felt it was too drastic) formed the basis of a government resolution passed by the Commons in June 1907.[5]

It was a tribute to Churchill's confident energy and to the less rigid 'departmentalism' of those days, says Roy Jenkins, that, while a mere parliamentary under-secretary for the colonies, he was able to appear as one of the government spokesmen in a debate on a major constitutional issue (the debate on the Campbell-Bannerman resolution). It was an uncompromising performance, in which he denounced the House of Lords as 'one-sided, hereditary, unpurged, unrepresentative, irresponsible, absentee'. The Lords were the Conservative Party's 'obedient henchmen', the second chamber was 'not a national institution, but a party dodge', the instrument of 'aristocratic and plutocratic domination'. Churchill took a swipe at the presence of the Church of England bishops in the Lords as violating ideas of religious equality – it helped 'to make quite sure that official Christianity shall be on the side of the upper classes'. The House of Lords had never been right on

29

all the historic settled controversies of political and constitutional development, he argued (citing Catholic emancipation, the 1832 Reform Act and the
Ballot Bill, but side-stepping Home Rule as 'a matter which lies in the
future'). And now, 'to dispute the authority of an elected body fresh from its
constituents is a deliberate incitement to the adoption of lawless and unconstitutional methods'. 'If we persevere,' he concluded, 'we shall wrest from
the hands of privilege and wealth the evil and ugly and sinister weapon of
the Peers' veto, which they have used so ill so long.'[6]

The Lords did not back down, however. In November 1908, after their
rejection of the Licensing Bill, Churchill (by then president of the Board of
Trade in Asquith's cabinet) was reported as furiously commenting at a
private dinner party that 'they have started the class war, they had better be
careful'. 'We shall send them up such a Budget in June as shall terrify them.'
In a belligerent speech in January 1909 he taunted the Lords and, in effect,
dared them to reject the forthcoming budget. He was willing to admit that
there should be 'a chamber of review' and 'counter-checks upon a democratic Assembly', but they should be 'in the nature of delay and not . . .
arrest', and should operate evenly and equally against both parties, not just
one of them. The 'abuses and absurdities' of the present set-up had now
reached a point where 'effective and far-reaching' reform was necessary and,
after an election, no Liberal government should assume office 'without
securing guarantees that reform shall be carried out'. He was willing, he
said, to see the stakes raised: the Lords had the power, but not the constitutional right, to bring the government of the country to a standstill by
rejecting the budget. That would be a 'constitutional outrage' but he would
in any event be eager to see battle joined on the issue of 'aristocratic rule
against representative government'.[7]

It would be wrong, though, to see Lloyd George's 1909 budget as a deliberately set trap for the Lords, designed to provoke them into an
unprecedented veto and so engineer a constitutional showdown. The chancellor and the prime minister aimed to circumvent the Lords' veto, not
destroy it, and did not plan for a decisive constitutional conflict. In fact, the
great majority of cabinet ministers – although apparently not Churchill –
seemed to have hoped until the last that the Lords would pass the budget.
The Treasury needed to raise large sums to pay both for naval expansion

(new dreadnoughts) and for old age pensions. The 'People's Budget' was certainly a radical stroke, challenging the Tory tariff reformers by linking increased taxation and social benefits, and provoking howls of outrage from aristocratic and landed interests about the new 'supertax', increased death duties and income tax, and new land taxes. At this time Churchill and Lloyd George were allies in promoting New Liberal social welfare reforms (pensions, labour exchanges, unemployment and health insurance, and so on). Later, in 1910, Churchill (by then a reforming home secretary) even said that he wanted to get the House of Lords issue 'shunted' off the agenda because it was a distraction from dealing with 'boy prisoners, truck, [the] feeble-minded'. He seems to have had some doubts about the 1909 budget – being to some extent 'Blenheim-minded' and concerned for his rich friends and relations – but, valuing his partnership with Lloyd George and wanting to maintain his profile as a radical reformer, he did support the chancellor in the cabinet, going on to act as a combative propagandist as president of the Budget League. So eager was he in fact that Asquith had to slap him down in July 1909, after a speech in which he jumped the gun by saying, without consultation or authorization, that if the Lords rejected the budget there would be an immediate dissolution and an election.[8]

Churchill did not pull his punches. Back in 1908, he had laid into the House of Lords as 'filled with old doddering peers, cute financial magnates, clever wirepullers, big brewers with bulbous noses. All the enemies of progress are there – weaklings, sleek, smug, comfortable, self-important individuals'. Joining battle on the budget, he called the Lords (in September 1909) 'a miserable minority of titled persons . . . who only scurry up to London to vote in their party interests, their class interests and their own interests'. Rejection of the budget by the Lords would be 'a violent rupture of constitutional custom and usage extending over 300 years . . . It would amount to an attempt at revolution, not by the poor but by the rich, not by the masses but by the privileged few, not in the name of progress but in that of reaction'. If the Lords were to win the struggle, they would have asserted their right to control not only legislation but the finances of the country. If the Commons came out on top: 'we will smash to pieces their veto'. Accepting the right of the Lords to reject budgets would mean, he said, in October 1909, accepting the claim of a non-elected and unrepresentative chamber to make and unmake governments, and the Lords would then become 'the main source and origin of all political power under the Crown'. 'Our whole system of government,' he declared, would 'crumble to pieces' if the representative assembly – the Commons – lost sole control over finance; that power was the 'keystone' of the constitutional structure. It was a risky strategy for the Lords to 'violate the constitutional tradition of our land', he warned, for after all it was respect for constitutional tradition upon which their existence depended.[9]

By November 1909 – after the Commons had finally passed the Finance Bill, and as the Lords were girding themselves up to reject it, which they did on 30 November, leaving the government with no alternative but to call an election – he was virtually inciting them to 'commit an act of violence against the British Constitution' (not that the Tory peers needed his provocation). The House of Lords' 'existence in its present form finds absolutely no justification', he said, 'except in the grey yet not inglorious past of British institutions'. The Lords were 'utterly unfit . . . to have any concern with serious affairs'. 'This headstrong freak' might 'go mad' and 'put a stone on the track', which would 'throw the train of State off the line'. A budget veto would be 'an outrageous and malevolent act'. 'They will have broken the Constitution.' The 'vast majority' of the chamber of hereditary peers 'do not understand either the [budget] proposals or the arguments by which those proposals are advocated or opposed'. The bulk of them, after all, were just 'quite ordinary people of the well-to-do class'. Lloyd George had been even more insulting, talking of 'five hundred men, ordinary men chosen accidentally from among the unemployed', but as the political temperature rose, it was Churchill – the grandson of a duke and someone who would weekend at Blenheim Palace – who was usually singled out for special abuse as a traitor to his class, and he gave as good as he got.[10]

Behind the scenes, however, Churchill's tone was more moderate and constructive. In October and November 1909 the cabinet began to review its policy on the Lords, ministers circulated memoranda and Asquith (probably still attracted by the 'joint session' idea or the Ripon plan) had the papers of the 1907 cabinet committee reprinted. At this stage Churchill was willing to go along with the Ripon plan, though he believed that 'no statement of a detailed plan before the election seems likely to be useful'. He set out his views in a confidential note on 9 November. The key problem, he argued, was the lack of any means of resolving a constitutional deadlock when the Lords and Commons differed; any remedy should provide such a means 'with the least possible change in constitutional custom and appearances'. He accepted, too, that a second chamber should be able to impose 'a real check' on the Commons. Joint sessions, held in Westminster Hall, had some advantages:

> [They] would be productive of debates of the highest value, not only to guide and inform public opinion, but also to mitigate the crudeness of party controversy and to afford an entirely fresh opportunity of conciliatory settlements. The infusion into an elective Chamber, controlled on strict party lines and gripped increasingly by party organization, of an element of eminent men free from such trammels, would . . . be an immense advantage in itself . . . The new Assembly, properly constituted from both existing Houses, would be stronger and wiser than either, and more free than the House of Commons.

Churchill ruled out excluding any MPs from the joint session (which would mean effectively disenfranchising their constituencies, he argued). The tricky question was the size of the Lords' delegation and, significantly, Churchill was willing to see one of 120 with the aim of reducing the parliamentary clout of the Irish Nationalists. The Lords' delegation 'should be at least strong enough to prevent any Government obtaining *absolute* legislative mastery by means of the Irish Nationalist vote' (emphasis in original). To try to prevent the Lords' bloc being overwhelmingly Conservative, he recommended that it should include peers from both parties who had held important public offices (such as ministers; distinguished military, naval or civil service figures; certain colonial governors; those with at least fifteen years' membership of the Commons or with long and responsible service in local government), and that there should be a process of (internal) election to secure 'fair representation' of the rest of the House of Lords. There would be a power of delay to the extent that a joint session would be held by agreement between the Commons and the Lords in the same year in which the legislation giving rise to the disagreement was first presented, and failing agreement the Commons could insist on one being convened if a bill was presented for a second time in a second year. There would thus be a mechanism for arriving at a definite decision, and (perhaps optimistically) Churchill did not think that the public would view it as 'novel, artificial or far-fetched'. Unless there was a deadlock serious enough to justify a joint session (and Churchill believed that they would only be held in 'very exceptional circumstances'), 'everything would go on exactly as at present': there would be no repudiation of the hereditary principle, peers would have the same voting and speaking rights in their own chamber, and there would be 'the least possible disturbance of existing custom, and . . . no break in the historical continuity of our constitutional development'.[11]

This memorandum seems to mark the first occasion on which he made the proposal that peers should have the right to renounce their peerages ('for periods of not less than ten years at a time', he said) and 'enjoy all the rights of a commoner', including standing for election to the Commons. Ministers should be able to speak in both Houses, he recommended. In the years ahead, he was to repeat both of these proposals. (Perhaps there was a personal motive? For a short time in the 1890s Churchill had actually been heir presumptive to the dukedom of Marlborough and if he had inherited the title, his career would have been different and he would almost certainly never have become prime minister. Churchill's first-ever vote as an MP, in February 1901, had been cast against the formal sessional order forbidding peers to take part in parliamentary elections – he voted with the Irish and Radical MPs and against most of the leading Tories.) It is also interesting that he was prepared to contemplate a Lords' delegation larger than that envisaged in the original Ripon plan and one that – whatever safeguards he tried to build in – would have increased the Conservatives' voting strength in any joint session, and so the size of a Liberal Commons' majority needed to carry controversial legislation. Later, in the summer of 1910, there were understandable inter-party differences on this point when the idea of joint sessions was broached at the Constitutional Conference held to try to break the log jam on the Lords issue, the Conservatives wanting a bigger Lords' group than the Liberals could or would accept. Lloyd George was clearly unwilling to accept a peers' delegation of the size Churchill had in mind. Churchill, on this aspect of the House of Lords issue at any rate, was less of a radical than his general public speeches might have led many to suppose.[12]

34

On the election campaign hustings in December 1909 and January 1910, he was characteristically unrestrained. 'Five hundred men have cast out [the budget], but . . . five million men will drive [it] through,' he declared. The House of Lords was 'a lingering relic of the feudal order . . . a solitary reminder of a state of things and of a balance of forces which has wholly passed away'. It was 'a prejudiced chamber, hereditary, non-elected, irresponsible, irremediable, and all composed of one class, and that class, as Mr Bagehot said, not the best class'. The time had come to relieve 'hereditary legislators armed with an arbitrary veto' of their functions and responsibilities. He mocked the 'four to five hundred "backwoods" peers all meditating upon their estates upon the great questions of Government – studying Ruff's Guide [to the Turf] and other blue books, or resolving the problems of Empire and Epsom; every one of them a heaven-born or God-granted legislator, who knows what the people want by instinct'. When Lord Curzon made a speech claiming 'all civilization has been the work of aristocracies', Churchill's response was devastating. 'They liked that in Oldham,' he said. 'There was not a duke, not an earl, not a marquis, not a viscount in Oldham who did not feel that a compliment had been paid to him.' To loud cheers, he went on: 'it would be much more true to say that the upkeep of the aristocracy has been the hard work of all civilizations'. (He was later to scoff at 'a house of superior persons, a house of Lord Curzons and Lord Milners, a house of swells'.)[13]

The actions of the House of Lords had posed a challenge to 'the tradition of hundreds of years, that usage of common sense and of respect for old forms and old customs which is such an important part of our unwritten Constitution'. From the monarch down, there was not an official of the state who was 'unchecked or uncontrolled': 'the House of Lords presents the solitary exception of uncontrolled power'; it was responsible to nobody and represented no one. The outcome of the constitutional crisis, he asserted, could only be 'fatal to the veto and to the character of an hereditary House of Lords'. The Lords had 'come face to face with the electors in a fierce collision which must involve a constitutional change'. The Lords' veto over finance must be abolished altogether, that over legislation restricted 'so that the will of the people's representatives can be carried into effect within the lifetime of a single Parliament'. 'Either finance must be given wholly to one Chamber as it has been in the past or else both Chambers must be elected simultaneously,' he argued in one speech (4 December 1909). In another (10 January 1910), he was outspoken, but less specific: 'The people have the right to vote, and as they vote so the action of the legislature and of the government should follow. We are not a lot of savages and Hottentots in the depths of Africa. We are not children in the schools.' To impose some check or delay upon hasty legislation, and for the purpose of revision by another body 'differently constituted to the House of Commons', there should be, 'within proper limits and under proper conditions of constitution', a second chamber. But he stood for 'the effective supremacy of the House of Commons', he insisted.[14]

The January 1910 election advanced Churchill's own career – he was promoted (in February 1910) to become home secretary, aged only thirty-five – but was a setback for the Liberals, who lost their great majority of 1906, and were reduced to 275 seats, only two ahead of the Conservatives. Asquith now depended for his continuance in power on the support of Labour (40 MPs) and the Irish Nationalists (82) – the very situation Churchill had wanted to guard against in his November 1909 plan (see page 33). That Lords reform would, in these circumstances, open the way to Irish Home Rule stiffened the opposition of the Conservatives. Churchill (and many others) had assumed during the election campaign that a new Liberal government would have a mandate and full powers to deal with the Lords and their veto. He had not been told that, before the election, the King had made clear to Asquith that he would not assent to the mass creation of new peers if that were necessary to swamp (or threaten) the Lords and overcome their resistance until after another, second election. Later, in August 1911, Churchill was to tell MPs that he believed that a second election was not constitutionally required to justify the use of the Crown's prerogative (to create new peers) – the December 1910 election, he said, was 'a voluntary and additional proof on our part'.[15]

The budget now became, as Churchill saw, a secondary issue (it was eventually passed in a single day by the Lords in April 1910). But while some politicians, including Churchill, wanted to see a major reform of the House of Lords, others, including the Irish Nationalists, were simply anxious to abolish the Lords' veto and opposed any broader scheme to produce a less anachronistic second chamber that might be more likely to use its powers. In a January 1910 cabinet memorandum Churchill argued that the best course of action would be for the government immediately to bring forward a measure to secure the undivided authority of the Commons over money bills, to define the relations of the two Houses so that the will of the people, as expressed by the House of Commons, should prevail within the lifetime of a single parliament, and 'to establish an elective second chamber based upon the parliamentary franchise'. The prime minister, he said, should formally ask the King for a guarantee that he would be prepared to create sufficient new peers – and if he refused, the government should resign, saying that 'the constitution as it stands is so unfair that we cannot be responsible for the conduct of affairs. We can raise the anti–hereditary issue in opposition'. He was clear that a radical policy on the Lords was called for: 'The CB [Campbell-Bannerman] resolution does not go far enough. No election can be fought with enthusiasm except upon the abolition of the principle of hereditary legislators. No one can Un-Radical the man who means that . . . I am for our adopting the policy of the CB resolution plus an elective second chamber.'[16]

'The time has come for the total abolition of the House of Lords,' Churchill went on to declare dramatically in a further cabinet memorandum, on 14 February 1910.[17] In opposing the principle of a hereditary legislative assembly, the fundamental question was: one chamber or two?

> I would not myself be frightened by having only one. The stability of this country does not depend upon its form of Government, but upon the general balance of the nation, the diversity of interests, the ever-widening diffusion of property, and the intelligence and strong character of the British people. The masses of wage-earners have only to vote once or twice with some approach to solidarity to do anything they like with our Parliamentary machinery.

Lloyd George was a 'single chamber man'[18] but Churchill acknowledged that the cabinet would not agree on unicameralism. Unity was vital and he accepted therefore the case for a 'properly constituted and duly subordinated Second Chamber, to revise legislation . . . from a non-party point of view, or at least from a differently constituted party point of view, and to interpose the potent safeguard of delay'. He also recognized a two–chamber system's 'soothing effect upon large classes, who fear that their special interests may be ill-treated by the modern House of Commons'. However, the problem with the 'CB' plan of tackling the veto and not the composition of the Lords was that 'on the first return of the Conservative Party to power the Lords would be reformed in the Conservative interest and their veto restored to them. To make any victory permanent in this field the captured ground must be strongly occupied by a new institution erected upon the ruins of the old'.

What was needed was 'a symmetrical and logical system', 'a plan based on broad principles', but also one 'producing the right results in practice'. The parties had different goals, after all: 'When we speak of a reformed Second Chamber, what we mean is a Second Chamber which will enable us to pass Home Rule, Welsh Disestablishment, Plural Voting, and other Party Bills. What the Conservatives mean is a Chamber which will enable them more effectually to resist these measures.'

Any second chamber must be subordinate, democratic and fair, he insisted. That is: the Commons must be supreme; the second chamber must be based on the votes of all electors – 'though a different grouping should be sought'; and all parties must have 'an equal chance'. He did not claim originality for his plan. He envisaged a second chamber of 150 members, 100 of whom would be elected from fifty big two–member constituencies (a feature that would have enabled the Liberals and Labour to work together in some areas and continue their electoral pact).[19] They would sit for eight-year terms (the Commons terms being reduced from seven to five years), 'retiring by halves', and would be chosen from a 'panel of public service' (including those with experience in 'certain great offices', ten years in either House of Parliament, or special municipal service). The 100 elected members would co-opt an additional fifty from the same panel 'by a system of voting which enables the strict party proportion to be preserved'. (This would open a route for 'distinguished men not suited by health or temperament to popular election'; Churchill also proposed that two representatives 'of each of the great Dominions' should have the right to speak but not vote in the second chamber.) The new second chamber would have no power to touch money bills but would possess a suspensory veto on all other legislation 'to the third year' – after which, if there was still disagreement, there would be a simple majority vote in a joint session of both chambers. Along with all this, he proposed – as before – that peers should be eligible to sit in the Commons and ministers have the right to speak in both chambers. With the existing House of Lords disappearing, the future of the law lords was an issue, and he recommended the creation of a 'Supreme Court of Appeal for the British Empire'.

Churchill's reform plan would have certainly eliminated the built-in Conservative majority in the Lords and opened up the possibility of a Liberal second chamber that could, one day, harass, check and delay the measures of a Conservative government, as Paul Addison notes. But the plan got nowhere. There was, to be sure, a powerful 'reform' faction in the cabinet, including Grey and Haldane and – up to a point – Lloyd George (it has been suggested that Churchill's scheme was developed in collaboration with Lloyd George). But other ministers did not want to be diverted from immediate action to deal with the veto and opposed what one called 'fanciful schemes . . . for a new heaven and a new earth'. That was also the view of the bulk of Liberal MPs and the party in the country. The government's position and resolve were shaky and, after Asquith rocked the Commons on 21 February 1910 with the revelation that he had been given no assurances by the King about the creation of peers, the cabinet teetered for a while on the brink of resignation (Churchill, though, was for fighting on). In a speech in the Free Trade Hall, Manchester, on 19 March Churchill supported the abolition of the veto as a first move, winning cheers when he stated that the Liberals stood for the supremacy of the Commons and that 'a stronger Second Chamber must mean a weaker House of Commons' – but (repeating his cabinet memorandum almost word for word) made the case also for a reformed second chamber. By then, however, the cabinet had decided that the only practical course open to it was to proceed with the Campbell-Bannerman plan to limit the veto and restrict the powers of the Lords, tabling resolutions (in late March) and then introducing the Parliament Bill (in April 1910). Under its terms the Lords would not be allowed to amend or reject a money bill (as defined and certified by the Speaker of the Commons); over other legislation they were given the power of delay for two years, a bill passed by the Commons for a third successive time would become law without the assent of the peers; and the duration of parliaments would be reduced from seven to five years. As a concession to the 'reformers', the bill had a preamble with a vague commitment stating the intention to substitute for the House of Lords a second chamber 'constituted on a popular instead of hereditary basis' at some time 'hereafter'.[20]

The constitutional crisis dominated politics during 1910. In March, Churchill made a speech in which he talked about the 'the Crown and the people against this oligarchy' and 'the Crown and the Commons acting together against the encroachment of the Lords', provoking complaints from Buckingham Palace. King Edward VII thought in fact that the government's policy was tantamount to the destruction of the House of Lords. But in April, after fraught cabinet meetings in which Lloyd George and Churchill threatened resignation unless the issue of a royal guarantee was faced up to, Asquith made it clear that if the Lords were to reject the Parliament Bill then there would be another election, and if the Liberals won the King would be expected to act on the advice of ministers and, if necessary, create peers (or let the government use that as a threat) to ensure that the bill reached the statute book. Edward's death in May and the accession of King George V led Asquith to try a different approach, exploring the grounds for an agreed solution with the Conservatives through talks in a Constitutional Conference (June–November 1910). Churchill was not a member of the Liberal delegation but apparently thought that a compromise settlement might be possible on the constitutional issues dividing the parties – he was willing, for instance, to go along with Lloyd George's scheme at this time for a political truce and a national coalition, but it came to nothing. The 'Ripon plan' resurfaced in the talks, but too much was at stake for the parties to hammer out an agreed formula regarding the arithmetic of parliamentary joint sessions, and, given the bitterness of party politics since 1906 and irreconcilable disagreements over Home Rule, it was probably not surprising that the Constitutional Conference broke down. Its failure led back inevitably to the more open politics of the ballot box. Asquith had extracted a secret commitment to create peers from the reluctant King George V in November 1910 and called another election. Once again the invective flowed from Churchill: the Tories acted as if they had a divine right to rule, the Lords' veto would be 'shattered into fragments'. The results of the December 1910 general election were virtually unchanged from January (the net effect was that the Liberals lost three seats and the Conservatives one, giving them 272 each, while the Irish Nationalists and Labour each gained two seats), but the government now had a clear and indisputable mandate for the Parliament Bill.[21]

Churchill took a considerable part in conducting the Parliament Bill through the House of Commons over 1910 and 1911, acting as Asquith's lieutenant, winding up debates and active in the committee stage. 'They were stormy days and nights, and early mornings,' he later recalled. (Churchill was frequently in charge of business in Parliament after dinner – Asquith often 'dining well', in the euphemism of the time.) He was notably more belligerent than the prime minister. Asquith hoped and believed that it would not in the end be necessary to swamp the upper house (though the King's guarantee was made public in July 1911 and the PM did draw up a list of 249 men to be ennobled if the Lords proved intransigent and opted to die in the last ditch). Churchill was more willing to see the threat carried out and to 'clink the coronets in their scabbards', as he put it in a letter to his chief in January 1911:

We ought as early as possible to make it clear that we are not a bit afraid of creating 500 peers . . . Such a creation wd be in fact for the interest of the Liberal party, & a disaster to the Conservative party . . . We should at a stroke gain a great addition of influence in the country. The wealth & importance of British Society cd easily maintain 1000 notables – much more easily than 300 a century ago. The enlarged Peerage wd serve as an admirable panel from wh a working body of 200 to 400 cd be chosen. As we shd have a majority in the panel, we shd obtain a majority in the chambers; & our representatives wd be far more capable & determined politicians than the Tory nobles. We shd then at any rate for some years be able to dispense through the agreement between the Liberal majorities in both Houses with any of the inconveniences (to us) of the two year delay & the three sessions procedure.

Later, on the eve of the final crucial vote in the House of Lords, in August 1911, he asked in the Commons: 'Why should we shrink from the creation of 400 or 500 peers?' The use of the 'reserve forces of the Crown' to help

41

create 'a fair and even Constitution' and 'an impartial Second Chamber evenly balanced in which Liberal legislation will have some chance' was now, he said, 'overpoweringly justifiable and indisputable'. Rattling the gilded cage in this way helped to concentrate minds, and the government's brinkmanship worked in that the Conservative leaders blinked first and pulled back from seeing the Lords swamped, the Parliament Act being finally passed over the opposition of the Tory 'diehards' in the Lords by 131 to 114 votes.[22]

Churchill accepted but was not altogether happy with the veto policy and did not want to lose sight of the broader issue of House of Lords reform. He sounded off in private to fellow ministers, and in the Commons debates on the Parliament Bill in 1910–11 argued that it was the first word and 'not necessarily the last word' – he took the bill's preamble seriously. There would be no absolute veto but the Lords, he pointed out, would still have 'great powers and functions', with an effective power of delay that amounted to 'a tremendous power of correction and discrimination' in the last two years of a government's term of office (and only a Liberal government would really face that problem). The Lords would possess significant 'powers for bargaining and for revising legislation'. If the Lords continued to be a partisan body, overwhelmingly Conservative in composition, he warned, then there would still be in the future the potential for 'mischief and friction'. 'While the House of Lords remains unreformed, it will always leave [the Conservatives] possessed of exceptional advantages' – the constitution might be 'tolerable and workable' after the passage of the Parliament Act, but it would still not be entirely 'an equal Constitution'. After the veto had been abolished, he said, he wished 'to see the House of Lords as at present constituted swept away entirely'. He was certain, he told MPs, that 'the second step in this policy will have to be taken, and that the powers which are now relegated to the House of Lords cannot be exercised in perpetuity by a body which is so unfairly and improperly constituted as they are'. He wanted to see 'a more fair-minded . . . a more competent and more evenly constituted' second chamber and one that was 'democratic in its foundation'.[23]

'When the veto has gone reform [of the Lords] will take its place among the three or four most important practical issues of modern politics,'

Churchill argued in a March 1911 speech. He recognized that reforming 'the present lopsided and obsolete Second Chamber . . . could only be accomplished by a very large measure of general agreement between all parties in the State'. He had written to Asquith in January 1911 urging that 'We should state at the proper time that after the Veto has been restricted we shall be quite ready to discuss the future composition of the Lords with the Conservative leaders'. The government should pursue '*une politique d'apaisement*', he said, and 'offer to confer with the Conservatives not only on the Reform of the Lords but on Ireland'.[24] But with the Parliament Act on the statute book, political attention turned to other issues – Churchill became first lord of the Admiralty in October 1911 and absorbed by defence issues; the bitter and divisive Home Rule struggle (1911-14) came to the fore. The Parliament Act had resolved the immediate constitutional crisis over the power of the House of Lords. Churchill wanted it to be the first instalment of the reform process, but he could hardly have guessed in 1911 just how long that supposedly interim measure and what he thought was only a half-reformed House of Lords would, in their essentials, last.

Non-reform of the House of Lords in the 1920s

'A wave of negativism. People don't want anything done in any direction. "fed-uppism",' Churchill scribbled during a cabinet meeting in June 1927 when it was becoming clear that the latest attempt to reform the House of Lords was going to run into the sands. In public in the 1920s he insisted that he still supported the preamble of the 1911 Parliament Act.[25] Behind the scenes, as a National Liberal in the Lloyd George coalition after the First World War and then as a Conservative in Baldwin's government in the mid-1920s, Churchill was active on cabinet committees set up to consider the question of the second stage, as it were, of House of Lords reform. He was imaginative and ingenious but now also rather more conservative than in 1909-10 in his ideas and plans about the second chamber.

Churchill knew as well as anyone that the political context in which these issues were being discussed and handled was very different from that faced before the war. 'The scene is completely transformed. We have a new electorate, a new generation . . . a new world, and undoubtedly the opinion of this new generation, of this new electorate, must be the supreme factor in any modification of our Constitution,' he said, in a parliamentary debate on the Lords in 1927. On the right of the political spectrum, there was Conservative pressure to restore at least the pre-1911 powers of the House of Lords as a counterweight against the new mass electorate of 1918 and – on a partisan level – as a bulwark against the advance of the Labour Party. Reform of the powers and/or composition of the Lords would strengthen its reputation, its legitimacy and its ability more effectively to thwart or delay threatening 'socialist' measures, and some Tories believed that ultimately this might require an elected second chamber (though others disagreed). Liberals and Labour did not want to put back the constitutional clock, however, and were adamantly opposed to any increase in the blocking or veto powers of the Lords; the 1918 Labour manifesto actually called for the total abolition of the House of Lords (a pledge repeated by the 1927 party conference and later in the 1935 manifesto). That different party views and agendas (including differences *within* parties) would frustrate attempts at reform became apparent from the time when the all-party Bryce Commission of 1917-18 was unable to agree on the composition of a reformed second chamber. In the end, Lords reform in the interwar period was by default, as Churchill put it (in 1923), 'relegated to a remote, hypothetical, and nebulous futurity'.[26]

'It is only right that we should approach this question along the path of historical continuity,' Churchill argued, in 1927. What he meant was that the 1911 Act should be regarded as 'the foundation and the starting point of all modern constitutional reform'. 'The Parliament Act must remain as the instrument to regulate the relations between the Houses, unless or until some Second Chamber utterly different in composition from what exists today were actually called into being.' In a November 1923 speech, he had talked of the House of Lords as 'securely entrenched upon the foundation – I hope the irremovable foundation – of the Parliament Act'. 'In those [prewar] days the Parliament Act was the most fiercely controverted measure of Liberal and Radical reform,' he said in 1927. 'Now it is accepted widely and generally; for good or for ill, it is accepted as having taken a lasting and almost an unchallenged place in the Constitution' – although this was not in fact a view shared by all Conservative MPs or peers, as he knew. By stressing his support for a 'Chamber of review, a revising Chamber', equipped with 'the weapon of delay', aiming to 'ensure a reasonable amount of revision', and to 'safeguard the country against sudden and precipitate action, against laws passed in passion and in violence', he also claimed continuity with the 1911 Act – but, in public at any rate, glided over the arguments and controversy about the scope and terms of the delaying power.[27]

The grievance of the Liberals in their pre-war dispute with the Lords had been about 'constitutional inequality', argued Churchill. 'Their objection was not so much to a brake on the wheel, but that this brake was in the hands of one particular Party and was applied only in accordance with one view of the national interests . . . [which] divided the State into two sets of citizens each numbering many millions, one of which possessed superior and the other inferior rights under the Constitution.' In the post-war world, 'We shall be safe only as long as we march along the high road of fair play to all parties,' he warned. 'I feel profoundly the need not only for prudence in the degree of action, but for continued contact with Constitutional equality.' 'Loading the dice' too blatantly would enable non-Conservative parties to make common cause and go to the electorate with a new and populist 'equal rights under the Constitution' appeal. Political realism and not just constitutional principle thus came into it. Narrowly partisan-inspired constitutional changes would backfire, he suggested.[28]

Churchill therefore urged a cautious line in 1921-2, when Conservative pressure led Lloyd George to appoint a cabinet committee to consider Lords reform, chaired by the Tory grandee Lord Curzon. Curzon favoured a complicated part-hereditary, part-elected and part-nominated House, with provision for joint sessions to resolve disagreements with the Commons – but Churchill believed that his plan was too transparently anti-Labour in motivation and design to succeed. 'Parliament exists as a vehicle for giving effect to the public will, and not, as one would imagine, to read some of the proposals put before us, to tie down the public and prevent the passage of legislation which they have demanded,' he argued, in a memorandum to the House of Lords Reform Committee in December 1921.[29] A Curzon-type scheme would be more likely to provoke the socialist wild men than to head off the threat of direct action or a general strike then felt to be rumbling in the background.

It will arm Labour with a cry which will appeal far outside collectivist circles. It will rob the responsible leaders of Labour of their one great argument against direct action, namely, that Parliament is the vehicle. I do not see what was the use of extending the franchise as was done by the War Cabinet if on the morrow of such extension the rights conceded are to a very large extent to be taken away. The greatest difficulty now is to make the people look to Parliament for the redress of their grievances instead of to strikes and violent measures. It is essential that a clear constitutional path should exist for the redress of popular grievances and for giving timely effect by constitutional means even to mistaken views if demanded by great numbers.

'I cannot conceive anything more dangerous,' argued Churchill, 'than to let it be said that even if the Labour Party win a majority of more than a hundred at an election the House of Lords by joint session will be able to veto all their legislation.' The 1911 Parliament Act 'provides machinery which secures the vital breathing space for consideration and for the more stable forces in the community to assert themselves,' he declared. A Labour government, he predicted, would probably be 'a well-meaning and respectable body', which would in time 'disappoint their friends', 'make enemies' and 'quarrel . . . with their violent supporters'. Strategically, therefore, it was better (and more in accordance with 'true Conservative interests') for Labour to assume office on the basis of the checks and limitations imposed by the Parliament Act than to arrive in power pledged to destroy 'the new instrument which, as they would assert, the classes had invented to tie them down'.

In a further cabinet paper in June 1922, Churchill criticized Curzon's proposed new second chamber as based on 'fancy franchises or selection'. This meant that it would have two vital drawbacks, he argued: '(1) that it cannot compare with the present House of Lords in antiquity and tradition and that it will be shorn of much of the strength arising from history, custom and long usage; (2) that it cannot compare with the democratic credentials of the House of Commons'. Although he had supported the general idea before 1911, he was now scathing about the proposed 'joint sessions': the Commons would be 'mutilated' because on Curzon's scheme half of MPs would be left out of the sessions, and the Lords representatives would be chosen on an 'arbitrary and artificial' basis. This mechanism would hamstring any non-Conservative government unless it had a majority on the scale of the Liberals in 1906–10: the Conservatives would otherwise enjoy in effect 'continued, absolute, over-riding control', amounting to 'a denial of the power to legislate to any Labour Government that may take office, except under the very conditions when restraint is most desirable, viz., those of an overwhelming populist landslide'. 'Powers such as are claimed for the Second Chamber by Lord Curzon could never be exercised over the House of Commons except by a body possessing an equally authoritative basis,' Churchill insisted. This might be achieved, he said, by adopting proportional representation, an electorate of the over-thirties, and different term-lengths for the second chamber relative to the Commons. But starting down this path, he warned, would in the end probably involve sweeping away altogether the hereditary principle.[30]

In his December 1921 paper he had stood by the Parliament Act as fixing the proper relations of the two Houses but had indicated that he would support some limited reforms. He would accept the setting up of a 'tribunal' rather than relying on the Speaker to rule on money bills (a change favoured by Conservatives anxious about confiscatory socialist budgets – although Churchill thought that it would 'not give any real protection in view of the powers of the Executive in regard to printing paper money'). The selection or election from within the House of Lords itself of 'a smaller number of its abler members and the elimination of the backwoodsmen' would strengthen 'the influence and efficiency of the House of Lords as a chamber of review', but he gave no details of how this might be done. He was also, he said, not opposed to ministers being able to speak in both Houses, though he anticipated that MPs would not welcome non-elected ministers at the Commons despatch box. His ministerial colleagues must have either chuckled or groaned when they read the line: 'I should be quite willing to offer my advice freely to the House of Lords if at any time they felt they desired my assistance.' But he soon concluded that closing down the issue and doing nothing, rather than stirring up a hornets' nest, was probably the safest course. It would be wiser, he was arguing by June 1922, 'to stand on the ancient, historic prescription of the House of Lords, reformed by any internal process they may think fit, and equipped with the immense delaying

47

power of the Parliament Act'. In the end, the political drive and momentum necessary for major constitutional reform were missing. The cabinet agreed that 'substantial modification of the main features of the Parliament Act' would be highly contentious and alienate the government's Liberal supporters, and that there could be no constitutional reform without reference to the people (i.e., after an election). A cabinet committee (on which Churchill sat) killed off the 'joint sessions' idea and the issue shortly fizzled out (for the moment), with an inconclusive debate in the Lords on some sketchy government resolutions for reform in July 1922.[31]

Although the short-lived minority Labour government of 1924 was eminently 'safe', respectable and unrevolutionary – increasing some politicians' scepticism about whether second chamber reform was really needed – there was continued Conservative pressure to do something about the House of Lords. The Baldwin government set up a new House of Lords Reform Committee in June 1925, chaired by Lord Cave (the lord chancellor), on which Churchill (now chancellor of the exchequer) sat. As before, it soon became apparent that everyone had his own pet scheme: backbench MPs and peers on the Second Chamber Committee were divided about elections and the hereditary principle; on the cabinet committee, as Lord Birkenhead (Churchill's friend, F. E. Smith) noted, ministers put forward 'very divergent proposals'.[32] The minutes of the cabinet committee and the extensive material in the Churchill papers show that Churchill was actively and seriously engaged with the issues over 1925-6.

In November 1925, at a meeting of ministers and Conservative peers, Churchill said that 'the country wanted a House of Lords which could always be trusted to take a middle course between violent revolution and extreme reaction. The House should be conservative with a small "c"'. That same month he spelt out his thinking on Lords reform in considerable detail in a lengthy memorandum circulated to the cabinet committee. It was an incisive paper, if not particularly original because the arguments were by then becoming familiar to the various protagonists, and showed that he was a politician prepared to think in broad and constructive terms about the constitution.[33]

'So long as the changes proposed to be made in the powers of the House of Lords are not important and do not challenge the main structure of the

Parliament Act, viz., the right of the House of Commons to legislate freely within the lifetime of a single Parliament, no serious question is raised about the composition of the House of Lords,' argued Churchill. The cabinet committee had been discussing whether, if they were deadlocked, disputes between the Commons and the Lords should be settled by recourse to referendums. 'F. E.' (Birkenhead) was doubtful about this idea, but Churchill was prepared to support it – although he insisted that if the House of Lords were to have such a far-reaching checking power, then its composition became 'the main issue in a great controversy'. 'There are millions of people outside the Conservative Party who wish to be protected against sudden, violent, irreparable changes in the structure of the State and of society, who would not be prepared to entrust this protection to the leaders at any given period of the Conservative Party,' he argued. If the 'Chamber of review' was to have great powers, it must be 'placed upon a national and not upon a Party basis' and 'be so clothed with representative authority and animated by the public will as to be above sectional partisanship'. While 'we must have some provision in the Constitution which will prevent the violent and revolutionary overturn by legislative action of the whole basis of society', the Conservatives should not (again) put themselves on the wrong side of a 'people versus the peers' controversy.

He then dissected the various options for reconstituting the House of Lords. A system of *direct election* could yield an authoritative second chamber, he admitted, perhaps chosen on the basis of proportional representation from 'grouped constituencies' with a different franchise from the Commons (electors aged over thirty or thirty-five). This would give the second chamber 'an authority not indeed co-equal with the House of Commons, but a different measure of the same kind of authority', and would not be open to objection on the score of class or party inequality. But, Churchill argued, a system of direct election 'would certainly not meet the highest requirements of good government':

Many of the elements on which the dignity or wisdom of a Second Chamber depends would never face the whirlpool of popular election. The idea of a Chamber of Elder Statesmen, in itself inherently sound, just and logical, would never play its part under such a system. The Second Chamber would be very like the First. The exigencies of electioneers would rule it in as great a degree. The State and Empire would not gain the invaluable influence of age, experience and pre-eminence in the varied walks of life. Nor would it possess that detached view, or that superiority to passing moods and vulgar errors inseparable from a great senate.

He also ruled out a purely *nominated* chamber. The new 'senators' would owe their position solely to the favour of a party leader. 'The present House of Lords, in spite of every anomaly and defect, stands as an august institution of the Realm, second only to the Monarchy itself. But once a chasm has been cut between past and present and it is sought to create a new Assembly with novel powers and new relationships, mere nomination would be found a trumpery foundation.'

Indirect election by local authorities or by groups of them – whether county councils or county boroughs – was open to objection too, Churchill thought, and would not provide a strong or representative or dignified basis for an effective second chamber. The county councils were mostly Conservative. There was the danger of distorting the purpose and transforming the character of local authorities and local elections. Either county council politics would become nationalized or the members of the new second chamber would sit as a consequence of an electoral choice that had no relation to the matters on which they were to deliberate. A body elected on such an irrelevant basis could not wield a moral authority comparable with that which 'antiquity and custom' gave to the present House of Lords. Indirect election by MPs in the Commons, as recommended by the Bryce Committee, had some advantages, however. It would put the Lords 'in contact with the authority of the electorate'; the machinery of election would be 'swift, simple and convenient'; the choosing body would not only wield and confer electoral legitimacy, but would be well informed ('men's reputations and services are fairly well known at Westminster'). But there was the danger that 'apart from influence exerted by the organization of the Conservative Party, there would be no force tending to the selection of Peers'. Many peers might soon drift out of public life. 'The Peerage, shorn of all connection with legislative function, would sink, as in France, to a mere titled class divorced from all connection with Government.' Any system of election that did not operate mainly within the limits of the existing hereditary peerage would in fact lead to 'the obliteration of that order as a political reality'. But because the peerage was overwhelmingly Conservative, there were few Labour peers and 'the multiplication of hereditary peerages to suit the changing requirements of political parties would be absurd', the peerage had to be allied to other 'elements of distinction fairly representative of the nation as a whole'. Thus was Churchill led to advocate the creation of a 'Panel', larger and far more representative of the whole country than the existing House of Lords, from which there should be chosen 'a smaller working body associated with the movements of the electorate to transact public business'.

Churchill proposed an upper house of 315 members to be chosen from a panel of 1200. The panel would consist of all the hereditary peers, all privy councillors present and future, persons who had held important public or municipal offices (such as chairman of a royal commission, county council chairman, lord mayor, or lord provost), MPs who had sat in the Commons for twelve years or more, and other nominated figures. Regional groupings of MPs (there would be fifteen areas) would choose a quota of 'Peers of Parliament' from the panel by proportional representation, who would serve for twelve-year terms, one-third of them standing down at each dissolution of Parliament or every four years, whichever was the shorter period. (Peers not chosen would be able to retire from the panel and be eligible to stand for election to the Commons, and hereditary peers not elected a 'Peer of Parliament' would still be entitled to sit and speak but not to vote in the second chamber.)

This plan had many advantages, claimed Churchill. 'It provides an Assembly which rests on and moves, albeit slowly, with the national will,' and which 'would increasingly adapt itself to the settled purposes of the electorate' as its composition would, over the long run, reflect the party balance in the Commons. (As Paul Addison comments: 'A sequence of Labour majorities in the Commons would certainly have translated, under Churchill's plan, into a Labour majority, albeit a very staid and respectable one, in the upper House.')[34] It would be an 'assembly of notables' different in character from the House of Commons, but possessing the legitimacy necessary to justify wielding the power of delay subject to referendum. It secured the representation of 'all the vital elements in the present Assembly' and exposed no one to the strain and burden of electioneering. It would involve 'the smallest possible change in appearances', retaining the form and much of the substance of the existing House of Lords. And it would be fair to all parties in accordance with their strength in the Commons over successive elections (the important principle of 'constitutional equality').

Churchill knew all the basic arguments, the pros and cons of the various possible reform schemes. He acknowledged that his plan 'contains the defect of undue influence by the party machines'. 'With the best will in the world to solve the problem', he admitted, 'everyone who tries must feel the obstinacy of the objections to every plan.' But he then did not help his own case in the cabinet's House of Lords Reform Committee, and in some ways undermined himself, by going on to raise a wider set of issues and linking Lords reform to the idea of devolution, and proposing the creation of a new tier of government in the form of sixteen local parliaments or provincial councils (renewing an argument he had first advanced before 1914 – see chapter 3). There was certainly a powerful constitutional logic in the idea of the local or provincial assemblies in a federal or quasi-federal system choosing or linking in to the second chamber (Churchill argued that they would choose representatives from a panel made up of their own members plus the hereditary peerage). Peers might see a partial diminution of their traditional rights at the centre, but federalism would open up to them a new sphere of activity and influence in the provinces, he said. This idea would involve presenting the reform of the House of Lords 'not as an isolated episode in our constitutional history . . . but as an integral part in a broad and salutary reconstruction of our constitutional machinery'. All of this would greatly enlarge the sphere of action, he admitted, and it was a far-reaching proposal but, he asserted with sublime over-optimism, it would probably require no more than the two or three years then at the disposal of the government.

Neither version of Churchill's scheme made any headway in the cabinet committee. Within a month in fact, Lord Birkenhead was telling the committee that he felt all the proposals they had considered (including, presumably, Churchill's) were 'necessarily unfamiliar . . . artificial . . . could be effectively riddled in parliamentary debate and could be massacred upon the platform'. Eventually, what came out of the committee was a plan for a mixed House of 150 elected representative hereditary peers, 100 indirectly elected members chosen by local electoral councils, and fifty nominated peers. The whole process was then derailed. The proposals were made public in June 1927, but more important than Labour attacks on what it called the attempted 'gerrymandering' of the constitution, were the continued divisions and doubts on the Conservative side – at all levels among ministers, MPs and peers. A significant number of Conservative MPs, it became apparent, believed that the danger (to their seats) of an election fought on the issue of the Lords powers was more real than the bogey of a 'revolutionary' threat that a new second chamber would somehow prevent. Baldwin – who had anyway never been keen on reform – was only too glad to be able to kick the issue into the long grass. Churchill was fielded to wind up for the government in a censure debate on the issue, and took the line that 'if the relations between the two Houses are satisfactory – if they are regulated by the Parliament Act and are satisfactory to the House of Commons – the composition of the House of Lords becomes definitely less important'. There was no question, he said, of a 'brand new elective Senate which would be a rival to the House of Commons' – the objective was an assembly that could better and more fairly discharge the functions it had under the 1911 Parliament Act. The government dropped any idea of new legislation.[35]

The 1911 Act was not, in the end, bad ground on which Conservatives might stand, it could be argued. Churchill always said that under it the Lords had 'limited but . . . effective', even 'tremendous' powers. The power of rejection and delay (for two years) might only be rarely used because of its two-edged potential, but the Lords' ability to amend and modify the details of legislation within that limitation was considerable, as the 1929–31 Labour government found to its cost. The issue of Lords reform did not go away, however. Paul Addison is not quite right to say that Churchill's bold 1925 blueprint 'vanished without trace' because in March 1931 in his Rectorial Address at Edinburgh University he resurrected the proposal for a reformed and strengthened second chamber or senate based on and linked to a wider scheme of federal assemblies (and alongside his plan for an Economic Sub-Parliament – on which see chapter 5). Reform ideas still bubbled away in Conservative circles in the early 1930s and Churchill, anxious about the weakness of checks and balances in the constitution, from time to time stressed the need for a 'strong and effective second chamber'. He welcomed proposals brought forward by Lord Salisbury (the fourth Marquess) in 1932, for instance, and in 1934 argued that 'The House of Lords in its present form cannot play the part which a second chamber should do'. He called for 'the building up of a new strong second chamber of notables, not to be a rival of the House of Commons, but to give assurances that the fundamental principles of our national life cannot be suddenly changed'. In 1931 he had made the novel suggestion that a joint committee of the Commons and the Lords be set up to examine the Statute of Westminster, tapping what he called 'the unequalled legal authority and constitutional knowledge' of the Lords. But out of office he could do nothing, of course. Where Baldwin wanted to defuse the issue, it has been suggested that Neville Chamberlain – who, by 1931, was convinced that it was 'impossible' for the Lords to remain unreformed – might well have tried to take action as prime minister if the international crisis of the late 1930s had not dominated his agenda, although, as before, it would probably have been difficult to secure broad intra- and inter-party agreement on any fundamental reconstruction.[36]

Peerages and Disappearages

Contrary to both left- and right-wing expectations in the inter war period, the Conservative-dominated House of Lords did not after the Second World War clash with a Labour government elected with a large Commons majority and a radical programme. The upper house operated largely in its textbook role between 1945 and 1951 as a useful and subordinate revising and amending chamber, with Lord Salisbury (the fifth Marquess), the Conservative leader in the Lords, emphasizing the need to respect the mandate of an elected government. This experience made any idea of a fundamental reform of the Lords seem less necessary or important. However, controversy over iron and steel nationalization, and a fear that the Lords' two-year delaying power might become a problem towards the end of the government's term of office, led the Attlee government to introduce in

1947 legislation (it became the 1949 Parliament Act) that reduced the power of delay to one year only. Churchill opposed this. 'I shall always be proud of my association with [the Parliament Act of 1911],' he said in a speech in October 1947. 'I was in favour of it then, and I am in favour of it now.' He noted that the government had admitted that it had 'no complaint against the conduct and behaviour of the House of Lords', and accused it of 'reopen[ing] the Constitutional settlement which was reached in the Parliament Act of 1911, and which has formed the basis of our Constitution for the last 36 years'.[37]

In the debate on Labour's Parliament Bill in November 1947 Churchill argued that the object of the 1911 Parliament Act was 'to give effect, not to the spasmodic emotions of the electorate, but to the settled will of the people. What they wanted to do they could do, and what they did not want to do they could stop'. The second chamber on this view was a 'brake . . . it prevents an accident through going too fast'. He rejected the argument that the 'present Second Chamber is a biased and unrepresentative body; that it does not act evenly between the two sides or parties in the State'. He mocked the government's stance: 'As the Socialist Government now stand, they maintain the hereditary principle. The hereditary Chamber is to have one year's suspensory veto but not two. One year's suspensory veto by a hereditary assembly is the true blue of Socialist democracy; two years is class tyranny.' What Labour wanted, he argued, 'is virtually . . . single-Chamber Government'. No major free countries enjoying democratic institutions, he said, had a single-chamber system – the overwhelming majority of states had a second chamber 'mostly with lesser powers than the popular assembly and with a different outlook and function'. The key argument for bicameralism, he went on, was 'that between the chance vote of an election on universal suffrage and the permanent alteration of the whole slowly built structure of the State and nation there ought to be some modifying process'. The constitutional aim was 'that the persistent resolve of the people shall prevail without throwing the community into convulsion and disorder by rash or violent, irreparable action and to restrain and prevent a group or sect or faction assuming dictatorial power'. In a situation where there was no constitutional or legal bar upon the right of a government to propose any legislation whether or not it had figured in its election manifesto, the people 'have no guarantee, except the suspensory power of the House of Lords' that measures to which they object will not be imposed upon them. Moreover, single-chamber government was especially dangerous in a country without a written constitution and with parliaments elected for as long as five years. Labour, he argued, 'wish to keep the present Second Chamber on the hereditary basis so they can abuse it, insult it and attack it and yet cripple its powers'. 'If they do not like the character of the brake,' Churchill declared, 'why do they not propose the reform of the Second Chamber?' The Conservatives, he said, were 'quite ready to confer with them and to help them in such a task'.[38]

By trying vehemently to characterize the government's modest proposals as a 'deliberate act of socialist aggression' against democracy and the constitution, Churchill was in truth overstating his case. The functions of the Lords were not being touched, and the halving of their delaying powers was actually criticized as too little by some Labour backbenchers who wanted only a three-month delaying power or the total abolition of the upper house. The King was not alarmed by the far-from-menacing proposals, although the Lords did throw them out and they had to be forced through under the terms of the 1911 Act. Churchill's proposal that there should be inter-party discussions about the future of the Lords was, however, taken up and a conference of party leaders met in February–April 1948. Attlee and Herbert Morrison led for Labour and Clement Davies for the Liberal Party, but Churchill was not a member of the Conservative team, which included Anthony Eden and Lord Salisbury. Broad agreement was reached in these negotiations on the future composition of a reformed House of Lords that would have ended the domination of the (overwhelmingly Tory) hereditary peers, its membership to be a mix of selected hereditary peers, appointed life peers and women peers, with no permanent majority for any one party, and with hereditary peers able to stand for election to the Commons. But the conference broke down after disagreement over the extent of the delaying powers that the new upper house would have before it was overridden by the Commons, the final sticking point ostensibly coming down to a three-month difference between what Labour and the Conservatives said they could accept. In the end, for Labour the priority was always curbing the Lords' possible veto power in the last two years of the government's term of office, while the Conservatives were ultimately not being offered enough in 1948 in terms of powers to justify moving away from the hereditary principle as the basis for membership of the second chamber.[39]

In both the 1950 and 1951 elections the Conservatives pledged to call an all-party conference to consider proposals for the reform and powers of the House of Lords. But little was achieved during Churchill's peacetime government, 1951-5 because the Conservatives were in practice divided and the Labour Party was unwilling to co-operate. 'Salisbury and Churchill are very keen on reform, Butler and Eden don't care either way and there are some younger Tory ministers who are dead against any reform at all,' Lord Hailsham told Anthony Wedgwood Benn (Tony Benn). Churchill, however, ruled out in November 1951 the idea of allowing ministers who were peers to answer questions or take part in debates in the Commons – which he had favoured years before. In February 1953 Attlee refused to join in talks on 'the proper part to be played by the House of Lords as a Second Chamber under the Constitution', citing what he called the fundamental difference in views revealed in the 1948 all-party talks. According to Lord Moran, Churchill said: 'We may revoke the Parliament Act [meaning presumably, the 1949 Act], if they are not too timid. Everyone is timid nowadays. It is all appeasement. I don't like it . . . We may do better on our own. At any rate we should restore the two years [delaying power].' A cabinet committee on House of Lords reform, chaired by Lord Salisbury, was set up, but it made little progress, holding only four meetings between May 1953 and March 1955, ruling out increasing the existing powers (the one-year delaying power), and revealing sharp differences of ministerial opinion about the composition of a reformed second chamber. In February 1955, Churchill told MPs that the government was 'actively examining [the] difficult and important subject' of Lords reform, repeating that great constitutional change was best done with inter-party agreement – but Labour would still not play along. After nearly half a century of involvement in the debates and controversies over the House of Lords, any chance of a final role for Churchill in the process of significantly reshaping that chamber was thus gone.[40]

For all that references to Churchill as a 'romantic reactionary' or a 'paternalistic Whig aristocrat' capture important aspects of his social and political outlook at certain times in his career, and while he had been 'avid for medals' as a young army officer, as a world-famous statesman he was not particularly interested in titles and honours. He was proud to be the Great Commoner and had no desire to sit in the House of Lords. He had declined King George VI's offer of the Order of the Garter in 1945, although he accepted it from Queen Elizabeth II in 1953. He would have liked, however, to have had it both ways, in the sense of remaining plain 'Mr Churchill' rather than becoming known as 'Sir Winston'. As he said to Norman Brook: 'I don't see why I should not have the Garter but continue to be Mr Churchill. After all, my father was known as Lord Randolph Churchill, but he was not a Lord. That was only a courtesy title. Why should not I continue to be called Mr Churchill as a discourtesy title?'[41]

'The House of Lords means nothing to him,' Lord Moran had noted in February 1953. 'I am afraid he regards us in the Lords as a rather disreputable collection of old gentlemen,' Lord Salisbury had remarked the year before. With concerns mounting about Churchill's fitness for the premiership, Salisbury, John Colville (Churchill's Number 10 private secretary), Moran and Lascelles (the Queen's private secretary) had discussed the idea of recreating something like the old 1895-1902 Salisbury-Balfour arrangement,* with Churchill being sent to the Lords while formally remaining prime minister, and Anthony Eden becoming leader of the House of Commons and, in effect, a virtual joint party leader and joint PM. 'In 1952 no one but Winston could be Prime Minister in the Lords,' said Colville. 'He would be the grand old man of politics, coming down from time to time and making a great speech to their Lordships.' 'Nobody but Winston could go to the Lords and remain Prime Minister, but he could,' Lascelles agreed. 'He is a law to himself and is still a great figure in the country.' The catch was, as they soon realized, that Churchill would not agree. As he quipped when surprise was expressed at a particularly undistinguished figure being sent to the Lords, 'It isn't just a peerage, it is a disappearage.' He himself was not going to be 'disappeared' so easily. The idea that the Queen might be brought in to persuade him to accept this plan was also a non-starter.

---

* The third Marquess of Salisbury had been prime minister and (until 1900) foreign secretary; his nephew Arthur Balfour had been first lord of the treasury and leader of the House of Commons, succeeding to the premiership in 1902.

Eden would probably not have been attracted by anything other than the full premiership. It is also doubtful whether the Labour opposition in Parliament would have accepted such a set-up in view of the loud Labour complaints about Churchill's ministerial 'Overlords' (see chapter 7) and the later storm when Lord Home became foreign secretary (in 1960).[42]

When he did finally retire, in April 1955, the Queen offered Churchill a dukedom, the highest rank of the peerage (the 'going rate' for retiring prime ministers at that time normally being an hereditary earldom – as accepted by Baldwin, Attlee and Eden, for instance), but only after discreet enquiries confirmed that he would refuse it. There was, by all accounts, a last-minute 'wobble' when it seemed – to the Queen's alarm – that he might, after all, accept it, but he did decline the honour. He said that if he was unable to stay in the Commons, he would be proud if the offer could be reconsidered, but through the bleak years of his retirement and decline he never did ask for it to be renewed. At various times, Churchill had toyed with titles like 'the Duke of London' and the 'Duke of Chartwell', but never very seriously. He reportedly felt that a dukedom without a great estate might be an embarrassment. He said that he did not want to interfere with his son Randolph's political career, although in truth his political prospects were zero by that time, and Churchill's reverence for his famous ancestors was perhaps not matched by a wholly positive view of his own immediate heir's character and political abilities; certainly their relationship was known to be bad. According to Anthony Montague Browne, Churchill once expounded the intriguing idea that the heirs to an hereditary peerage should, each generation, descend one level unless they rendered such service to the nation as to justify retaining their father's rank. 'Thus the undistinguished son of a Duke would be a Marquess, and his equally undistinguished son an Earl and so on, until in WSC's words, they would not only be undistinguished but extinguished.' On this (hypothetical) basis, Randolph Churchill (or, indeed, anybody else) would have been hard pressed to retain any dukedom conferred on his illustrious father.[43]

Three years after Churchill left Number 10, the 1958 Life Peerages Act was passed, producing the most significant reform of the composition of the upper house until the expulsion of all but ninety-two of the hereditary peers by Tony Blair's Labour government in 1999, envisaged as the first stage of its reform plan for the House of Lords. In 1953 Lord Simon had introduced a Life Peers Bill which had made no progress and which the government had not supported at the time. Life peerages were finally introduced under Harold Macmillan, a politician who, like Churchill, had ducal connections (in his case by marriage) and an aristocratic style, but who often seemed to hold the House of Lords in low esteem as a place where old politicians were put out to grass (it was 'not worth belonging to', he once loftily said), and who himself refused an hereditary peerage (an earldom) and the Garter on his retirement as prime minister in 1963 – although he finally relented and became Earl of Stockton in 1984. Pride and arrogance might have been involved, and perhaps, as Anthony Sampson speculated, (some) prime ministers, who can effectively make peers, can also see through them – puppet-masters do not want to become puppets?[44]

Churchill had a small walk-on role in another reform of the Lords, which turned out to have some significant political consequences. He had long supported the idea that peers should be able to renounce their peerages and stand for election to the House of Commons. Since the 1890s there had been various attempts to change political practice and the law in this area, which had all failed. But the issue only came alive when Anthony Wedgwood Benn, an ambitious Labour politician elected an MP in 1950 and heir to a viscountcy (bestowed on his father in 1941), started a campaign to change the law to allow him to stay in the Commons. Benn wrote to Churchill about his predicament and got a sympathetic reply in September 1953, which had to remain confidential, Churchill said, because he was prime minister. In 1955, he tried to introduce a private 'Wedgwood Benn Renunciation Bill' but was blocked, though as a trump card made public a letter from Churchill (written on 9 April 1955, four days after he had resigned as prime minister), repeating what he had said in 1953: 'I certainly feel yours is a very hard case, and I am personally strongly in favour of sons having the right to renounce irrevocably the peerages they inherit from their fathers. This would not of course prevent them from accepting another peerage, if they were offered one, later on.' It was undoubtedly helpful to Benn to be able to show that 'the greatest living Conservative' supported his long campaign to change the constitution – support that was 'of great practical value', Benn later commented. 'You must carry on,' Churchill once said to Benn, and in 1959 the 'wonderful old boy', as Benn called him, gave permission for further use to be made of that letter of support. When in 1960 Benn's father died and he was evicted (as a new peer) from the Commons only to fight the by-election opened in his Bristol constituency, Benn made sure that all Conservative MPs received a copy and that 10,000 copies were distributed to voters – something which greatly embarrassed the Conservative candidate. Churchill even made a donation (of ten pounds) to Benn's election campaign fund. It is ironic in view of Benn's later political trajectory that he must be the only Labour candidate able to claim that he had the personal backing of Winston Churchill. Further embarrassment to the Conservatives ensued when Benn won the 1961 by-election but was debarred from taking up his seat. He finally returned to the Commons and was able to pursue his political career after the 1963 Peerages Act was passed, a measure that, of course, also enabled Lord Home to renounce his hereditary peerage and unexpectedly become Conservative prime minister in October 1963.[45]

Conclusion

Although he believed deeply and profoundly in the established institutions of the British constitution, there is a sense in which Robert Rhodes James was right to point to Churchill 'having no time whatever for the [House of] Lords'. His own unwillingness to accept a peerage and go to the Lords in the 1950s is very revealing. He never wavered from the view that the House of Commons was and should be constitutionally and politically supreme. His belief that the Commons was the centre of the action is seen in his long commitment to the idea that peers should be able to renounce their peerages and stand for election as MPs. In his 1909 memorandum on the Lords (quoted on page 34) he had talked about this producing 'the possibility of an excessive movement on the part of persons who take a leading part in party government towards the House of Commons' – adding 'if that be an evil' in a way that suggested he did not feel it would be. He could mock the Gilbert and Sullivan aspects of the Lords – 'this comical anachronism', he called it in 1910, a place stuffed with 'generals, proconsuls, masters of foxhounds, and all those other responsible and important persons'. But there was real and serious feeling in his attacks on the peers during the struggles for the Lloyd George budget and the Parliament Act.[46]

Although he did say in 1910 that he would not be 'frightened' by having a unicameral or single-chamber system, and talked then about 'abolition' of the Lords, Churchill was not really a 'single-chamber man'. In his February 1910 cabinet memorandum he said that he supported a two-chamber system 'both on merits and tactics'. In parliamentary speeches he insisted: 'I do not believe the bicameral system is necessary for the stability of the State. I think it is necessary for the passage of good laws.' 'I am in favour of a double Chamber,' he said, 'because it is to my mind a much more convenient and much more effective Parliamentary machine.' 'It is a more convenient Parliamentary apparatus to have the revising influence of another body which can add Amendments and within certain limits check and correct the original draft and form of a Bill.' He pointed out, though, that we had in effect 'a single-Chamber system in respect of nearly all the fundamental matters of State – war, peace, treaties, Supply, police, and so forth'. The Lords' veto was not needed for 'vital national interests', he argued, because 'those national interests are not covered by it'. The Conservatives were really fighting, he asserted, to sustain the veto 'for class and party questions'. Whenever the Conservative Party was in power, he argued in 1910, single-chamber rule was anyway the norm because the Lords could be guaranteed to be quiescent. What was important, if there were to be two chambers, was that the two Houses of Parliament 'must work together in general harmony unless the whole Constitution is to go awry'.[47]

His views on the Lords were, to an extent, tied in to and reflected his wider political stance. Before the First World War, as a radical reforming Liberal, he saw the Lords as a barrier or obstacle to progressive and democratic reform. 'As the nation advances, as the democracy becomes more numerous, and more educated, as culture and comforts spread more broadly, as the structure of our civilization becomes more complex,' he argued in 1911, 'it is absolutely necessary that the influence and control of the Peers of the Realm should become less and less, and not more and more.' What the Conservatives were trying to do, he claimed, was deliberately to undo and reverse the effects of 'the great extensions of the franchise' made in 1867 and 1884. Behind the defence of the peers' veto was a desire 'to diminish the share of the Government now enjoyed by the wage-earning classes'. 'Now when small tradesmen, school teachers, trade unionists, co-operators are all being elected, the House of Lords and London society does not feel much liking for or confidence in the House of Commons.' In this sense, he portrayed the 1911 Parliament Act as 'marking a moderate, but at the same time a definite, advance in the democratic character of our institutions'. And in social and political terms, by putting the House of Lords in its (subordinate) place, he regarded that measure as 'territory conquered by the masses from the classes'.[48]

Moving to the right and adopting a more conservative (and Conservative) attitude from the 1920s, Churchill stressed, as we have seen, the role of the House of Lords as a political and constitutional long-stop. He defended the second chamber as providing a means to secure 'the vital breathing space for consideration and for the more stable forces in the community to assert themselves'. The Lords were a barrier against 'sudden, violent, irreparable changes in the structure of the state and of society'. But he did not want to roll back or undo the Parliament Act and restore to the Lords the place and powers they had had before 1911. He was not in that sense a reactionary on the House of Lords issue. He said that he wanted a 'strong and effective' second chamber but he did not want or intend it to be a rival to the House of Commons. And he insisted on the need for 'constitutional equality'. The Labour Party had to feel that the system was basically fair and not loaded too much against it. Many socialists, he knew, wanted to abolish the House of Lords altogether and it would be wrong and foolish to play into their hands. Any further reform of the House of Lords had to be on the basis of inter-party agreement if it was to be durable.[49]

Back in 1911, Churchill described the Parliament Act as 'not by itself a final solution of constitutional difficulties'. He felt that, in truth, only a moderate change had been effected by that measure. 'It may work for a good many years,' he admitted, but in the end he believed that the parties should and would have to get together to work out the composition, role and powers of a new second chamber.[50] He clearly felt that that would happen during his political lifetime. Even in the 1950s, as prime minister, he had not given up hope that progress might be made on this issue and that the promise of the Parliament Act's preamble might be fulfilled. But in his time it was not to be. Far from being a dyed-in-the-wool, reactionary or nostalgic defender of the peers and the House of Lords, Churchill was always, on some level, a frustrated would-be reformer of that ancient institution.

THREE

Home Rule, Devolution and the Heptarchy

Churchill and Irish Home Rule

The British-Irish connection was an important aspect of Churchill's personal background and upbringing. His family was strongly Unionist, his grandfather (the seventh Duke of Marlborough) serving in Disraeli's Conservative government as Lord Lieutenant of Ireland 1876–80, and he had Anglo-Irish ascendancy relatives (Londonderrys, Leslies). His earliest memories were of Ireland, where he lived for three years when his father Lord Randolph Churchill served as secretary to *his* father, the viceroy. *My Early Life* reports childhood impressions and recollections of the viceregal lodge in the Phoenix Park, Dublin Castle, British soldiers, warnings given to the young Winston about the 'wicked' Fenians and complaints about the 'ungrateful' Irish. But his grandfather's and father's strict Unionism was combined with conciliatory and progressive policies towards Ireland (on land, education and the avoidance of coercion). Lord Randolph's approach to politics was flexible, tactical and opportunistic. He certainly played the 'Orange card' in 1886 – 'Ulster will fight and Ulster will be right' – but the champion of Protestant Ulster and the Union might have toyed at various times with ideas of devolution, federalism and Home Rule, although Winston rather skirted round this in his own biography of Lord Randolph. Wilfrid Scawen Blunt believed that Lord Randolph had really been been more of a covert Home Ruler (in 1885) than Winston seemed to know or was prepared to admit.[1]

Churchill entered politics as a Conservative rather than a Liberal because of Home Rule – 'to which I will never consent', as he wrote to his mother in

1897. His desire to maintain 'the Legislative union as at present established' overcame his bitterness towards the Tory high command for what he felt was their mistreatment of Lord Randolph after his political self-destruction and resignation as chancellor of the exchequer in December 1886. As a young man he had witnessed from the gallery of the House of Commons the dramatic scene as Gladstone wound up the second reading debate on his second Home Rule Bill in 1893. Many years later (in his *History of the English-Speaking Peoples*), Churchill seemed to view its ultimate defeat as a missed opportunity, commenting on the House of Lords' rejection of the Home Rule Bill: 'Thus perished all hope of a united self-governing Ireland, loyal to the British Crown. A generation later civil war, partition, and the separation of the South . . . were to be Ireland's lot.' However, in his early political speeches he can be found calling Home Rule a 'millstone' round the Liberals' necks and an 'odious measure'. 'I defy you to produce a workable measure of it,' he had written to an American friend, Bourke Cockran, in 1896, referring to the 'demand for Confederate independence' in a way that suggested Home Rule would be a similar fundamental challenge to the state. He did not deny that 'England has treated Ireland disgracefully in the past', as he told Cockran. But he felt that the Irish problem 'is nearly solved'. 'There is no tyranny in Ireland now,' he argued: 'the Irish peasant is as free and well represented as the English labourer. Everything that can be done to alleviate distress and heal the wounds of the past is done – and done in spite of rhetorical attempts to keep them open.' Not for twenty years could a Home Rule measure pass the English people, he predicted, and by then it would 'as likely as not . . . be merged in a wider measure of Imperial Federation'.[2]

As he moved over to join the Liberals in 1904, however, Churchill began to edge away from this clear-cut anti-Home Rule position. He was still of the opinion that 'the creation of a separate Parliament for Ireland would be dangerous and impracticable', he insisted. But he was helped by the fact that the Liberals at this time felt that Irish Home Rule was divisive and an electoral liability, and were not committed to introducing a bill. Patricia Jalland suggests that Churchill was attracted by the idea of 'administrative devolution' partly because of its tactical uses as a 'stepping stone' on his move from Conservative Unionism to the Liberals. But in fact as early as

1901 Churchill was already thinking more widely than just of Ireland and (working with Lord Hugh Cecil) had prepared a scheme of devolution to 'provincial councils', arguing that 'the reputation and efficiency of Parliament almost entirely depends upon its being cleared of the over-press of minor duties on which so much time is wasted, and which prevents any detailed and effective criticism being brought to bear on the affairs of a world-wide Empire'.[3]

Over 1904–05, Churchill carefully marked out his middle-way position. He emphasized that a definite proposal to create a separate parliament in Ireland would put him 'in a position of hideous difficulty' and create 'a most hateful and monstrous dilemma'. He looked forward, he said, 'to the day when the Irish will be, as they are not now, free to control and influence the course of their own government' – he looked forward to 'Ireland free, as England, Scotland, and Wales are free' – but he opposed a Dublin parliament that would be 'a rival of, and perhaps an enemy of, the central Parliament here at home'. He had a clear sense of what had to be kept at the centre in a quasi-federal system and what could be devolved. 'For all the effective purposes of government – for Customs, currency, defence, for the fundamental principles of law and justice – the United Kingdom must be one country.' The 'system of centralized government from Dublin Castle', which operated in Ireland, was, he maintained, 'a very bad, vicious, and wasteful system'. It 'was not democratic, autocratic, or even oligarchical'; the land was 'hag-ridden by forty-one separate semi-independent administrative boards, which overlapped in all directions'. The present system in Ireland gave the people 'no sense of ownership in government similar to that existing in this country'. It should be replaced by 'greater powers of local self-government for the Irish people'. He spoke of 'securing to the Irish people a more effective and intimate control of their own purely local and domestic concerns, of their private bill legislation, for certain portions of their local legislation, and for the spending and auditing of their own money'. Writing to John Morley, he defined administrative home rule as a system of county councils and the delegation of education, rating, drainage and railways to 'the Irish people to manage or *mis*manage as they choose'.[4]

Although willing to talk of giving 'a fair and unprejudiced consideration to Irish national claims', Churchill insisted that he 'did not think that the question of Irish devolution stood alone'. There were also Wales and Scotland to consider. But an 'extension of self-government' was vital 'not only in the interests of nationalities which were cramped within our larger political organization', but also 'in the interests of Parliament' and the imperial centre. The 'Imperial Parliament' at Westminster was becoming 'gorged to suffocation with business', suffering from 'congestion', 'increasingly choked with an ever-expanding volume of business'. Parliament was losing the capacity to consider legislation effectively, pass necessary bills, scrutinize public accounts and the details of expenditure, or (in revealing remarks) 'debate the most exciting questions' and properly discuss 'urgent Imperial matters'. He anticipated the overload at the centre getting worse year by year because of the 'complexities of modern life' and 'the manifold possibilities of the King's Dominions'. This was the context in which he saw the need for a 'process of devolution' and 'the delegation of administrative and legislative functions to provincial or national boards in the four parts of the kingdom, and the handing over to them of large slices and blocks of business which could not properly be dealt with at Westminster'.[5]

In these years Churchill was also engaged in writing his father's biography (published in January 1906) in which he signalled that he believed the issue had moved on since 1886. 'A proposal to establish by statute, subject to guarantees of Imperial supremacy, a colonial Parliament in Ireland for the transaction of Irish business may indeed be unwise,' he wrote, 'but is not, and ought not to be, outside the limits of calm and patient consideration.' Such a proposal was 'not necessarily fraught with the immense and terrific consequences which were so generally associated with it', he continued. Indeed, 'A generation may arise in England who will question the policy of creating subordinate legislatures as little as we question the propriety of Catholic Emancipation and who will study the records of the fierce disputes of 1886 with the superior manner of a modern professor examining the controversies of the early Church.' But as he stated explicitly in an election campaign speech in January 1906, he was 'not prepared to support any legislation which, in my opinion, will affect or injure the integrity of the United Kingdom, or which would lead to a separation between England and Ireland'. However, there was a case for a 'measure of devolution', 'administrative reforms' and the 'reform of Dublin Castle'.[6]

It has been fairly said that in suggesting a devolution scheme in this way, Churchill was attempting to have the best of both worlds: in constitutional terms maintaining the Union and the supremacy of the UK parliament while acknowledging national/regional differences and meeting demands for self-government, and in personal terms distancing himself from but not breaking with his Unionist inheritance. In going down this road he was not taking up an original position. A scheme of limited Irish self-management and devolved administration had been proposed by Lord Dunraven (a liberal-minded Unionist friend of Lord Randolph Churchill) in 1904, which Churchill had broadly welcomed, but which had aroused bitter Unionist opposition. Federal ideas had been discussed in British politics since the 1870s, and linked to the Irish issue as well as Scotland and Wales in the guise of 'Home Rule All Round'. Joseph Chamberlain had flirted with this in 1886, largely for tactical reasons as he manoeuvred to smash Home Rule. Both Rosebery and Lloyd George favoured 'Home Rule All Round'. The idea that devolution was an antidote to over-centralization and 'congestion' at Westminster was also not new. Neither was the case for viewing the Home Rule issue in a wider imperial context: indeed, while a schoolboy at Harrow, Churchill had been impressed by a lecture on the subject of 'Imperial Federation'. As Patricia Jalland comments, devolution had some of the qualities – and weaknesses – of a 'universal panacea', an 'all things to all men' idea. It appealed to 'faint-hearted Liberals as a device to submerge Irish Home Rule in a massive theoretical scheme, which might postpone the Irish measure indefinitely'. (That was why the Irish Nationalists and those Liberals loyal to Gladstone's Irish Home Rule project distrusted the notion.) And it is possible, as Ian Chambers says, that this was why Churchill favoured it. But his commitment to the broader devolution idea, dating from before his switch to the Liberals (the 'provincial councils' idea of 1901) and later, in 1911–12 and in the 1920s and 1930s, suggests a genuine interest in the concept, and that it was not for him just a tactical expedient or diversion.[7]

Churchill's aim, in a sense, was to reform the Union in order to preserve it. In her book *Churchill and Ireland*, Mary Bromage argued that his basic principle and unwavering aim in approaching the Irish question was 'simply what was good for England'. Paul Addison agrees that 'Churchill's Irish policies were driven at all times by a conception of British interests'. That he looked far beyond the 'dreary steeples of Fermanagh and Tyrone' and conceived of those interests in a broader imperial framework has been emphasized by Andrew Muldoon, who argues that Churchill came to see and support Irish Home Rule as a step towards federating, binding together and strengthening the British Empire. He was never an enthusiast for Ireland and the Irish cause as such, and later on never became a whole-hearted Home Ruler, as Patricia Jalland notes. Like Lloyd George, he wanted the issue settled in order to free up ministerial energy and parliamentary time for other important issues on the political agenda (social reform, defence). Later, in his book *Great Contemporaries*, he remarked on the 'baleful, extraneous influence of the Irish feud', which had 'poisoned nearly forty years of our public life'. What, asked Addison, did he believe or feel about Ireland? 'Little, perhaps, except that the Irish were difficult, depressing, and deserved to be manipulated for the benefit of Churchill and the British State.'[8]

The decisive Liberal victory of 1906 and the noncommittal 'step-by-step' line promulgated by Campbell-Bannerman put the Irish issue on the back-burner. Yet by April 1908, Churchill was saying to an audience at Manchester: 'Don't let us be afraid of the words Home Rule.' Why the apparent change in views? The 'catalyzing factor', as Henry Pelling put it, was the Manchester North-West by-election, which Churchill was obliged to fight (as was the rule in those days) on his appointment as a cabinet minister. Churchill narrowly lost, the Irish Catholic vote going against him, mainly on the education issue, and he had hurriedly to take himself off to Dundee (another seat with a sizeable Irish community), which he won. He trumpeted what he called his 'new and advanced position on the Irish question' in the Manchester by-election in an (unsuccessful) attempt to shore up the Liberal vote. On 30 March 1908 Churchill had voted with the government in support of a resolution introduced by the Irish Nationalists calling for 'the Irish people [to be given] legislative and executive control of all purely Irish affairs', to which had been added a government amendment: 'subject to the supreme authority of the Imperial Parliament'. As Colonial Office under-secretary (1906–08), Churchill had been heavily involved in the moves to extend self-government to the defeated Boers of the Transvaal and the Orange Free State in South Africa. He now seized on that analogy to make the case for 'a settlement of national difficulties with Ireland in a similar spirit', though with the qualification that it would not necessarily be achieved by 'similar methods'. He claimed that his opinion on the issue had 'ripened' over the previous two years, and that he was now convinced that 'a national settlement of the Irish difficulty on broad and generous lines must be indispensable to any harmonious conception of Liberalism'. Home Rule had not been abandoned or shelved, he insisted. The Liberals were bound so far as the current parliament was concerned, but at the next election – and he said this with the new prime minister Asquith's explicit approval – the Liberals would claim 'full authority and a free hand to deal with the problem of Irish self-government without being restricted to some measure of administration and devolution of the character of the Irish Councils Bill'.[9]

As everyone knew, the veto power of the House of Lords still stood as a huge roadblock in the way of Home Rule for Ireland. The Liberals' motives for engaging in their battle with the Lords in 1909-11 were overwhelmingly about domestic politics (see chapter 2), but the implications for the future of the Irish issue were apparent to all. The two constitutional issues were inter-related because, with their veto curbed, the Lords would not be able to prevent Home Rule, as they had done in 1893. Loreburn, the lord chancellor, argued that a policy of 'Home Rule All Round' (to which he was sympathetic) would go even further, and effectively destroy the Lords' powers in all delegated matters: they would only retain power over non-financial 'Imperial' legislation.[10]

'In relation to his manifold other interests,' Robert Rhodes James cautions, 'Ireland counted for very little.' Churchill's 'devotion to the cause of Irish Home Rule . . . was not very profound,' he maintains. 'The matter did not really occupy his attention until the two 1910 general elections showed the Liberals that they were dependent upon the Irish votes for their majority in the House of Commons.' The Liberals were in fact left in a similar situation to Gladstone in 1892, about which Churchill had written (in 1906) that 'concessions to Ireland made by any British Government which depends for its existence on the Irish vote, will naturally and necessarily be suspect'. We have seen that in his November 1909 memorandum on Lords reform (chapter 2), he had wanted to retain safeguards against the power of a government dependent on the Irish Nationalists. Looking back years later, Churchill was blunt about their leverage power: it was the Liberal government's dependence on the support of eighty Irish MPs that was 'the spur which alone exhorted action' on Home Rule.[11]

John Redmond (the Irish Nationalists' leader) claimed that Churchill had once told him that it was 'the ambition of his life to bring in a Home Rule Bill as Chief Secretary' (the cabinet minister in day-to-day charge of Irish government). But when Asquith offered Churchill that post in February 1910, he refused it (with the exception of Balfour in the 1880s, it had been a graveyard for ambitious politicians).[12]

Nevertheless Churchill was well to the fore in the Home Rule struggle, 1911-14: vocal, inventive and energetic, as he had been on the House of Lords issue (see chapter 2). Typically, when he took up an issue he threw himself into it and sought a leading role. He gave the government's Irish Home Rule Bill full public support but at times took an independent line, to the consternation and embarrassment of his colleagues and the Irish Nationalists. He was a prominent spokesman in Parliament and on public platforms up and down the country, even – in an audacious move – taking the campaign to Belfast in February 1912, where he planned to speak in favour of Home Rule in the Ulster Hall in a strongly Protestant area (the scene of his father's famous anti–Home Rule speech of 1886), although the threat of unrest forced him to address instead an audience of five thousand at a football ground in a working-class Catholic district. With soldiers guarding the route, large and hostile crowds had mobbed Churchill's party in the streets and his cousin (Freddie Guest) attended the event with a revolver in his pocket. Churchill took plenty of political risks too, particularly in his repeated attempts to find a solution to the Ulster problem – he was an early and strong advocate of the exclusion of the north-east counties of Ireland from Home Rule, putting himself at odds with the prime minister and creating problems for himself in the cabinet, the Liberal Party and with the Irish Nationalists. He combined an active role and private moderation in behind-the-scenes contacts with the Conservatives to try to broker a compromise deal with tub-thumping belligerence in his public speeches – something which also ate into his political capital and fed Tory mistrust and dislike of him.[13]

'An Irish Parliament, loyal to the Crown, and free to make the best of the Emerald Isle' was how Churchill summed up Home Rule. 'The separation of Ireland from Great Britain is absolutely impossible,' he declared in his Belfast speech in February 1912. 'The interests and affairs of the two islands are eternally interwoven.' Home Rule would not involve 'a divorce of the two Kingdoms', he told MPs in April 1912, or 'separation from the United Kingdom or . . . from the British Empire', or 'the termination of the Parliamentary Union', or anything like 'Colonial autonomy'. Home Rule was 'a measure which implements, amplifies, and carries out the union of the two countries under forms which for the first time will receive the assent of the Irish people'. The Irish, he said, 'have too much power in this country and not enough in their own'. It was a limited and moderate step. Westminster retained its full sovereignty and would still 'have not only the legal but the moral right to legislate. The Imperial Parliament can resume its delegated powers in whole or in part. It can legislate as it chooses for Ireland'. As he had spelt out in December 1910: Home Rule 'would give the Irish people the power of dealing with purely Irish affairs through an Irish Assembly, and with an Irish executive responsible to that Assembly, but that would not include Imperial matters. It would not include matters which affect the United Kingdom as a whole, and the Imperial Parliament would . . . . possess an overriding power which would effectively secure its supremacy'.[14]

Churchill justified Home Rule on a number of grounds. He made the case for it as a first step in a 'general scheme of Parliamentary devolution' so that the House of Commons could 'hold its position as the great representative Assembly of [the] British Empire'. Over-centralization, he argued, 'exposes the supreme organization to stresses and shocks which derange and disturb its action, and chokes with a mass of unsuitable business the highest council of a world State'. In historical terms, he argued, 'Irish Home Rule is no longer as big a question for Great Britain as it used to be.' The old danger of a Continental invasion of Britain through Ireland had long passed: Home Rule would not weaken British strategic security or power in wartime. In economic and trade terms, Irish and British interdependence would remain a unifying force. The population balance had changed dramatically since the time of the Union in 1800: then, Ireland had had five million people compared to Britain's 10.5 million, but by 1911 Ireland had just over four million to Britain's 41 million. 'That is a prodigious change in the balance of affairs and in the proportion of the question,' said Churchill. He stressed also the advantages for the Empire: Home Rule would 'have the effect of adding to our imperial strength and pave the way perhaps for a great measure of imperial federation'. Moreover, Britain was 'hampered at the present time in the progress of our Colonial policy by hostility and distrust in every one of the great English-speaking dominions, which, traced home to its source, arises from the presence of unreconciled Irish in positions of prosperity and honour in their midst'. As well as being 'an adverse force' in the colonies, Irishmen had 'on more than one occasion unfavourably deflected the policy of the United States'. Home Rule would therefore bring diplomatic benefits to the UK, he claimed, and improve British relations with the USA.[15]

Rather than a bitter party fight to the death over Home Rule, Churchill wanted a bipartisan settlement so that Irish issues could be taken out of British politics. He thought that a solution of the Irish question was in the interests of both the Liberal and Conservative parties. From an early stage, therefore, he was flexible, seeing a wider quasi-federal devolution scheme and/or special treatment for Ulster as the way forward. In early 1911 he presented devolution proposals to the cabinet committee on Home Rule (of which he was a member, along with some other supporters of 'Home Rule All Round', notably Lloyd George, Edward Grey and Haldane). In his first paper (dated 24 February 1911), he argued that it seemed to him 'absolutely impossible that an English Parliament, and still more an English Executive, could exist side by side with an Imperial Parliament and an Imperial Executive'. This was so for several reasons. The first was that 'Imperial affairs could not in practice be separated from English party politics, which consist principally of domestic questions'. 'The external sphere touches the internal at almost every point,' argued Churchill. 'The fortunes of the country abroad and at home are interdependent and indissoluble . . . No separation of the ["external" and "domestic"] issues is possible in practice, and none is desirable.' Equally, there could not be two separate classes of politicians: 'The persons who are prominent in British party politics will be so mainly because of their following in England on internal questions; and it is not conceivable that such persons, having acquired mastery in the decisive field of home politics, would be willing, or would be able, to surrender the control of foreign, colonial, military, and naval affairs to another class of Ministers or politicians.' Another reason for the unworkability of a federal model based on a separate English parliament was the likelihood of disabling party clashes if the Imperial and English parliaments were in different hands, something that at worst could 'tear the State in half' and at best would not be conducive to 'good government'.[16]

A week later, on 1 March, Churchill put forward his radical solution to the English problem. The 'Imperial Parliament' at Westminster would remain unaltered 'except by a strict numerical redistribution between countries' (which would reduce Irish representation). The United Kingdom was to be divided into ten areas, 'having regard to geographical, racial, and historical considerations', each area having a separately elected legislative body and an administrative structure. In Ireland, Scotland and Wales the devolved bodies were to be 'clothed with Parliamentary form so far as may be desirable in each case'. Women would have the right to vote and serve on all these bodies, except in Ireland where the national parliament would decide. These bodies would have significant powers and responsibilities, taking over all the powers currently exercised by county councils and certain powers exercised by municipal bodies, together with powers devolved from Westminster, including: education, licensing, land, housing, police, local judges and magistrates, the poor law, agriculture, fisheries, private bill legislation, roads, local government boundary questions, and 'such further powers as Parliament shall from time to time devolve on any or all of them'. The imperial parliament would retain all powers not specifically devolved. Churchill envisaged the policy finding shape in two bills, simultaneously announced but with legislation for Ireland being tackled a year ahead of a bill dealing with Great Britain.[17]

Such a 'Home Rule All Round' or federal scheme (these terms were used interchangeably and loosely in political debates at that time) had a number of potential advantages. By dividing England itself into different regions (in this case, seven), it avoided the problems inherent in a lopsided federal system necessarily dominated and unbalanced by the sheer size of England relative to the other parts of the UK. It preserved the Union and headed off separatism while not giving any sort of special treatment to Ireland distinct from other parts of the UK – and he hoped that this might mean that the Conservatives and the Ulstermen would be able to swallow it. It provided a solution, too, to what a later generation would call the 'West Lothian question' (or what might equally be called the 'West Cork question', and one that had baffled Gladstone): the problem of representation at Westminster after devolution or Home Rule. The status of Irish MPs in the Westminster parliament in a federal system would be the same as MPs from Scotland, Wales and England.

Churchill's colleagues, however, saw only drawbacks and problems, and his plan never took off. Augustine Birrell, the chief secretary, and the Irish Nationalists suspected the federalists' motives and would not accept anything that might delay, complicate or wreck the chances of securing Home Rule for Ireland. Courtney Ilbert, the clerk of the House of Commons, told the cabinet committee that Churchill's scheme was not 'expedient or practicable'. The situation was different in the different parts of the UK: unlike Ireland, Scotland and Wales mainly demanded or required administrative, not legislative, devolution. There was no evidence of support in England for devolution, no demand for English provincial councils, or any developed provincial consciousness or homogeneity in groups of English counties. Lloyd George argued that while devolution might work for Scotland and Wales, 'the people in England were wholly unprepared for such a scheme'. 'The progressive North would never submit to be placed under the control of the semi-feudal south,' he said. 'England could not be divided,' Asquith agreed: 'we could not go back to the Heptarchy.' England did not need 'a welter of parochialism', said John Burns. Lloyd George's ingenious but more limited idea for English, Scottish and Welsh parliamentary grand committees with full legislative powers (to deal with the problem of Irish MPs at Westminster otherwise still having voting powers over English, Scottish and Welsh domestic affairs after Home Rule) made a little more progress, actually featuring in the first draft of the 1912 Home Rule Bill before it, too, was dropped.[18]

Churchill's description (in April 1912) of the Home Rule Bill as 'the forerunner of a general system of devolution in the United Kingdom' was echoed in a distinctly lukewarm fashion by Asquith, who was willing for tactical reasons to pay lip service to the idea that it was the first step in a devolution process, partly to keep the federalists in the cabinet and on the Liberal backbenches happy and partly in case it might later be useful as a bargaining counter in compromise talks with the Unionists. But Asquith and other ministers were horrified when, without giving them any warning at all, Churchill gave a speech in his constituency in Dundee in September 1912 that went far beyond the minimalist official line. Citing the cases of federal systems like those of the United States, Germany, Canada, South Africa and Australia, Churchill declared that he was 'not in the least disturbed by the prospect of seeing erected in this country ten or twelve separate legislative bodies for the discharge of the functions entrusted to them by the Imperial Parliament'. Though many politicians thought otherwise, Churchill maintained that 'there would be no difficulty in setting up a thoroughly workable federal system throughout the country', cheerfully hinting at parliaments for Yorkshire, Lancashire, the Midlands and Greater London (provoking one critic to sneer at the idea of England's 'robe of national unity' being replaced by a 'patchwork quilt dragged out of the cupboard of the Anglo-Saxons'). It was one thing for Churchill's ideas to be presented to and turned down by a secret cabinet committee: now he was summarizing the arguments on the public platform, generating a major controversy and a press storm. This was because the questions of federalism and Ulster could not be separated, and there was now more at stake than a frankly rather academic debate about devolution. Churchill was convinced of the need for special treatment and the (temporary) exclusion of Protestant Ulster from Home Rule. By conjuring up a vision of ten or twelve parliaments, he was opening up a breach in the government's position because his speech was widely interpreted as an attempt to resolve the growing crisis over Ulster by offering it a parliament of its own, separate from Dublin.[19]

In fact Churchill made persistent attempts to defuse the Irish crisis in the years before 1914 by trying to reach a compromise deal with the Conservatives and accommodate the concerns of Ulster. He supported Lloyd George's coalition overtures in 1910, a plan (ultimately abortive) that had the attraction of freeing British politicians from the constraints imposed by dependence on Nationalists or Orangemen, perhaps opening the way to the imposition of an agreed settlement on Ireland as part of some sort of 'Home Rule All Round' scheme (which Lloyd George floated, only for Balfour to reject). Churchill was disappointed at the failure of the 1910 Constitutional Conference, which he seems to have attributed partly to the Liberals' determination to 'stick to Home Rule', although it was also clear that the Conservatives would not compromise on the issue of the Union. Undeterred, in January 1911 he urged what he called a policy of appeasement upon Asquith, arguing that the government should confer with the Conservatives on Ireland and on House of Lords reform. Later, he met with leading Conservatives – Bonar Law, Austen Chamberlain, F. E. Smith – to discuss the Irish/Ulster issue and seek common ground on various occasions in 1913-14. Addison describes Churchill as 'the principal go-between in a number of secret moves to bring about a compromise between the parties'.[20]

The chances of such a settlement were perhaps never particularly high and an increasingly ugly and bitter political situation developed as the party warfare over Home Rule intensified and as the Ulster Protestants, led by Sir Edward Carson, mobilized for armed resistance (forming the paramilitary Ulster Volunteer Force), encouraged by the Conservative opposition. Bonar Law, the Tory leader, warned that 'there are things stronger than parliamentary majorities . . . I can imagine no length of resistance to which Ulster will go in which I shall not be ready to support them'. Churchill was shocked and appalled at what he called these 'threats of armed rebellion so recklessly and lightly made', accusing Bonar Law of coming 'very near the borderland of treason'. Did the Tories think they would never come back to power? Was their policy to make Ireland ungovernable? By their intransigence and threatened defiance of Parliament, they were playing with fire. 'The principle and doctrine lately enunciated would dissolve the framework not only of the British Empire, but of civil society,' he argued. He condemned such incitement to 'unconstitutional resistance' to laws properly passed by Parliament. (However, looking back years later he was of the opinion that 'if Ulster had confined herself simply to constitutional agitation, it is extremely improbable that she would have escaped forcible inclusion in a Dublin Parliament'.)[21]

The cause of Ulster had been taken up by Lord Randolph Churchill, as by Bonar Law, as a way of opposing Irish Home Rule as a whole. For his part, Churchill was sympathetic to Ulster's concerns, believing that Ulster should and could not be coerced into a united Home Rule Ireland. But he would not accept it blocking Home Rule for the rest of Ireland: 'Half a province cannot impose a permanent veto on the nation.' He was ahead of the rest of the government in being willing publicly to acknowledge (in April 1912) that 'the perfectly genuine apprehensions' of the Ulster Protestants were a 'serious obstacle' to a settlement, and that it would be 'impossible' for the government to ignore them or to treat them 'cavalierly or contemptuously'. He rejected the claim that 'Home Rule means Rome Rule'. There would be safeguards and guarantees for the Protestants of Ulster and Ireland. The Home Rule parliament, both in its House of Commons and its Senate, would be 'fully and fairly representative of the Irish nation, and of Protestants as well as of Catholics, of urban interests as well as of agricultural interests, of minorities even more than majorities'. He listed other protections: the Crown would be able to refuse assent to an unjust bill; the imperial parliament at Westminster would be able to repeal such a bill or enact its own measures; there would be explicit safeguards for religious freedom; the Privy Council would be able to strike down a law passed in Dublin that transgressed the limits of the Home Rule Act; the Home Rule system would be 'worked in the face of Great Britain as well as of Ireland' and Westminster had 'unquestioned' powers to intervene if necessary. Privately, however, his view was that 'There is not the slightest danger . . . of Protestants in Ulster being persecuted for their religion under a system of Home Rule. The danger is entirely the other way, viz. – that the very strong and aggressive Protestant majority in parts of North East Ulster will maltreat and bully the Catholics in their midst'.[22]

Writing in the 1920s, Churchill claimed that 'From the earliest discussion of the Home Rule Bill in 1909 the Chancellor of the Exchequer [Lloyd George] and I had always advocated the exclusion of Ulster on a basis of a county option or some similar process'. In fact, as Patricia Jalland argues, it was probably Augustine Birrell in August 1911 who first planted the idea in Churchill's mind of local ballots and a temporary, or transitional, five-year exclusion from Home Rule for any Ulster counties that so voted, followed by fresh referendums, as a way of heading off the threat of civil war. In February 1912, two months before the legislation was introduced, Churchill and Lloyd George argued in the cabinet for Ulster exclusion but were overruled (as was Churchill when he tried again the next month), and the government's Home Rule Bill dealt with a united Ireland, making no special provision for Ulster. Subsequently Asquith told Churchill (in September 1913) that he had always thought that, in the end, a bargain would have to be made about Ulster as the price of achieving a settlement, but that as a matter of tactics the concession should not be made too soon (and the prime minister made no formal offer until March 1914). Churchill claimed not to understand the logic of this stance, and Jalland argues that the Liberals would have been in a stronger position and far wiser to have followed Churchill's (and Lloyd George's) line, in a sense retaining the initiative by making definite and reasonable proposals at the start to deal with Ulster. This might have taken the wind out of Ulster's opposition to Home Rule, wrongfooted the Conservatives, and helped with British public opinion. But there is also the possibility that if concessions had been made at an early stage, then the opposition and the Orangemen might have simply raised their demands and pressed for more.[23]

Straining the convention of collective cabinet responsibility to the limit (if not beyond), Churchill pressed both publicly and privately for concessions to Ulster. We have already noted his flying of the Home Rule All Round kite in September 1912. Before that, in April 1912, he had controversially asked in Parliament: 'Do they claim separate treatment for themselves? Do the counties of Down and Antrim and Londonderry, for instance, ask to be exempted from the scope of the [Home Rule] Bill? Do they ask for a Parliament of their own, or do they wish to remain here?' In August 1912 he had proposed both to Lloyd George and to Redmond that the 'characteristically Protestant and Orange counties' should be given the option of a 'moratorium' of up to five or ten years before acceding to a Home Rule parliament, a view that angered the Nationalists, who opposed the break-up of Ireland. In December 1912, when Carson tabled a wrecking amendment to exclude all nine Ulster counties from Home Rule, Churchill (and Lloyd George) argued unsuccessfully in cabinet for the door to be left open for some sort of compromise over exclusion. At the time, Churchill professed to believe that any Ulster exclusion would be temporary, writing in an open letter to the chairman of the Dundee Liberals (in September

1912) that once an Irish parliament was set up and seen to be working as a successful body it would engender feelings of confidence and, with economic pressure from the rest of Ireland upon Belfast, overcome Ulster's misgivings and win over a majority of Orangemen 'in the course of a few years'. In March 1914 Asquith finally offered county plebiscites by which Ulster counties could exclude themselves for six years – in other words, until after two successive general elections had taken place. The Unionists rejected this and Carson said that Ulster did not want 'sentence of death with a stay of execution for six years'. But a few years later, in 1920, Churchill let slip that the Liberals by that stage knew that agreeing that Ulster was not to be compelled against its will to join a Home Rule parliament on those terms was 'tantamount to saying she could never join a Dublin Parliament' – in other words that exclusion would involve or lead to an act of partition that might well be permanent.[24]

Churchill was willing to go to exceptional lengths to conciliate Ulster and find a compromise, but he strongly resented the blank rejection of the government's offer and the continued threats of, and preparations for, illegal and unconstitutional resistance. He wanted to treat Ulster fairly, but he also wanted to give it a lesson about threatening civil war and the use of force against the government. As Patricia Jalland comments: 'Churchill could be the strongest ministerial advocate of Ulster exclusion, but also the keenest to use firm methods to control the illegal preparations of the Ulstermen.'[25] Fundamental constitutional principles were now at stake, Churchill believed, but he also had personal political reasons of his own for 'mingling actively in the Irish controversy' at this time, as he later put it. His stance over Ulster and a general drifting towards the right had weakened his position in the Liberal Party. A bitter cabinet dispute about his naval spending plans over the winter of 1913-14 had left him further isolated and on the brink of resigning from or being forced out of the government. Asquith patched together a compromise, and Churchill seems consciously to have decided to build bridges and strengthen his party standing with some stage-managed and theatrical provocation over Ulster.

Addressing a crowd of three thousand at St George's Hall in Bradford on 14 March 1914, he warned that the Ulster Protestants and the Unionist party had a clear 'constitutional remedy'. 'They should obey the law,' he insisted, and if they disliked a law passed by Parliament, 'let them agitate for a majority when an election comes, and then, if they choose, they can amend or . . . repeal a law against which the country would then have pronounced.' Bonar Law and Carson's brinkmanship, treasonable conspiracies and threats had raised the issue of 'whether civil and Parliamentary government in these realms is to be beaten down by the menace of armed force'. 'It is the old battle-ground of English history,' Churchill declared to loud cheers. 'It is the issue fought out 250 years ago on the field of Marston Moor.' 'There is no lawful measure from which this Government will shrink . . . there are worse things than bloodshed,' he thundered. 'Let us put these grave matters to the proof.'[26]

The government's bluff was called. Rather than having any plans to coerce Ulster, it was actually on the defensive, rattled and alarmed about what the Ulster Volunteers might be about to do (such as seize arms depots and barracks). Churchill sat on a cabinet committee to co-ordinate precautionary military preparations and, as first lord of the Admiralty, he ordered warships to take up position at Lamlash on the Scottish coast, a few hours' sailing distance from Belfast. It is claimed that Churchill threatened that, if Belfast fought, 'his fleet would have the town in ruins in twenty-four hours'. However, it was the war secretary, Jack Seeley, rather than Churchill, who was entangled in (and paid the price for) the mixture of muddle, incompetence and military disloyalty of the so-called 'Curragh Mutiny'. That episode showed that the government could not ultimately rely on the army to 'put these grave matters to the proof' and enforce Home Rule on Ulster. For the Conservatives, Churchill was the arch villain who had been plotting an 'Ulster Pogrom'; in return, he dismissed their attacks as 'like a vote of censure by the criminal classes on the police'. The wilder accusations against Churchill were untrue. But it was certainly the case that he believed that armed rebellion against the state would make the use of force to put down an insurrection in Ulster legitimate and justified.[27]

With events rapidly spinning out of control, large quantities of weapons being illegally shipped into Ulster, paramilitary militias drilling and civil war apparently looming, Churchill still clung to the hope that a compromise solution might be found on terms acceptable to the Unionists. In April 1914 he held out an olive branch to the Ulster Unionists, urging Carson to 'run some risk for peace' by accepting a settlement that would 'safeguard the dignity and interests of Protestant Ulster' and make 'Ireland an integral unit in a federal system'. In the March–May 1914 period Churchill also worked behind the scenes with F. E. Smith and the (Unionist-inclined) Round Table Group on a plan for Ulster exclusion as part of a wider federal scheme for the UK. These efforts were fruitless, as was a conference of party leaders meeting at Buckingham Palace in July 1914 on the eve of Armageddon in Europe, which broke down, unable to agree on the details of a settlement. Churchill urged 'splitting the outstanding differences, if possible with Irish acquiescence, but if necessary over the heads of both Irish parties'; and he now talked frankly of 'partition'. The outbreak of war brought down the lid on the crisis: the Home Rule Bill was put on the statute book in September 1914 but suspended for one year or until after the war, and Asquith promised to introduce an amending bill dealing with Ulster exclusion (Churchill had wanted both bills enacted together).[28]

Churchill won more enemies than friends in this period with his role in the Irish question. To some critics his switch from an anti- to a pro–Home Rule stance seemed opportunistic. Then, as the political temperature rose, his confrontational and aggressive public approach towards the Conservatives and the Ulster Unionists fed the opposition's great hatred of him – Churchill's scalp was to be one of the Tories' principal conditions for joining a coalition government under Asquith in 1915. On the other hand, his constant promotion of compromise and Ulster exclusion antagonized the Irish Nationalists and left him exposed in the Liberal Party. His broader federalist enthusiasms seemed to many government colleagues at best impracticable and unrealistic, and at worst (as in his Dundee speech in 1912) damaging and unhelpful. In December 1913, after discussing the Irish problem with Austen Chamberlain, Churchill commented that 'It is so easy to talk vaguely about Federalism, but few people try to face the obvious difficulties, or to provide answers to the first questions which arise'. He showed Chamberlain his two 1911 cabinet papers on the subject, but in truth those memoranda were themselves pretty vague outline papers, recognizing some of the key issues but sketchy, and Churchill's imaginative 'heptarchy' plan had been quite easily pulled apart at the cabinet committee in 1911. His strict line on upholding the authority of the government and Parliament, the rule of law, and constitutional methods against threats of armed rebellion looked to his opponents like a purely rhetorical stance in the explosive atmosphere of the Ulster crisis in 1914, when Unionists regarded him as akin to an *agent provocateur*. Ironically, he wanted to placate Ulster but discovered the hard way the destructive potential of the Irish issue both for his own reputation and for his basic conception of politics and the constitution.[29]

The Irish Treaty and After

'Whatever form the Irish question may take, it no longer comes to us in the fierce and tragic guise in which it presented itself to our forerunners who sat here in the early [eighteen] eighties,' Churchill had said in a Commons speech in 1911. 'Rebellion, murder, and dynamite – these have vanished from Ireland,' he continued, in remarks that were to prove horribly wrong after 1916. The Easter Rebellion, the sweeping success of Sinn Fein – which set up its own parliament in Dublin, the Dáil, and declared Ireland a republic – and the IRA guerrilla war against the British transformed the situation. The chances of a Home Rule settlement on the Gladstonian or Asquithian model vanished (Churchill was subsequently to write wistfully of the 1886 version of Home Rule as offering a better solution to the Irish question than the ultimate outcome). By 1920, as Churchill later wrote, 'Ireland had become ungovernable except by processes of terror and violent subjugation deeply repugnant to British institutions and to British national character.' As secretary of state for war (1919–21) he certainly supported a tough, ruthless and militaristic approach – including martial law, police reprisals, and the use of irregular forces (the infamous 'Black and Tans') to meet terror with terror. He believed that the IRA could be crushed, if enough soldiers were deployed for long enough and the war intensified, but this view was probably unrealistic in the immediate Irish context and Churchill was very conscious of the damage being caused to Britain's international reputation and interests. Following the declaration of a truce in July 1921, Churchill was a member of the British delegation that negotiated the Anglo–Irish treaty, playing a major role in negotiating the clauses allowing Britain to maintain naval bases in the south and patrol the coastal waters.[30]

Realistically, Churchill recognized that 'something more than nineteenth-century home rule . . . had to be given as the solution for Ireland', says Mary Bromage. From July 1920, at least, he had been prepared to consider 'full Dominion Home Rule', as he called it in a cabinet meeting. However, like his father, he seems to have rejected a full parallel between Ireland and, say, Canada, not least because Ireland was on Britain's doorstep, and he always insisted that there were 'special reservations' contained in the treaty, relating to Ireland's status and relations with the UK. Bromage comments that 'The difference between the old status implied by home rule and the new status of dominion self-government was, in his mind, small'. 'In Churchill's heart,' she argued, 'he did not accept the fact that Ireland had to be regarded as a full-fledged dominion.' What he does not seem to have appreciated is that in *their* hearts the Irish leaders did not accept dominion status, oaths of allegiance to the Crown, and so on, as anything other than a temporary halfway house to complete national independence. Churchill opposed the 1931 Statute of Westminster (giving the dominions full legal autonomy from Westminster) in part because of his concerns about India but also because he feared that it would allow the rulers of the Irish Free State to repudiate the treaty and any formal link with the Crown and the Commonwealth – as, indeed, happened in stages in 1937 and 1949, Ireland eventually becoming a republic and leaving the Commonwealth.[31]

Ulster had had a separate Home Rule parliament of its own since the 1920 Government of Ireland Act. During the 1921 treaty talks, Churchill was apparently willing at least to consider the Irish offer to give Ulster a provincial legislature, with special protections, under the Dublin parliament – Ulster would 'hold autonomy . . . from them instead of from us', he said – but he recognized that the British were not free agents in that respect. He regularly said he hoped that 'some day' Ulster would, 'of her own free will, and in her own time', join with Southern Ireland – achieving the national unity of Ireland 'within the British Empire' (which would be unacceptable to the leaders of the south). But Ulster could not and should not be compelled to sever the ties that bound it to the UK or be forced to integrate into a united Ireland. His offer to de Valera in 1940 that, in return for Ireland coming into the war on the British side, there would be a British declaration accepting the principle of a united Ireland (the constitutional and practical details to be worked out later) is probably best seen, like the offer of perpetual union with France also made in 1940, as 'a grand gesture at a desperate time, rather than a considered proposal for constitutional change', as John Ramsden says. In any case de Valera rejected it, and the Northern Ireland prime minister sounded off about 'treachery to loyal Ulster' and rushed to London to be reassured by Churchill that, of course, Ulster would never be coerced by London. After the war, Churchill felt that Eire becoming formally a republic 'dug a ditch' and 'opened a gulf' between the two parts of Ireland. In September 1953 he met de Valera in Downing Street – their first and only meeting – and when the Irish leader spoke of unification, Churchill replied bluntly that 'they could never put out the people of the Six Counties so long as the majority wished to remain with them'. There were also, he added, 'political factors which no Conservative could ignore' – an allusion to the support of the Ulster Unionists MPs for the Conservatives at Westminster.[32]

The people of Ulster were 'part of our flesh and blood', Churchill once said to Anthony Montague Browne. He had been a long-term champion of their rights and of Ulster's status as part of the UK. But, it would seem, as Ian Wood comments, that he 'never could grasp the depth and destructive venom of sectarian divisions under Unionist rule'. Back in 1922, as colonial secretary, although he had legal powers, he had refused to veto the Ulster Unionists' decision to abandon proportional representation for local elections in Northern Ireland – a move designed to reduce the representation of the minority Catholic population and ensure Protestant domination. It was symptomatic of a general British unwillingness not to lift the lid on what was going on in the province. So far as London was concerned, Ulster appeared politically settled, as was the case in Churchill's 1951–55 administration, when the later civil rights campaign and descent into political violence were unforeseen. Blindness at Westminster was among the negative consequences of devolution to Stormont.[33]

The Missing Tier of Government

'The present Government is much too centralized,' Churchill told Lord Riddell in July 1920. He was 'firmly convinced', he said, 'that the only remedy is devolution'. In the 1920s and early 1930s Churchill still clung to ideas of Home Rule All Round, devolution, federalism or regional government. In a 1918 election speech he had said that he was in favour of Home Rule for Ireland, Scotland, Wales and four big regions in England. In 1922 (in a speech in Dundee) he repeated that he favoured Scottish Home Rule, if Scotland demanded it – but, noting that Scots found the UK and the Empire a great field for ambition and activity, added that 'Scotland so far has been inclined to think it is better to rule the British Empire'. As Ian Wood notes, Churchill was here to an extent telling Home Rule-supporting Scottish Liberals what they wanted to hear. And it is true that after 1922, when he lost his Dundee seat and left the Liberals, there was no longer 'any pressing need for him to speak on the Scottish constitutional question'. He found that this was a non-issue for the Conservatives. Some Scottish Unionists had been supportive of UK devolution in 1919-20, but their interest in federalism and Scottish Home Rule quickly disappeared after the Irish settlement. Scottish nationalism was a minor force in the interwar period.[34]

The idea of devolution was given some support immediately after the First World War by a Speakers' Conference in 1919-20 (albeit divided on whether the sub-parliaments should be directly elected), and by a vote carried (by 187 to 34) in the House of Commons in June 1919 in favour of the creation of subordinate legislatures in the UK to ease parliamentary congestion. But in truth there was little political impetus behind these schemes. The Irish question had largely been the driving force behind federalism before 1914, and its separate treatment in 1920-21 removed any sense of urgency and exposed the limited support for Home Rule All Round – that cause further suffering with the decline of the Liberals and the rise of the Labour Party, with its centralist politics. The mood of the country after the war was not supportive of far-reaching constitutional change, as Vernon Bogdanor notes, and no government sought or could claim a mandate for remaking the UK constitution.[35]

Although there was no real market for the idea, Churchill remained convinced of the value and practicability of devolution. 'Is there not a storey missing in the fabric of our national life?' he asked in 1925. 'Could not the top-heavy character of the present structure be remedied and the whole edifice vastly strengthened if the missing storey were properly built in?' With Baldwin's Conservative government discussing House of Lords reform (see chapter 2), he tried, unsuccessfully, to create some leverage by linking the two issues. There was a need, he argued in a cabinet memorandum, for 'the erection of far larger, more powerful and more strongly characteristic local bodies than any we have yet devised, except in London or in Northern Ireland'. He repeated the familiar argument that 'the attempt to transact all affairs great and small at Westminster is attended by grave inconveniences'. Overloaded by 'a multiplicity of business . . . [and] ill-assorted and dispro-portionate functions', Parliament could not 'really fulfil the functions of an Imperial or even of a national assembly'. He now proposed the creation of sixteen (not ten, as in 1911) 'Provincial Councils or Local Parliaments, repre-senting all the well marked historical and geographical areas of Great Britain'. These 'local parliaments', like the states of the USA, would choose the second chamber, he proposed, and – in a measure resembling the French notion of *cumul des mandats* – he would allow politicians to be a member simultaneously of the House of Commons or Lords and of a local parliament. Nothing came of Churchill's plan, although in March 1931 he alluded to it again in his Rectorial Address at Edinburgh University and, in the same month, told the Select Committee on Procedure that he supported devolution of 'the machine work' from Parliament to larger local bodies.[36]

Wales and Scotland post-1945

Although it featured as part of his federal schemes, and Home Rule All Round implied some sort of Welsh parliament, Churchill does not seem to have had a strong sense of Wales as a separate national political entity or to have paid much attention to Wales. He belonged to a generation which took for granted that Wales was, in a sense, part of England – as indeed it basically was in constitutional terms. For instance, until 1967 the term 'England' in an Act of Parliament was explicitly held to include Wales too. 'Almost certainly [Churchill] did not think of it as being any more materi-ally different from England than was, say, Yorkshire,' as John Ramsden puts it. He rarely went there. Labour gibes about Tonypandy and his role in the alleged shooting of Welsh miners obviously rattled him. And as

Conservative leader it was alien territory in that while before the First World War Wales had been a Liberal stronghold, from the 1920s Labour had become the dominant party, and there were only four Conservative MPs there in 1945, rising to six (out of 36) when Churchill became prime minister for the second time in 1951. The Conservatives under Churchill 'had little to gain from wooing the Welsh', as Ramsden notes. In the Liberal heyday, Home Rule had actually been a divisive issue in Welsh politics, nationalists concentrating on cultural issues. The Labour Party was centralist, Aneurin Bevan famously dismissing Welsh devolution as 'escapism'. In the 1930s Neville Chamberlain had rejected the idea of a minister for Wales, as had Attlee in 1946. In opposition, however, responding to Welsh national sentiment, and trying to outbid Labour, which had created a rather feeble Council of Wales, the Conservatives promised (in 1949) to appoint a minister for Welsh Affairs. But symbolically, the minister who was thus appointed in 1951 turned out to be a Scot sitting for an English seat – the home secretary, Sir David Maxwell-Fyfe. Churchill made it clear to MPs that this part-time minister for Welsh Affairs did not have executive powers, the role really boiling down to making regular visits to and speeches in Wales, and little came of this initiative in terms of policy co-ordination or big initiatives. 'It is a step on the road that they wish to tread,' was all that Churchill would say – but it was a pretty limited step and wider measures of Welsh devolution were a non-starter. Churchill refused to appoint a royal commission to inquire into government in Wales and English-Welsh relations. The creation of the Welsh Office had to wait until Labour returned to power in 1964.[37]

Scotland was a rather different matter: the tradition of Tory Unionism was still strong at this time and (unlike the position later, particularly in the 1980s and 1990s) the Conservatives were successful north of the border and not seen as 'anti-Scottish'. They were in a much stronger electoral position than in Wales, winning 44.8 per cent of the Scottish vote and 31 seats in 1950, rising to 48.6 per cent and 35 seats in 1951. In the 1955 election, a few months after Churchill's retirement, the Conservatives won 36 seats (out of 71) and 50.1 per cent of the vote (they were in fact the only party in the twentieth century to win over 50 per cent of the vote in Scotland). The Conservatives were helped in their battle with Scottish Labour in this period by the Liberals' poor showing and the inability of the SNP to translate widespread but vague and shallow nationalist sentiment into actual votes. The later long-term decline and then collapse in the Conservatives' position in Scotland was not foreseen in Churchill's time.

During the war, the Scottish Office had enjoyed a great deal of autonomy and Churchill had got on well with, and given strong backing to, his Scottish secretary, Labour's Tom Johnston. In 1945 Churchill had rejected the idea of a referendum on the establishment of a Scottish parliament. He believed that Scotland's future was inextricably tied up with England's ('Scotsmen would make a wrong decision if they tried to separate their fortunes from ours,' he said in a 1950 speech: the union was in both England and Scotland's interest). However, in opposition he took up a populist stance, seizing the chance to 'play the Scottish card'. In a case of 'Tory Unionism bedecking itself in tartan' (Andrew Marr), he 'flirted outrageously with nationalist sentiment' (Paul Addison). But it is doubtful if it was ever much more than a useful propaganda stick with which to beat Labour. Back in power after 1951, Churchill's real interest in Scottish affairs was in practice, says Anthony Seldon, 'minimal'.[38]

Churchill aimed to capitalize on and link together anti-Labour and nationalist tides of opinion. Welfare-state nationalization and socialist planning meant centralization and London rule, was roughly the argument. During the 1950 election, in a speech in Edinburgh, he really stirred the pot, condemning 'the supervision, interference and control in the ordinary details of Scottish life and business by the Parliament at Westminster':

> The principle of centralization of government in Whitehall and Westminster is emphasized in a manner not hitherto experienced or contemplated in the Act of Union . . . If England became an absolute Socialist State, owning all the means of production, distribution and exchange, ruled only by politicians and their officials in London offices, I personally cannot feel that Scotland would be bound to accept such a dispensation . . . I would never accept the view that Scotland should be forced into the serfdom of Socialiam as the result of a vote in the House of Commons.

But this indignant and exaggerated language did not mean that he endorsed Home Rule, and (along with Attlee) he refused to meet representatives of the Scottish Convention, who had gathered nearly two million signatures in support of its campaign for a Scottish parliament.[39]

The Conservatives' plans for Scotland were in fact moderate and limited. James Mitchell talks of 'window dressing' and 'minor palliatives': 'not for a moment were they considering establishing any meaningful institutional arrangements likely to promote autonomy'. 'Scottish control of Scottish affairs' was the slogan adopted in 1949. Churchill talked of 'further guarantees of national security and internal independence' for Scotland. With the idea of a Scottish parliament ruled out, however, all this meant was a programme of administrative devolution to give some more functions to the Scottish Office and gestures like the appointment in 1951 of the amiable Lord Home to the new post of minister of state, to act as a deputy to the secretary of state and man-on-the-spot in Edinburgh. 'Go and quell those turbulent Scots,' Churchill said to him, as if he were a pro-consul being sent off to govern some unruly and far-flung province, 'and don't come back until you've done it.' A royal commission on Scottish government was also set up, its report in 1954 producing some minor administrative changes and tidying-up. Churchill welcomed the report as largely endorsing the existing arrangements for the exercise of government functions in Scotland.[40] None of this was remotely like or intended to be the thin end of the wedge of a move to a quasi-federal Britain of the type Churchill had dreamed about forty years before. The aim was simply to reassure the Scots that they were not being ignored or forgotten, and to continue the process of government through the framework of the established institutions of the United Kingdom. With the benefit of hindsight it might look a complacent strategy, but it is understandable given the absence in the 1950s of deep popular discontent with the UK's governing arrangements, with Labour's face also set against legislative devolution, and with the lack of any serious separatist threat (all of these were to change in later decades, catching the Conservatives out).

Churchill and Local Government

'I refuse to be shut up in a soup kitchen with Mrs Sidney Webb,' Churchill remarked in 1908, rejecting the post of president of the Local Government

Board. He even told Asquith that he would rather remain a junior minister at the Colonial Office outside the cabinet than go there. 'There is no place in the Government more laborious, more anxious, more thankless, more choked with petty & even squalid detail, more full of hopeless and insoluble difficulties,' he wrote to the prime minister. He knew nothing, he said, of the 'basic subjects' – the poor law and rating issues (local government finance). Although interested in the idea of social reform (and accepting the Board of Trade), he pleaded that he lacked training and background in the details of domestic politics. The implication was clear: local government was too boring and tedious for Churchill to want to deal with.[41]

'Churchill knew little of local government', as Paul Addison says.[42] He paid relatively little attention to it throughout his career and – with one exception, in the 1920s – there seems to have been little detailed engagement on his part with issues of local government operation or reform.

In his reforming 'New Liberal' period, he at one time linked the need for 'active and increasing social construction and reconstruction' with the idea of 'skilled professional Mayors on the German model instead of our present happy-go-lucky amateur system'. He wondered whether this might go together with the creation of a national and unified organization of municipal and local government officials, 'animated by a high spirit of corporate honour'. Though these officials would doubtless be of a somewhat lower standard than the civil servants in Whitehall, he mused, the reform might provide 'more skilled advice to town councillors and provincial mayors' and 'enhance the dignity and efficiency of surveyors, electricians, boro [*sic*] architects, poor law officers, sanitary inspectors, and all that body of minor officials indispensable to modern local government'.[43]

Churchill was concerned about 'the over-centralization of government' and what he called in 1911 'the overpowering influence of London'. He wondered how the country's 'great cities' could 'effectively correct and resist the undue dominance and predominance of this great centralized capital'. Between the House of Commons and the municipalities and counties, he said, 'there is under our system nothing at all – nothing but a growing system of bureaucratic control'. Bureaucratic control, he warned, could stifle local initiative. 'Centralized control might give guidance, might be a corrective, might be a complement to, but it can never be a substitute for local effort.' But he also saw the need for consolidation of the fragmented and patchwork structure of local government. 'I have no hesitation in saying larger units of local government are required for the welfare and active development of our country,' he stated in 1912. As a minister at the Board of Trade and at the Home Office, says Paul Addison, he had been 'impressed by the chaotic multiplicity of minor local authorities'. This was linked to his devolution ideas. As a backbencher in 1904, he had called for 'the expansion, elevation, and aggrandizement of local bodies, until they strain provincial proportions and perhaps even national proportions'. Devolution in this light involved for him 'an extension of local government, far beyond the limits which we have at present'. His 'heptarchy' scheme of 1911, as presented secretly to his cabinet colleagues, would have seen the new provincial assemblies take over all the functions of county councils and some of the powers of municipal councils (though he did not mention this point when he 'went public' in his September 1912 Dundee speech). Some reformers might have welcomed this sort of rationalization, the *Manchester Guardian*, for instance, commenting in 1912 that 'for fully one-half of the work of local government the present units are too small for efficiency'. The *Municipal Journal* realized, however, that Churchill's scheme would involve the breakdown of counties, which were among the oldest parts of the constitution and the oldest local governing units in the land. This challenge to local vested interests would surely have met fierce resistance from many councils and local political networks.[44]

In 1925, as noted above, Churchill returned to this issue, linking the proposed reform of the House of Lords with a move to a quasi-federal system, based around a number of 'Provincial Councils' or 'Local Parliaments'. 'The need for larger units of local government is deep and obvious,' he argued in a cabinet memorandum about this plan. 'I have for twenty years wished to see Great Britain equipped with modern bodies of great local authority. I believe such a system might be attended by a diminution in the multiplicity of elections and by much simplification over the whole field of local government.' With 'a far more spacious structure of local government', as he put it, 'these larger local bodies' could take on responsibilities and powers 'much beyond those which are conferred at present'. Along with this would go a recasting of the system of local finance. Noting the plans to move to a new system of 'block grants' to local councils, which he approved of (Whitehall grants accounting for about a quarter of local government expenditure in the 1920s), Churchill wondered 'Ought we not to go further?' 'The spending by one authority of funds provided by another is bound to be subversive of thrifty housekeeping,' he warned. 'Ought we not to assign them . . . a share in revenues they do not now possess, but which revenues rise or fall with the general prosperity of the nation?' he asked, hinting at wider tax-raising powers for these bigger local councils, relieving the national exchequer of what he called 'ill-adjusted burdens'.

Nothing came of these (very sketchy) ideas. Neville Chamberlain, minister of health in the Baldwin government (1924–9), was the cabinet's local government expert and had his own agenda, centred on rating reform, poor law reform, and more centralized financial control through block grants. He was not happy at Churchill's involvement and interference in his schemes. Lloyd George once damned Neville Chamberlain as a good lord mayor of Birmingham in a lean year (he had actually been a successful leader of the council). But Churchill argued that British politics would benefit by an influx of people like him, 'who had attained eminence . . . not merely by House of Commons sword-play or successful electioneering [Churchill's own route] . . . but also by records of administrative achievement, by years of service and of proved capacity in powerful local bodies'. He paid tribute to the patriarch of the Chamberlain clan: 'We have not seen, since the days of Mr Joseph Chamberlain, a man attain the first rank in politics by municipal service and move like him quite easily and naturally from the head of a great municipal body to a situation in the Cabinet.'[45]

Neville Chamberlain and Churchill clashed seriously over Churchill's 'big idea' about derating reform in 1927–8. Chamberlain was (accurately enough) concerned that his impetuous colleague was more interested in forging ahead with large and bold schemes than in grappling with the details and practicalities of local government finance, a subject about which he was largely ignorant ('Of course, I know very little about the rating system,' Churchill once told Baldwin). Although he shared Churchill's declared aim to 'establish a sound relation between national and local finance, with proper incentive to economy and real responsibility for local bodies', Chamberlain was not won over by Churchill's talk of a reform of 'the whole system' of local government 'as famous as that of 1834'. Churchill's plan was basically to exempt industry and agriculture from local taxation, transferring the burden (amounting to about a quarter of the total raised through the rating system) to national taxation, and raising the new central government revenue needed to fill the gap mainly from defence cuts, a new fuel tax and a profits tax on industry. Churchill wanted, he said, 'to take the Producers out of the Medieval Rating system'. He revealed a markedly centralist attitude, however. The rates were 'dependent upon the caprice of local elections' and varied in different parts of the country ('handicapping businesses which ought to have an equal chance on economic merits'). In contrast the Treasury wanted the profits tax to be paid at a uniform rate over the whole country and then the funds to be redistributed from the centre. 'True economy can only be achieved by an administrative machine like the Treasury, well removed and carefully protected from electoral influences,' one of Churchill's civil servants told him – a view completely subversive of the principle of local government independence. Chamberlain feared that if local industry was freed from local taxation, it would cease to have any direct interest in 'good' (meaning economical) administration. To which Harold Macmillan (advising Churchill on the scheme) replied: 'If the fat kine [cows] are taken away, the lean kine will have nothing left to devour but their own proletarian hides.' But Churchill was as concerned as Chamberlain about the need to check 'the forces making for extravagant expenditure on social services'. Rather than the 'spasmodic influence' that local industry might or might not be able to exert, however, he argued that his plan would place a 'more powerful, direct and continuing pressure' on the mass of local government electors, 'who would experience in greater measure than at present the ill-effects of extravagant administration and on the other hand enjoy in greater degree the fruits of thrifty management'. (Decades later, in the 1980s, a similar argument was used to justify the 'poll tax'.) After fierce arguments over the details (Chamberlain insisting that the reduced industrial rate should still be raised by local councils, for instance), a derating scheme was introduced in Churchill's 1928 budget. The whole complex and tangled controversy did nothing for Chamberlain's estimation of Churchill, who certainly showed a considerable degree of ignorance and inexperience in the local government field.[46]

As prime minister, Churchill seems largely to have confined himself to platitudes on the rare occasions when he mentioned local government at all. 'The government are . . . very much alive to the need for avoiding any weakening of the structure of local government,' he told MPs in 1943, ruling out at that time 'a comprehensive inquiry into the machinery of local government'. In the later 1940s he echoed standard Conservative attacks on Labour centralization and the transfer of local functions like health to unelected boards – 'much has been done to injure and even, in some cases, to destroy local government,' he told the 1949 party conference. 'We shall strive to invest local government with renewed confidence in itself and with full responsibility,' he said. 'Our guiding aim will be to stimulate rather than to strangle, to liberate rather than to hobble, all the energies of local government . . . Above all, Conservatives will take care that local government remains local – and remains a true reflection of the communities which it exists to serve, rather than become a mere appendage, or even utensil, of any government that rules in Westminster.' He pledged that a Conservative government would 'consult with all local authorities in the overhaul of their areas, functions, and financial arrangements'. However, his local government minister after 1951, Harold Macmillan, while aware of the problems and the need for a reorganization of local government structures and functions, had few definite ideas about what to do and was wary of the host of vested interests making any reform difficult. Large-scale local government reorganization was effectively shelved until the Maud Commission in the late 1960s followed by the 1972 Local Government Act, introduced under the next Conservative prime minister but three, Edward Heath.[47]

Conclusion

In October 1913 Churchill made a speech in his Dundee constituency in which he talked about the 'establishment of a federal system in the United Kingdom', one in which 'Scotland, Ireland, and Wales, and, if necessary, parts of England, could have separate legislation and Parliamentary institutions to enable them to develop in their own way their own life according to their own ideas and needs'. He was speaking, he said, of a 'subject which lay for the moment outside the immediate sphere of practical politics'; he was 'raising a question for reflection and discussion rather than for prompt action'. It was a subject, he argued, currently 'beneath the threshold of national consciousness', but 'it will some day spring into full and vigorous reality', he predicted. 'The day will most certainly come,' he told his audience, and 'many of you will live to see it come, when a federal system will be established in these islands, which will give Wales and Scotland control, within proper limits, of their own Welsh and Scottish affairs.' And such a system, he thought, would be 'the forerunner and the nucleus of a general scheme of Imperial federation', gathering together 'in one indissoluble circle the British peoples here and beyond the seas'.[48]

Over eighty years – a rather longer period than Churchill had anticipated – were to pass before this prediction was fulfilled, with the creation of the Scottish Parliament and the Welsh Assembly, which held their first elections in 1999. And only in 2002 did the Labour government publish a white paper setting out cautious plans for elected assemblies in the English regions, which might in practice be slow to get off the ground and then only in a few regions at first (depending on local referendums). What Churchill had called (in 1925) the 'missing storey' of the UK's institutional structure has been very slow to appear, and then in an incomplete fashion. It would be wrong, of course, to view Churchill as a uniquely far-sighted and original statesman in this respect, or the structures that started to emerge and take shape after 1997 as being in a direct line of development from his long-ago ideas and schemes. The idea of a grand imperial federation has long vanished, and was in any case at odds with the counter-tendency towards looser ties. Many people and organizations had been devising and pressing for schemes of UK devolution, federalism and Home Rule before Churchill came on the scene, alongside him (particularly before 1914) and afterwards. He was interested in these ideas but never himself developed anything like a detailed federal blueprint. Ireland before 1914 apart, in Churchill's time the forces of political nationalism were weak. For instance, the Scottish National Party won only 0.5 per cent of the Scottish vote in the 1955 election, just after Churchill finally left Downing Street. Only in the 1970s did the SNP emerge as a serious electoral force, with Plaid Cymru in Wales lagging behind. Events, politics and politicians long after Churchill's retirement and death are responsible for the process of UK devolution now under way, but it is a process he would have understood and broadly welcomed.

The debates and events and problems of his time still have a fascination and relevance, however. Ireland is an intriguing 'what if' issue. It is *possible* that if the proposals for Irish Home Rule together with special treatment for Ulster (exclusion or a separate sub–parliament) that Churchill (along with Lloyd George) had supported in 1912 had been adopted, then the twenty-six counties of the Republic of Ireland, and not just the six counties of Northern Ireland, might still be part of the United Kingdom (or might have remained part of the UK for longer than they did). There is something to the argument that the spring of 1912 was the last chance for a Home Rule settlement of the Irish question, and that Carson and Bonar Law might at that stage have been open to and been able to deliver a compromise – but they were not by 1914, by which time the situation had spiralled virtually out of control.[49]

As for contemporary relevance, it is clear that Churchill recognized that the creation of English regional assemblies would have consequences for local government in the country's towns and counties, not least because his devolution ideas involved not just a transfer of powers and responsibilities *down* from Westminster and Whitehall, but also *up* from local councils to the regional level. Local politicians and commentators in 1912 were quick to spot this, and it remains an issue today. The implications of the contemporary move to elected regional assemblies for the structure and functions of English local government will be controversial and possibly destabilizing in some areas. A rolling process of devolution is currently envisaged with some regions perhaps pushing ahead to set up assemblies ahead of others. At some times Churchill seemed to be expecting a sort of 'top down' imposition of a regional structure on the country; at other times, he seemed more tentative – in 1912, for instance, identifying Yorkshire, Lancashire, the Midlands and London as 'four great areas in England which might well have a conscious political identity, an effective political machinery, bestowed upon them'. 'There are other parts of England which it is not nearly so easy to deal with,' he admitted. Without wanting to over-interpret his remarks, it could be that they contain the germs of the seed of rolling regional devolution. Then, as now, in Churchill's words, 'The questions which are raised by the adoption of a federal system in England are very difficult' – but we will have to see whether he was right to believe that they were 'not insoluble'.[50]

For all his involvement with the Irish question, however, and his long-term interest in federalism, Churchill was pre-eminently a Westminster-centred English politician with national, international and imperial interests. His remark in 1904, quoted above, about how devolution would stop the House of Commons from being clogged with minor details and provide more opportunities to debate 'the most exciting questions' and 'urgent' matters tells it all. He was consistent in his concern to uphold the political and constitutional supremacy of Westminster and the central state. Although he sat for a Scottish seat from 1908 until 1922, Churchill's real interest in the UK's 'Celtic fringe' (Scotland, Wales and Ireland) was limited. The language he used to describe the UK's political and constitutional structure is revealing: very often he can be found speaking or writing of the English monarchy, the English constitution, the English prime minister, Parliament as an English assembly, the English people or nation or race, and so on. Running together England, Britain and the United Kingdom in this way is a characteristically English practice. In terms of Jim Bulpitt's model of the United Kingdom as a 'Dual Polity', Churchill spent his career in, operated at, and was mainly concerned with the 'high politics' of the 'centre' rather than the 'low politics' of the 'territorial periphery'. He supported devolution to the 'periphery' to further the interests of the 'centre'.[51]

As a 'centre' politician of the capital city, he was also much, much too big a political figure to be bothered much about local government and local politics. In April 1956, a year after he left Downing Street, notes he prepared for a constituency speech read: 'Local govt is one of our oldest institutions, and it is important tt it shd continue to flourish and to attract responsible citizens. This cannot be if the Town Hall becomes a mere rubber stamp or local branch of Whitehall. You are elected to administer your Boro, and you must be allowed to do so w the least possible interference from the centre.'[52] These words were delivered in Hawkey Hall in Woodford, named after a distinguished local government worthy, who had combined long service on the local urban district council with a role as Churchill's constituency party chairman and right-hand man. Churchill could recognize the importance and value of local government and of this sort of local public service, but it goes without saying that he personally would have found its confines and limited scope maddening and intolerable.

FOUR

'Trust the People'

Churchill always made much of Lord Randolph Churchill's celebrated slogan 'Trust the people'. But what did this mean for political practice and governing arrangements under the British constitution? Who were 'the people'? How were they to exercise their power in the democratic government of Britain? For Churchill 'the people' were the electorate, and the main issues about them and their role that he faced during his political career concerned votes for women, the workings of the electoral system (including the question of proportional representation and electoral reform), and the referendum as a device of direct, rather than representative, democracy.

Votes for Women

In 1900, when Churchill first became an MP, the electorate consisted of 6.7 million men. By 1918 it had increased in size to 21.4 million voters, including 8.4 million women (40 per cent). By 1929 it had grown to 28.9 million, of which 15.2 million were women (52 per cent). (And by the time of Churchill's last election, in 1959, the electorate numbered over 35 million.) In October 1927, after the government had committed itself to an equal franchise for men and women, he told a constituency audience in Chingford that 'we must not only trust the people . . . but trust the whole people'. But he made no secret of his unhappiness about this extension and democratization of the franchise. And before the First World War he had, at best, been 'ambivalent' in his attitude towards the question of women's suffrage – or, according to more hostile accounts, 'downright hypocritical' on the subject.[1]

'I do not think our system less democratic because women are not enfranchised,' Churchill made clear at a meeting in Dundee in January 1910. Women, he argued, could make their influence felt at home and 'manage to fix it out somehow or other' with their menfolk. The House of Commons was a democratic assembly, he had argued in December 1909, because it represented over six million electors 'and a great many more who bring their influence to bear directly and indirectly' (presumably meaning women and the 40 per cent of men who were not enfranchised at that time).[2]

Neither Churchill's father, Lord Randolph, nor his mother, Lady Randolph, had supported votes for women. As a young army officer in India, Churchill had expressed (in 1897) some conventional chauvinistic views about women and politics. He opposed votes for women on the grounds that 'it is contrary to natural law and the practice of civilized states' and that 'no necessity is shown'. Only 'the most undesirable class of women' were eager for the right to vote, he maintained. 'Those women who discharge their duty to the state – viz. marrying & giving birth to children – are adequately represented by their husbands.' Unmarried women could only claim a vote on the basis of property, and he thought that such a 'claim on democratic principles is inadmissible'. The female suffrage movement was, he insisted, 'ridiculous'. He was disturbed by the idea that 'If you give women votes you must ultimately allow women to sit as members of Parliament'. 'Once you give votes to the vast numbers of women who form the majority of the community,' he concluded, 'all power passes to their hands.' And he was concerned that then 'every kind of hysterical fad would gain strength' and that 'religion would become much more intolerant'.[3]

He did support the 'extension of the Franchise to every male', as part of 'the creed of Tory Democracy', he told Lady Randolph Churchill. 'Ultimately "one man, one vote" is logically and morally certain,' he wrote in private notes at this time. But the question was 'the rate at which we move to so desirable a goal'. He believed that 'material comfort . . . and education should precede responsibility'. Votes should only be given to persons 'who can read and write and who are engaged in some fixed employment which brings in an adequate remuneration'. On this basis the unemployed and casually employed working men would not have the vote, or presumably the illiterate – and one estimate is that about 20 per cent of the poor working class were in practice illiterate in 1900. Churchill stated that he would extend the franchise 'not by giving votes to the ignorant and indigent, but by raising those classes to the standard when votes may safely be given'. 'This will take time,' he recognized. 'As each class becomes fit it can be enfranchised. The principle is one of levelling up.' Opposed to votes for women in 1897, he was thus also extremely cautious about extending the male franchise.[4]

Votes for women was a complex and tricky political question. It was not, as Geoffrey Best points out, 'the straightforward human rights issue simplistically imagined by the unhistorical'. Since 1869 women ratepayers had been allowed to vote in municipal elections, and women in the late nineteenth century had begun participating in local politics and became active in party organizations and as election canvassers. New Zealand (in 1893) and the Commonwealth of Australia (1902) had enacted women's suffrage, and at Westminster backbenchers had introduced suffrage bills in the Commons. But while many men had no vote (about 60 per cent had the vote after 1885) and some men (over half a million) had more than one vote – the plural voters, so qualified as university graduates or business property owners – difficulties arose over not just the principle but also the basis on which the vote could or should be given to women. Short of full adult suffrage there was, as Paul Addison notes, 'no simple or logical' way in which to proceed. Over four-fifths of men qualified for the vote as householders; any formula that enfranchised women on a householder or other propertied basis would be socially skewed in its effects – and skewed also in its likely party-political impact (although the politicians were inevitably coy about articulating this latter concern in public). The issue of women's suffrage was therefore bound up with broader questions about franchise reform.[5]

Churchill actually voted in Parliament in favour of a female suffrage bill in March 1904, a time when he was negotiating for the Liberal seat of Manchester North-West and in the process of crossing the floor. Addison suggests that his decision to support votes for women then might have been motivated by his need to stand well with Manchester radicals and Liberals. That city was also the birthplace of the Women's Social and Political Union (WSPU), founded in October 1903 by Mrs Emmeline Pankhurst. The suffragettes of the WSPU soon adopted militant tactics, disrupting public meetings, interrupting speakers and staging noisy demonstrations (later they became more violent: smashing windows and burning down houses). As a prominent figure, Churchill found himself on the receiving end of the WSPU's direct action. They caused a great deal of disorder and pandemonium at his election meetings in 1906, and later in Dundee in 1908, when a lady ringing a large dinner bell took to following him round and interrupting his speeches. And on two occasions later (in 1909 and 1910) he was physically attacked by WSPU supporters wielding whips.[6]

Churchill regarded the suffragettes' methods as undemocratic and counter productive. He told a 'Women's Freedom League' meeting in Dundee in October 1909 that 'In the beginning the militant tactics were of some advantage to them and their cause by directing attention to it'. But now, he continued, 'the effect of these tactics had been entirely unfavourable. They had practically made it impossible for either great party or any public men to come forward in their support.' At a meeting in January 1906, provoked by constant suffragette interruptions and uproar, he had lost his temper and burst out that 'having regard to the treatment I have received . . . nothing will induce me to vote for giving votes to women'. Calming down, he backtracked a little by saying that he was 'not so hostile to the proposal' as he had just said but that he was 'not going to be hen–pecked' on such an important matter. At the Dundee meeting in 1909 he said that his view of the merits of the women's suffrage question had not changed since his 1904 vote in favour. But he argued that the militant tactics of 'silly disorder and petty violence' were harming their cause and that the time was not ripe for enfranchising women while the militancy continued. The government and the House of Commons would not give them what they sought in these circumstances. The women's cause had 'marched backwards', he said. 'The frenzy of a few is no substitute for the earnest convictions and wishes of millions.' As he said a few months later, in January 1910: 'Some day I hope women will have votes too. But they will have to adopt another plan to get them.'[7]

Another method was adopted in the spring of 1910 when a pressure group, the Conciliation Committee, tried to promote female suffrage legislation on a non–party basis. The group's leaders, Lord Lytton and H. N. Brailsford, approached Churchill and other leading politicians, for support and he told them in April 1910: 'I do not wish to be committed at the present juncture to any special form or basis in or upon which the franchise is to be granted to women,' but he did also say that he was 'anxious to see women relieved in principle from a disability which is injurious to them whilst it is based on grounds of sex'. The Conciliation Committee's scheme would have enfranchised women with a household qualification and when the Liberal whips saw it they objected to that feature, Churchill telling Lytton that he had learned that his draft bill was 'open to many objections on the grounds of being partial and undemocratic'. Churchill also expressed to Brailsford doubts about the details of the plan, being concerned about the potential for so-called 'faggot voting' – wealthy men creating votes for their wives and daughters by letting to them pieces of property to the value of £10. Despite these warnings, the bill's sponsors were outraged when Churchill subsequently spoke out and voted against it in July 1910, and accused him of treachery.[8]

According to Lucy Masterman, Churchill – whom she described as a 'rather tepid' suffragist – had been intending to vote for the bill but at a crucial point his junior minister at the Home Office, Charles Masterman (her husband), told him that Lloyd George was opposed to it and put to him the arguments against.

> Winston began to see the opportunity for a speech on these lines, and as he paced up and down the room, began to roll off long phrases. By the end of the morning he was convinced that he had always been hostile to the Bill and that he had already thought of all these points himself . . . Charlie thinks that his *mind* had up till then been in favour of the suffrage but that his *instinct* was always against it. He snatched at Charlie's arguments against this particular Bill as a wild animal snatches at its food. At the end the instinct had completely triumphed over the mind.[9]

Churchill started his speech on 12 July 1910 by saying that he believed that there was 'a proportion of women capable of exercising the Parliamentary franchise, not merely for their own satisfaction, but to the public advantage . . . [and] the State would be the gainer if they had the vote and . . . [also] access in the fullest sense to all positions in our public life'. Then came the 'buts'. He argued that 'the grievance is greatly exaggerated', that women were not 'in any sensible degree losers by the disability under which they lie', and that the great mass of women did not want the vote. He denounced the bill as 'anti-democratic' and 'one-sided' because it gave 'an entirely unfair representation to property, as against persons'. The door would be opened to a great multiplication of 'faggot votes' which would be to the electoral advantage of the Conservatives. There would also be a number of other 'grotesque absurdities', he argued. Mothers and wives would be denied the vote unless they met the property qualification. The working man's wife would not be enfranchised, even if she were a wage-earner, but the young daughters of the well-off and the 'spinster of means' would be. A prostitute might qualify for the vote, he claimed, but would lose it if she married and became 'an honest woman', only to regain the franchise if she divorced. It was a violent and bitter speech, as Lucy Masterman said, tempered only slightly by his suggestion of alternative ways forward. The vote could be given, he proposed, 'to some of the best women of all classes', a 'comparatively small number of women' being enfranchised through a series of 'special franchises' relating to property, wage-earning capacity or education. Women would not have votes on the same basis as men, and it would not be a fully democratic proposal, he admitted, but it would provide for the representation of 'the strongest, most capable, and most responsible women of every class'. The only other scheme worth consideration, he asserted, would be 'a broad measure of adult suffrage . . . by which every person should have a vote over the age of twenty-five years'.[10]

The bill was carried on its second reading by 299 to 189 votes but it subsequently ran into the sands when the government refused to make any time available. Addison wonders whether Churchill's vehement attack on it revealed 'an underlying antipathy to female enfranchisement'. In public at any rate he stuck to the line he had taken up over the Conciliation Bill. 'The sex disqualification was not a true or logical disqualification,' he said at Dundee in December 1910, and he was in favour of the principle of women being enfranchised. 'But he declined utterly to pledge himself to any particular Bill at the present time.' It is certainly the case that he remained interested in the restrictive scheme he had mentioned in his July 1910 speech and limiting the number of women enfranchised as far as possible.

On 17 July 1910, a few days after his speech, Sir Edward Troup, his permanent secretary at the Home Office, sent him a memorandum adding some flesh to the bare bones of his idea, suggesting votes for certain categories of women: (a) those with higher educational qualifications, (b) those who had served on local authorities, and (c) those who – with husbands qualified for the vote by residence – had at least two children. The aim was to 'satisfy the strongest claims' but 'not add enormously to the mass of voters', noted Troup, who thought that groups (a) and (b) would add only about 20,000 votes and (c) less than a million. In a subsequent note, in August 1910, the figures and categories were slightly reworked, giving an estimate of 2.2 million out of the total of nine million women over the age of twenty-five getting the vote (some 200,000 professional and educated women, the rest with children up to fifteen years old). Nearly eighteen months later, in January 1912, Churchill told C. P. Scott, the editor of the *Manchester Guardian* that he would grant the vote to 'the women who really want and need it – graduates, doctors, poor law Guardians and members of town councils – by categories, as many as could be devised, perhaps 100,000 in all'. Churchill knew that this approach would not be widely acceptable – Lloyd George told him that he was 'on the wrong track' with his 'fancy franchise' idea – and it is possible that he was partly floating it as a 'wrecking' tactic because of resentment at the treatment meted out to him by the suffragettes. But it is of a piece with his generally elitist outlook on politics. He had claimed in July 1910 that he would be in favour of adult suffrage 'at the proper time and circumstances'. But as he told Lord Riddell in March 1912, 'The truth is we already have enough ignorant voters and we don't want any more.'[11]

Clementine Churchill was ardently in favour of votes for women and, according to Mary Soames, privately lobbied Churchill, but the most he would ever do was express support in general and carefully qualified terms. With the Liberal government embroiled in its struggle with the House of Lords and then preoccupied with Irish Home Rule, not to speak of other problems it faced and its social reform policies, he did not think that the issue was a priority. Ministers were split, with the prime minister, Asquith, opposed in principle to votes for women (and fighting a subtle obstructive and delaying campaign), while Sir Edward Grey and Lloyd George were among the supporters of the cause of women's suffrage. On becoming home secretary in 1910 Churchill had made concessions on prison discipline and routine, which had met many of the suffragettes' complaints about how they had been treated in prison, but he would make no concessions about forcible feeding of hunger strikers. The suffragettes' ire against him intensified after the virtual pitched battle between police and demonstrators in Parliament Square on 18 November 1910 ('Black Friday'), when there were hundreds of arrests and very aggressive and heavy-handed police treatment of suffragettes. Churchill claimed that his orders to the police had not been properly followed and ordered the immediate release of those taken into custody, but he refused calls for an impartial inquiry, and the events (followed a few days later by violent scuffles in Downing Street, during which Churchill showed up, shouting to the police: 'Take that woman away! She is obviously one of the ringleaders!') damaged both the government and him personally.[12]

In November 1911 Asquith announced that the government would introduce in the next parliamentary session legislation extending the franchise to (virtually) all men, leaving it to the Commons to decide whether it should be amended to give women the vote. The WSPU believed that this was a trick, designed to hold off votes for women as a general franchise extension scheme was sure to get bogged down in inter-party arguments, and suffragette militancy increased. Churchill, however, believed that votes for women was now a real possibility and was convinced that the government might break up over the issue. In December 1911 he frantically lobbied the prime minister, the chief whip and other top ministers (Grey and Lloyd George) with the argument that there should be a referendum on the issue (an idea he had floated at the December 1910 election). The Franchise Bill would not get through without a dissolution if it contained a clause adding eight million women to the electorate, and nor ought it to get through, he argued. Votes for women was so unpopular that by-elections would be unfavourable. The prime minister could not be expected to use the Parliament Act to force through a measure he had declared publicly to be 'disastrous'. The King would be entitled to refuse his consent, and could point out that the electorate had never been consulted on the measure. The government could fall, brought down by what he dismissed as 'petticoat politics'. With it would go down the Irish cause. (A year later, in January

1913, Churchill is said to have gone round Irish MPs, using the threat of Asquith's resignation, the fall of the government and the danger to Home Rule to stir up opposition to women's suffrage.) He did not conceal from Asquith his hope that a referendum would result in votes for women being 'smashed', although Lord Curzon warned him that the suffragettes would not necessarily accept the result of an unfavourable referendum and might then campaign even more violently. Churchill's alarmist arguments and his cynical referendum proposal do suggest that the suffrage campaigners were right to regard him as an enemy.[13]

The government pressed on with its plans for a Franchise Bill, however. Churchill repeated his argument for restricting the franchise to those aged twenty-five years, telling Grey in February 1912 that it would not be 'a violent reduction, but a perfectly reasonable improvement of our representation'. The assumption was that younger adults were more likely to be apathetic, politically unsophisticated, or irresponsible. (Since the qualifying age of twenty-one had been in place for 500 years, Churchill was planning to put the clock back in dramatic fashion in this respect.) In January 1913 he opposed the extension of the vote, under the terms of the bill, to soldiers living in barracks, warning in overheated terms of the dangers of stimulating a 'class campaign' for the improvement of soldiers' conditions and of soldiers acting like a trade union, able to enforce their will 'by the use of lethal weapons'. Later that month the Speaker of the Commons threw a spanner into the works by ruling that female suffrage amendments to the Franchise Bill would be out of order and the government decided to withdraw it. WSPU militancy continued and intensified but the Liberal government made no further attempts to deal with the women's suffrage issue before the outbreak of war. The stalemate suited Churchill.[14]

The dynamics of the suffrage question were changed dramatically in and by the war, and the 1918 Representation of the People Act extended the vote to virtually all men and to women over the age of thirty, Churchill not being in the government when the crucial decisions were taken about franchise reform in 1916–17. However, his attitude may be gauged from his comment in 1927 to his civil service private secretary that when the franchise was extended in 1918 'a whole mob of the worst class of voters was embraced'. About a third of women were left without the vote after 1918 – the politicians wanting to keep women in a minority in the electorate and to enfranchise only what they regarded as stable and mature family women. Nevertheless, it was recognized that an equal franchise and the removal of this limitation was in time inevitable – with Conservatives in particular hoping to delay any change.[15]

In March 1924, fighting the Westminster by-election, Churchill 'declared flatly against any further extension [of the franchise] for at least ten years'. In October 1924 his line was that 'while the principle of an equal franchise for both sexes was indisputable it was too soon to make a new large expansion of the electorate'. Baldwin had said in 1924 that the Conservatives favoured 'equal political rights for men and women' and promised an all-party conference to settle the matter. But speaking in Parliament in February 1925 the home secretary, Sir William Joynson-Hix, went beyond the agreed cabinet line, committing the government to action by pledging equal rights 'at the next election'. This triggered disputes within the cabinet, with Churchill and Lord Birkenhead (F. E. Smith) leading the opposition to legislation. Conservative Central Office was worried about the mill-girls' vote: that the enfranchisement of younger working women, subject to the influence of trade unions, would boost Labour in industrial areas and harm the Tories, something which concerned Churchill. Conservatives also had a low opinion of the political capabilities of the 'flappers', linked to a frankly pessimistic view of the electorate as a whole. For his part, Churchill was alarmed at the projected great increase in the size of the electorate and felt that with politics in a molten state in the 1920s – with the aftermath of the war, revolution abroad, the general strike at home, the advance of Labour – it was best to be cautious and prudent. 'Before any such plunge is taken there ought to be a reasonable certainty that the vast new electorate of 1918 has been digested and properly incorporated into the various Party organizations,' he argued, in a cabinet paper about the female suffrage in March 1927. There were echoes also of his views of 1897, when he described a decision to enfranchise five or six million new female voters as one which would 'finally . . . transfer the control of our affairs to a majority of women'. He wanted to put off action until after the next election. The idea of increasing the voting age also resurfaced. Many Conservatives would have liked to raise the voting age to twenty-five (for men and women), but that was unacceptable to the Labour Party and it was politically unrealistic to imagine that the vote could be taken away from men aged twenty-one to twenty-five. Churchill said that he would have been prepared to support as a compromise 'an equal residential qualification at 25 and an equal occupational qualification at 21 for both sexes'. This 'would involve the risk of universal suffrage at a later stage', he admitted, but 'would satisfy all legitimate demands without any real breach of principle'. The cabinet in the end decided in favour of equal votes at twenty-one, but Churchill insisted on having his dissent formally recorded in the cabinet minutes.[16]

In public speeches in 1927, Churchill said that he 'accepted' the decision of the cabinet, but strongly signalled his dissent. He privately told Baldwin in June 1927 that he hoped that the House of Lords would reject the Equal Franchise Bill and he described the prospect of having to vote for the measure as one 'which I should have more difficulty over and dislike more than anything that has ever happened in my public life'. He reluctantly accepted that 'the Flappers' Vote', as he called it, had become 'inevitable'. But he was deliberately absent (as were 134 other Conservative MPs) from the second reading vote in the House of Commons on 29 March 1928. By the end of 1928, however, he had come to the view (like many other Conservative MPs) that the change could well work out to the Conservatives' advantage: a large proportion of the new voters were 'of classes or in situations predominantly Conservative', he told Lord Rothermere, and women were 'on the whole . . . slightly more conservative than men'. And later, reflecting on the Conservatives' election defeat in 1929, he admitted that his earlier fears had been groundless: 'I do not think that the new electorate will in the long run prove adverse to Conservative interests . . . All the women have given very much the same verdict as in the same circumstances would have come from all the men.' 'It did not turn out as badly as I thought,' was his view by 1947, when he recognized that 'They are a strong prop to the Tories'.[17]

This analysis was correct: far from it harming them, the Conservatives prospered in the mass universal franchise electorate created in 1928, and particularly benefited from equal votes for women, a 'gender gap' in voting being detectable, with women being more likely than men to vote Conservative right up to the Thatcher era (the 'gender gap' disappeared in the 1980s). But if Churchill had had his way women in their twenties would not have got the vote until perhaps some time in the 1930s, and the Conservative Party would probably have been damaged, not least by being outbid in the franchise reform stakes by Labour on 'democratic' and 'equality' grounds. Before 1914 the influence of the supporters of women's suffrage had been weakened at cabinet level by Churchill's equivocations and his unradical stance – if he had been firmly allied with Lloyd George on the matter their cause would have had more political force (though still perhaps not enough to overcome the problems and obstacles).[18] In the 1920s, his stance was more one of trying to delay the inevitable, a reluctant democrat unhappy about the pace and scale of the franchise changes since the pre-war days. Even in the early 1930s there is evidence that he remained concerned that the young female voters enfranchised in 1928 were a potentially 'irresponsible' and destabilizing element in the electorate, and this view fed into his support for extra 'plural votes' for the more responsible citizens (see below). Churchill only slowly came to 'trust the whole people'.

Elections and Electoral Reform

In his essay 'Election Memories', printed in his 1932 book *Thoughts and Adventures*, Churchill claimed to have fought more parliamentary elections than any living member of the House of Commons – he had fought fifteen up to that time, and in fact over his whole career he fought twenty-one elections between his first, the Oldham by-election in July 1899 and his last, the 1959 general election. He won sixteen of these campaigns and lost five contests (including three in a row between November 1922 and March 1924). 'I do not like elections,' he admitted. Calculating that each election dominated about a month of his life apiece (including the campaign and a period afterwards 'when you are convalescing and paying the bills'), he worked out that by the age of fifty-six he had spent considerably more than a whole year of his life 'under these arduous and worrying conditions' (with more to come after 1932).[19]

He described the 1924 by-election campaign for the Abbey division of Westminster as 'the most exciting, stirring, sensational' election he had ever fought. (He drove around London's West End in a horse-drawn coach with a trumpeter on the box, was aided by the chorus girls of Daly's Theatre, whom he said sat up all night addressing envelopes and despatching his election address, and lost by only forty-three votes as an 'Independent Anti-Socialist'.) But he believed that on the whole by-elections were 'even worse than ordinary elections'. This was because, as he recalled in *My Early Life*, 'all the cranks and faddists of the country and all their associates and all the sponging "uplift" organizations fasten upon the wretched candidate'. 'All the woes of the world, all the shortcomings of human society' are laid upon the candidate, who is asked 'what he is going to do about them'. In a by-election 'all the discontents and any passing mood can be safely expressed by the voters', Churchill argued, and full vent can be given to criticism of the government without its opponents necessarily putting forward a constructive alternative policy. He was speaking from bitter experience for three of Churchill's five election defeats were in by-elections, two of these when he was a government party candidate.[20]

In 'Election Memories' he writes vividly of rushing round the constituency, meetings with small po-faced audiences in empty halls, which are 'a trial to the speaker', 'rowdy meetings' in front of packed and 'excited crowds', 'alarums and excursions in the local press', and all the 'clatter and the clamour', the 'exhaustion and suspense', and the 'strain and anxiety' of election campaigns. The 'ups and downs of politics' are directly experienced in and through elections: after several years' successful work as a leading minister in the Lloyd George coalition government, dealing with weighty and important national and imperial policy, Churchill found himself unceremoniously voted out by the newly enfranchised poor and working-class voters of Dundee in 1922, his career brought to a sudden halt by a surge of 'discontent and ill-will'. Nevertheless, as a democrat, he acknowledged that 'it is in my many elections that I have learnt to know and honour the people of this island'. 'It is the way the Constitution works,' he said. However inconvenient and bruising the encounters, Churchill believed that it was essential for statesmen to have practical experience of what he called democracy's 'rough and slatternly foundations'. 'No part of the education of a politician is more indispensable than the fighting of elections,' he argued in his book *Great Contemporaries*. 'Here you come into contact with all sorts of persons and every current of national life. You feel the Constitution at work in its primary processes.' It was one of Lord Rosebery's weaknesses, argued Churchill, that as the last prime minister who had never served at all in the House of Commons, he had no direct personal experience of electoral politics with its 'disorderly gatherings, its organized oppositions, its hostile little meetings, its jeering throng, its stream of disagreeable and often silly questions'. Rosebery disliked 'the caucus, the wire-puller and the soap-box'. He shrank from 'the laborious, vexatious and at times humiliating processes necessary under modern conditions to bring about great ends'.[21]

Elections were a vital expression of the workings and the will of a parliamentary democracy. But politicians and statesmen had also to govern. And although Churchill had supported the move in 1911 to five-yearly rather than seven-yearly parliamentary terms, he believed that too frequent general elections were 'highly detrimental to the interests of the public' (as he put it in 1925). 'To have a General Election every year, as the Chartists proposed, would deprive the House of Commons of much of its dignity and authority,' Churchill maintained. Rather than providing 'a stable foundation for the administration of the country', it would lead to short-termism and an atmosphere of permanent electioneering. As he robustly put it to MPs in 1953, 'elections exist for the sake of the House of Commons and not . . . the House of Commons . . . for the sake of elections'. It was a Whiggish and revealing order of priorities.[22]

Churchill cannot be numbered among the staunch and unwavering defenders of the British electoral system. Throughout his career he was interested in and advocated various reforms of the electoral system and election procedures. He believed that voting should be compulsory, for instance, with non-voters punished by a fine. In a universal franchise society voting was a civic or public duty, he argued, and 'no longer a privilege'. He was shocked and disturbed by examples of low turnout at elections, complaining in 1931 that 'vast numbers of electors take little or no interest in public affairs . . . they have to be almost dragged out of their houses to poll . . . millions of people treat the whole process on which the Government of the country rests with indifference'. 'When the vote was given to a few, all coveted it; when it was given to many, some coveted it,' he commented in 1934. 'Now it is given to all, you can hardly get them to go the poll.' 'If democracy is to maintain itself,' he wrote in 1935, 'there must be the conscious participation of the whole body of the voters in the responsibility for the good government of the country.' On the other hand he was equally concerned about the danger of voters voting in an irresponsible way, 'on some sudden wave of prejudice', and looked to various safeguards.[23]

One of these safeguards was a more drawn-out electoral process. In 1910 he had spoken out in favour of having general elections held on one day, but by the 1930s he looked back with nostalgia on the lengthy and elaborated elections of his earlier days. 'In the old days before the [Great] War,' he said in 1931, 'a General Election was spread over five or six weeks, and a far more closely reasoned decision was reached than is reached at present . . . The deliberate verdict of the country plainly manifesting itself after prolonged discussion is a considerable safeguard against incontinent decisions.' Now all electors voted blindly on one day, he argued (he was speaking, of course, in the days before modern public opinion polling, which gives voters a sense of which way the electoral tides are moving, though the polls are sometimes spectacularly inaccurate). 'One of the most alarming features of our present system,' said Churchill, 'is that the nation goes to bed on the night of the poll and wakes up to find that an irrevocable decision has been taken. No one knows what has been done until all has been done.' The old lengthy campaigns meant that 'national issues were really fought out' in detail and in depth by the parties and their leaders, and the staggering of the ballots in different constituencies allowed 'the national decision' to be 'reached in measured steps'. 'It would have been a wise and prudent feature in our constitution,' he argued, 'if a substantial proportion of the constituencies voted a few days later in the light of the situation resulting from the first ballots.' He supported proportional representation, he explained in 1931, but the 'next best' method was 'the second ballot'. 'There is no serious disadvantage in having 100 or 150 second ballot elections a few days or a week after the main part of the General Election is decided. On the contrary, there is a real advantage in enabling a portion of the electors to correct, if they choose, an undue landslide in either direction.' The second ballot system would be 'a powerful insurance against a too violent lurch in either direction' and 'would make for continuity and stability'.[24]

At times Churchill proposed moving away from the 'one man, one vote' principle, which he had seen as 'logically and morally certain' in 1897. In his radical Liberal days he had denounced plural voting – extra votes for businessmen and for university graduates – as an 'abuse', a 'scandal', and a 'great and gross swindle upon the electorate'. Later, as Conservative leader and with his party benefiting, the issue looked rather different and in 1948 Churchill criticized Labour's abolition of the university seats and the separate representation of the City of London. He pledged that a Conservative government would re-establish the university seats but in office after 1951 abandoned the idea of restoration of this particular type of plural voting.[25] In between these dates he became seriously interested in the idea of qualifications to the principle of universal suffrage, for reasons similar to those that had motivated the great liberal political thinker John Stuart Mill in the 1860s: concerned about the consequences of widening the franchise, Mill had backed extra votes for educated and professional people.

In the early 1930s Churchill argued strongly for the 'granting of additional, second or plural votes to the more active and responsible citizens in the community'. The franchise ought to be 'weighted', he believed, to make 'the total vote at the poll representative of the pulling and driving power of the country, instead of its more dependent and more volatile elements'. He had particularly in mind the need to '[correct] the effects of throwing an enormous mass of irresponsible voters into the scales as was done during Mr Baldwin's last administration' (i.e., the extension of the vote to women under thirty). During the debate on the Representation of the People Bill in June 1931 he proposed adding 'enormously' to the plural vote 'so as to increase the strength and vigour of the franchise':

Suppose, for instance, a second vote had been given to every householder or breadwinner at the head of a family, the man or woman who pays the rent or the rates, 7,000,000 or 8,000,000 additional votes would have been given. That, in my opinion, would have restored something of the quality of the old electorate. It would have drawn the true distinction which should be drawn between those wage earners who are really bearing the burden and their grown-up children or dependants who live in the same dwelling. It would have called back into being that specially responsible political democracy to whose exertions and keen discussions the health and the fame of our pre-war Parliamentary institutions were largely due.

The result would be 'a class bearing special political responsibilities' who would, he hoped, 'follow public affairs with more seriousness than at present'. Giving extra votes in this way to the more 'responsible' citizens or those with more of a stake in the country, as it might be said, was, however, simply not practical politics when the Labour Party wanted to sweep away the existing limited plural voting. But it does reveal the extent of Churchill's dissatisfaction with mass democracy in the early 1930s – similar reservations occasionally surfacing later in the 1950s, when he could still be found privately mulling over plural voting schemes.[26]

Churchill had a 'history of sympathy' with the issue of electoral reform and proportional representation (PR), as Peter Catterall puts it, one that can be traced from his time as a Liberal politician before the First World War through to his leadership of the Conservative Party. In part he supported PR as a safeguard in the context of the move to a mass democratic franchise, and in part because it fitted with his interest in the idea of a centrist bloc and coalition politics. There was also an argument for electoral reform in terms of government authority and efficiency as well in terms of justice for minorities, he believed. 'No Government which is in a large minority in the country, even though it possesses a working majority in the House of Commons, can have the necessary power to cope with real problems,' Churchill argued in 1931. 'A majority in the House of Commons should be based upon an intrinsic superiority of strength, I do not say always of numerical strength, in the country,' he maintained. Governments not based upon 'clear majority decisions' or backed up by 'a definite preponderance of the national will' were hobbled and constrained, he said.[27]

Issues about the representation of minorities, voter choice, the workings of the electoral system, and alternatives to the simple-majority (or plurality) system used in British elections had been debated since Victorian times. At a time when the Liberal Party benefited from the electoral system, it was not in favour of reform: after all, 49 per cent of the vote in 1906 had given them nearly 60 per cent of the seats in the Commons and a massive majority over the Conservatives. Proportional representation, they realized, would be likely to make them more dependent on the Irish Nationalists to put together a majority in Parliament. However, the emergence of the fledgling Labour Party (which elected twenty-nine MPs in 1906) raised the danger of the non-Conservative vote splitting, something which an electoral pact helped to prevent in 1906 and 1910, but which made some Liberals look more favourably on the idea of electoral reform – including Churchill. In January 1906 he supported the idea of the second ballot as 'essential to secure a proper majority representation'. 'We have evidently reached the end of the rigid two-party system in English politics,' Churchill wrote in December 1906, 'and we are bound to adapt our electoral machinery to the new conditions which the advent of new political forces have created.' He was concerned, he said, about 'triangular contests' resulting in the 'will of the majority' being 'defeated', and he expressed interest in devices such as the second ballot or the 'method of marking papers numerically' in single-member constituencies (i.e., the alternative vote [AV]) to combat this. In a 1909 speech he emphasized 'the broad democratic principle that a majority of votes in any electoral unit, acting together, shall be able to return their man'. The AV system (which was recommended by the Royal Commission on Electoral Systems in 1910) may ensure that individual MPs have majority support in their constituencies but its results may not be proportional at the level of party representation and the electorate across the country as a whole. On this broader level, Churchill indicated in May 1909 that he was prepared at least to consider 'proportional representation' in the 'great cities'. He argued that it was not necessary 'that the system by which representatives are elected . . . should necessarily be absolutely uniform over every area'. In 'country districts', he said, the 'personal connection' of the MP with each village in the constituency was the important factor. In the big cities, the community had a right to 'the collective expression of its own opinion'. In Birmingham, he pointed out, many thousands of Liberals across the city had been unable to return a single MP, and in Manchester the boot was on the other foot and 'the other side' less represented than their aggregate strength would apparently entitle them to. PR in multi-member seats would tackle such 'anomalies', he suggested.[28]

The Liberals saw no real need to introduce PR before 1914 but, in the shape of the single transferable vote (STV), it was recommended by an all-party Speaker's Conference in 1917 for larger towns and cities, with AV proposed for elsewhere. Advocates of PR had probably their best opportunity in the twentieth century to achieve their goal in the context of the massive extension of the franchise in 1918. But it did not happen. In a succession of votes in 1917–18, the Commons rejected STV but (narrowly) backed AV, only for the Lords to reject AV and vote for STV. The party leaders were suspicious of PR; the Liberals and Labour saw party advantage in AV not PR; and while Conservative peers supported PR, Conservative MPs mainly did not. In the end, the single-member plurality system survived by default.[29]

Churchill took no part in the parliamentary debates and votes on PR of 1917–18. But he took up the issue a few years later against the background of the uncertainties and swaying fortunes seen in the three-party politics of the 1922 and 1923 elections in particular, when small shifts in votes produced large increases or decreases in the number of MPs elected for the different parties. In the context of three-party politics, argued Churchill in 1923, the electoral system was 'faulty', 'absurd' and 'unfair'. A party could snatch the largest number of seats and form a government by split votes in 'triangular' contests and upon a minority basis. The danger of 'minority rule', he said, was 'one of the gravest constitutional issues' of the time. The existing electoral system was 'grossly unfair to moderate and central opinion' and it favoured 'the extremists both of the Right and of the Left'. 'The British people cannot get a stable government, nor a government representing a majority of the electors, nor in the long run the efficient and faithful conduct of their affairs,' he wrote in the *Sunday Chronicle*. 'We are no longer entitled to look down upon Continental Parliaments.' The two-party system, he argued, was 'the best foundation for Parliamentary institutions', whereas a three-party system was 'unquestionably the worst'. 'If we cannot have two Parties, it would be much better to have five or six,' he asserted. Instead of criticizing them for their weak and unstable governments, he painted a favourable picture of continental PR systems:

In any foreign country the majority of the electors in any Constituency or group of Constituencies would be sure of returning their candidates. The resulting Parliament would settle down in a semi-circular Chamber where every gradation of opinion from extreme Right to extreme Left could find its exact place, and a Government would be formed by making a block of the various groups most closely united, least seriously divided, which would truly represent the complexion of the Chamber as a whole and respond to the impulse given by the electors. With all the faults of the Continental systems, with all their inferiority to the old system in British government, it cannot be denied that their electoral and Parliamentary machinery offers both full expression to the will of majorities and free representation of sectional opinion. Here we have neither the one nor the other.

Either adoption of 'one or other of the many logical Continental systems of block Government by groups resting upon Proportional Representation, the Second Ballot or the Alternative Vote', or a return to the traditional British two–party system would be better than continuing with three–party politics combined with the existing plurality electoral system. 'Trust the people' meant, he argued, 'government in accordance with the will of the majority of the electors', and it must, he said, 'be the majority of the people and not the fortuitous combination of jealous and rival minorities'.[30]

When the May 1929 election turned out the Conservatives, produced another hung parliament and led to Labour forming another minority government (with 300,000 votes fewer than the Conservatives, Labour still had more MPs: 287 to 260), Churchill once again criticized the electoral system. In February 1929 he had met Lloyd George to discuss possible Conservative-Liberal co-operation and had been willing to accept the Liberal leader's demand for PR. Churchill was prepared publicly to admit that the Liberals had a legitimate 'grievance' about not being able to obtain representation in Parliament in relation to their voting strength. He was also worried about the anti–socialist vote being split, to Labour's advantage: 'the Socialists are the pampered darlings of our present electoral system,' he wrote in an article in *John Bull*.[31]

Another all-party conference on electoral reform (the Ullswater Conference in 1930) ended with no agreement. With the Tory leadership unwilling to make common cause with Lloyd George, the Liberals and Labour reached an understanding on the introduction of AV (in return for Liberal support of MacDonald's government) – something to which the Conservatives were fiercely opposed (fearing it would work against them) and the House of Lords threw out in 1931. Churchill was, once again, more sympathetic to electoral reform than many other Conservatives, including the party leadership. Speaking in the Commons in June 1931, he argued that it was not only a Liberal grievance but also 'a constitutional defect' that it took 20,000 votes to elect a Labour MP, 23,000 to elect a Conservative, but 100,000 to elect a Liberal. Abandoning his earlier support for it, he now condemned the idea of a move to the AV system as likely to lead to elections being decided by 'blind chance and accident', victory in constituencies being determined by 'the most worthless votes given for the most worthless candidates'. In line with what the Conservatives had been willing (without much enthusiasm) to accept in the Ullswater Conference, Churchill instead backed 'proportional representation [i.e., STV] in the cities' as 'incomparably the fairest, the most scientific and, on the whole, the best in the public interest'. The great cities like Manchester, Birmingham, Leeds, Liverpool, Glasgow, Edinburgh and Bristol should, through PR, be better able to express 'their collective personality', he argued, with their MPs carrying greater authority than if they just represented 'carved up communities of no integral strength' (the big cities 'are all carved up into meaningless blocks of houses', he later complained). The unspoken motive here was that PR for the big urban areas but not for the rural counties would boost Conservative support and representation, but not help Labour where the Tories were strongest.[32]

The collapse of the Labour government and the formation of the National Government in August 1931 effectively killed off the issue of electoral reform, despite the fact that the October 1931 general election produced a highly disproportionate result, with Labour winning only fifty-two seats for almost one-third of the vote and supporters of the National Government winning 90 per cent of the seats for two-thirds of the total vote. Labour was, however, adamantly opposed to PR and was committed to winning a majority through the existing system. As Churchill had seen in the 1920s, the three-party system could not last and in the 1930s the Liberals were splitting and being squeezed into irrelevance or swallowed up in a 'National' (i.e., Conservative) identity. All the same, some Conservatives remained interested in STV – including Churchill, who advocated it in his journalism in the mid-1930s and who was cited as a supporter of its cause by the Proportional Representation Society – but to little effect.[33]

Proportional representation was not on Churchill's agenda during the Second World War. He refused to see a deputation on the subject and wrote to one pro–PR MP in 1943: 'I do not see any possibility at the present time of taking up the question of electoral reform as distinct from electoral machinery.' Both main parties were hostile to electoral reform. The 1944 Speaker's Conference quickly and decisively rejected both the STV and the AV systems, and most of its attention was devoted to technical issues such as the electoral register, the services vote, counting arrangements and the redistribution of seats.[34]

However, electoral reform was an issue again in the late 1940s as Churchill became interested in the possibilities of forming an alliance with the Liberals in order to maximize anti-Labour support. Labour had won 61 per cent of the seats with 47.8 per cent of the vote in 1945 and Churchill complained that, even allowing for the usual winner's bonus at an election, it was over-represented and its majority exaggerated. Central Office was ordered to calculate the likely impact of STV in the cities (one paper in March 1950 indicating that the Tories could gain ten to twelve urban seats from Labour). In March 1950 Churchill spoke in the Commons of the 'anomaly' by which 186 MPs had just been elected on a minority vote in their constituencies (in the February 1950 election) and the 'constitutional injustice' by which 2.6 million total Liberal votes had produced only nine MPs. He proposed that a select committee be set up to inquire into the question of electoral reform. But he also warned that 'We do not wish to emulate some foreign Parliaments where small parliamentary parties are able, by putting themselves and their favours in the balance, to sway the course of considerable events' – exactly the sort of situation that could happen in the coalition politics produced by PR, of course.[35]

Back in office after October 1951, the arguments for taking no action soon seemed compelling. The Conservatives had benefited from the peculiarities of the 'first-past-the-post' system, winning 230,000 fewer votes than the Labour Party across the country as a whole but twenty-six more seats (for an overall majority of seventeen seats). Most Conservatives had not been keen on the idea of collaboration or a pact with the Liberals. There were concerns that PR would have the effect of 'artificially reviving the dying Liberal Party'. Rab Butler argued that PR could mean the Conservatives losing a good deal of middle-of-the-road support to the Liberals, for whom a vote would no longer seem wasted. And he warned Churchill that PR would give the Liberals a disproportionate influence in the House of Commons, which would be neither democratic nor in the interests of good government. Churchill's old Liberal friends like Violet Bonham-Carter still pressed the case for PR on him, but in August 1952 Churchill told the Liberal Party leader Clement Davies that electoral reform was 'not practical politics at this moment'. In July 1954 Churchill rejected calls to appoint a Royal Commission on the electoral system. Of proportional representation, he told MPs, 'logically there is a lot to be said for it but, in fact and in practice, it has brought to a standstill and to futility almost every Parliament in which it has ever been tried'. Later, in January 1955, he told Violet Bonham-Carter that his own opinion had 'hardened against it'. There was 'an overwhelming disapproval in the Conservative Party of any approach to PR in any form', he wrote. And he pointed to 'the ruin it has brought to every Parliament to which it has been applied. Look at the French Chamber with all its groups'.[36]

With the Liberals at an all-time low – polling only 2.6 per cent of the vote and fielding only 109 candidates in the 1951 election, winning six seats – two-party dominance seemed established (the Conservatives and Labour winning between them 96.8 per cent of the vote in 1951). As a Liberal before 1914 and then as a Conservative in the 1920s and 1930s, Churchill had essentially supported electoral reform when the two-party system seemed under threat and as a second-best device to cope with the dynamics of three-party politics, with its dangers of split votes in 'triangular' contests and minority rule. Partisan motives, to be sure, had never been far below the surface at those times, just as they were in the 1950s when he came to believe that PR would create more problems than it would solve. His changing views on this issue – as with other aspects of his constitutional thinking – must then be understood in the context of the developing political situation he faced. Electoral reform for Churchill, as for other politicians, was never and could never be an abstract and theoretical issue.

Churchill and Referendums

'Trust the people' was a consistent Churchillian cry, but that did not mean he favoured direct popular participation in government. He championed parliamentary democracy rather than direct democracy. Although on a number of occasions over his career he toyed with, supported or even proposed himself the use of the referendum, his motives in those cases were specific, short-term and tactical. The arguments of principle against referring political questions to the electorate for direct decision by a general ballot were, on the whole, compelling ones for him. 'We believe in democracy acting through representative institutions,' as he insisted in February 1911.

> We believe that Ministers should back their convictions by their offices. We believe Members of Parliament are representatives, and not delegates. We believe that Governments are the guides as well as the servants of the Nation. We believe that the people should choose their representatives, that they should come to a decision between men, party and policy, judging their character and judging the circumstances of the hour; that they should choose their representatives and then trust them and give them a fair chance within the limits of their commission for a period which should not be unreasonably prolonged; then these representatives should be summoned before their constituents, who should judge them in relation to all the circumstances proper to be considered, and in relation as well to the general effects of their policy, and should either confirm them in their places as representatives or choose other men to take their place.

Democracy, in this sense, was rule by elected politicians (a view later elaborated by the political theorist Joseph Schumpeter).[37]

The referendum was in fact a live issue in British politics in Churchill's first years on the scene. It had been seized upon by the leading constitutional theorist A. V. Dicey as a way of blocking Irish Home Rule in the 1890s – the 'sovereignty of the nation', in the form of a vote of all electors on this specific measure, being looked to as a last-ditch defence against Home Rule if the House of Lords caved in or was bulldozed into passing it. Dicey supported the referendum as a democratic and conservative check on the domination of the party machine over MPs and Parliament. The issue next surfaced in 1903–1904 during the controversy over tariff reform versus free trade when, aiming to appeal over the parties direct to the electorate, Joseph

Chamberlain called for a referendum on tariff reform (which Balfour refused). Then, in the constitutional crisis of 1909-11 over the powers of the House of Lords (see chapter 2), the Unionists/Conservatives proposed the adoption of the referendum on a number of occasions: during the 1910 Constitutional Conference as a way of resolving deadlocks between the Commons and the Lords; in the second 1910 election when Balfour announced that a Conservative government would call a referendum on tariff reform if the Liberals would put Home Rule to a vote of the people; and in 1911 when Balfour of Burleigh introduced a bill in the Lords which would have allowed 200 MPs to initiate a referendum.[38]

Churchill's main contribution to the debates about the referendum came in the 1910-12 period. He was sceptical about the Conservatives' motives, arguing that they were only posing as democrats and were not sincere in their advocacy of the referendum. Balfour was trying 'to rid his party of the incubus of Tariff Reform on the principle that one poison is used to expel another from the system', he claimed. In January 1910, at an election meeting in Dundee, Churchill had been emphatic, stating 'I am not in favour of a referendum'. However, in private notes, later that year, he hinted at a more flexible approach: 'Referendum procedure on constitutional questions would be unfair to the smaller nationalities, unless it were limited to questions affecting the United Kingdom equally as a whole. Insistence upon a referendum on Home Rule – even after the next election – must be fatal to settlement,' he wrote. 'It is not fair to submit questions like Home Rule & Welsh Disestablishment to Referendum, because tho [*sic*] they excite passionate interest in Ireland or Wales, they might not stir seriously one way or the other the English electorate,' he went on. 'A Referendum in such circumstances would be no less than a bludgeon of apathy to stun a sincere & vehement local demand.' The Liberals should refuse to agree to a referendum on such subjects at all costs. But constitutional questions that affected equally the whole of the UK were different, 'and this class comprises all the really great ones – Monarchy; the relations between the two Houses; the basis of the franchise. A referendum related to these Constitutional questions of general import might be agreed to.'[39]

There were 'some questions for which a Referendum might be an appropriate solution', Churchill admitted in a speech in November 1910. Female suffrage was one, he thought, that might well be the subject of 'direct appeal to the whole mass of the electors'. It was 'a moral and a social question at once', and one that applied to everyone in the UK and not to 'one part more than it does to another'. 'Every man [*sic*] in his cottage or in his house or in his palace' should form a view, he declared. Increases of taxation on wealth, property and land could probably be carried through by means of a referendum, he argued provocatively – not what Balfour and the Conservatives had in mind at all! But he insisted that 'the general adoption of a system of Referendum would not be a satisfactory method of conducting the government of the British Empire'. It would not 'conduce to the good government of our country'. He made the point that it would be 'very unfair on minorities like the Welsh or like the Irish or like the Scotch . . . which have a special point of view' to be brushed aside by the abstention or indifference of the majority of UK voters (who were, of course, English). And he was worried that progressive and reforming measures (dealing, for instance, with temperance, Sunday closing or contributory insurance) might be rejected by referendum 'before they were understood by the people if they were subject to a factious party attack'. In December 1910, he said that he welcomed Balfour's promise of a referendum on tariff reform ('I do not care how it is killed so long as it is killed, I welcome every new barrier in its path'). But he was adamant that the referendum was on the whole 'a bad and vicious system for a country to adopt'. 'It is altogether out of harmony with Parliamentary government,' he argued, 'and is destructive of Parliamentary responsibility.'[40]

During the debates on the 1911 Parliament Bill, Churchill continued to denounce the principle of the referendum. He was willing to tease the Conservatives with the idea that it could be used by demagogues and radicals to promote 'measures dealing with the redress of great inequalities in the distribution of property in this country, particularly of property in the land, on which a Referendum might be very effectively used'. Land nationalization might be carried by a referendum, he argued. There were 'perils from the point of view of property', as he explained to the King in one of his reports on parliamentary business. 'It would be a dangerous thing to put a great measure of a confiscatory character to the direct vote of millions of people, the vast majority of whom have only what they earn each week by constant toil. Yet that would certainly happen under the system sooner or later.' Regular recourse to referendums would undermine the stable foundations of the British system of government, he argued, in the Commons in February 1911, and would produce 'a tossing sea of frenzied electioneering':

> The mass of the people under the Referendum are forced to take a decisive part in a continuous process of lawmaking. Every Bill would have to be framed as if it were the campaign platform of an immediate General Election. Every clause would have to be drafted to secure an immediate popular vote . . . We should live in an unceasing stream of electioneering prejudice and abuse. Parliamentary debate would be swept aside for a series of organized electoral struggles. Ministers would be expected to retain office after the measures to which they had pledged their faith and honour had been rejected by the country. Governments would be expected to appeal to the country on one policy, and to remain in office to carry out the reverse.

Parliamentary and representative institutions, Churchill declared, would give way to 'the worst forms of Jacobinism, Caesarism, and Anarchy'.[41]

In May 1911 the Conservatives proposed an amendment to the Parliament Bill making provision for referendums on constitutional questions. In the event of a disagreement between the Commons and the Lords, it was proposed, matters affecting the Crown, Home Rule proposals, the powers or composition of both Houses of Parliament or relations between them, and the franchise would be subject to a referendum. Speaking for the government, Churchill rejected the idea of specifying in this way 'a class of questions apart from the ordinary general legislation of the country' that would be subject to 'an entirely different treatment from the ordinary Parliamentary treatment'. He quoted Dicey to the effect that in Britain 'constitutional' or 'fundamental' laws were not distinct from ordinary enactments. 'Although they appear fairly definite on paper . . .' argued Churchill . . . 'disputes and questions would arise in connection with almost every one of the categories', and this would 'require for their solution the intervention of a judicial body of some kind or other'. He was 'entirely opposed to the erection of any judicial body external to Parliament itself to sit on the proceedings of either House or both Houses of [the] Legislature, and to declare whether or not they have acted within a purely legal definition of the ever-changing needs of our constitutional system'. The Conservatives' proposal was in any case one-sided, he argued, because in practice it would be applied only to Liberal 'constitutional' measures and not Tory ones.

Balfour of Burleigh's proposal would potentially open up Conservative as well as Liberal legislation to the check of the referendum, Churchill acknowledged. But he ingeniously (if unconvincingly) argued that if a minority (200 MPs) in the Commons had the power to invoke a referendum on any important issue then 'it carries you directly to the abolition or nullity of the Second Chamber . . . What would be left for the Second Chamber to do?' There would be no need for 'a strong reconstituted Second Chamber' as a constitutional or legislative longstop. The referendum system, as proposed by the Conservatives, was a substitute for, not an addition to, a second parliamentary chamber, he claimed.

Churchill made great play of the problems that would arise after a minister or a government had received a rebuff in a referendum. How could they remain in office? 'After the Government had made a proposal of extreme magnitude and importance to which they had pledged their faith and their convictions, then when this proposal has been rejected, they are, we are told, to continue to administer the affairs of the country on an entirely different basis, and with an opposite purpose and opposite methods to those which they had been hoping and believing it would be right and proper for them to fulfil.' 'Politics may be a humble profession,' he quipped, 'but I am glad to say it is not quite so humble in this country as yet.' A referendum defeat and the reversal of ministerial policy, he maintained, 'would destroy the whole credentials of the Government and would render a General Election necessary as the inevitable and immediate consequence'.

The referendum was 'objectionable, not only in regard to the constitutional questions, but over the whole area of public affairs' was Churchill's conclusion. The only exception he would allow was in relation to 'questions which are non–party in their character' – questions 'for which you get no party and no Government to be responsible; questions about which it cannot be said that a single Member of the House [of Commons] was returned in consequence of them or prevented from being returned in consequence of them'. Even here he hedged and was careful to avoid an unequivocal commitment, but prudently left room for manoeuvre. 'I can conceive in certain circumstances, if there should be such a question that it might be a conceivable procedure to apply the machinery of a Referendum to ascertain the feelings of the country, which had not yet been decisively or effectively evoked through any of the ordinary proceedings of party representation.' Although he had earlier described the referendum as 'that form of bastard democracy which has the disadvantages of all political creeds without securing the results of any', he had with these remarks about 'non-party' questions left himself some 'wriggle room', as it were, on this issue should he ever need it.[42]

As noted earlier, Churchill believed that the female suffrage issue was one that could be handled via a referendum, which would get the government off the hook and avoid a party split. It was a way of pushing the issue to one side. As a non-party issue, Churchill argued in a letter to Lord Curzon in January 1912, it lay 'outside the scope of ordinary political machinery and of the usual tests whereby public opinion can be ascertained'. He wanted leading Conservative anti-suffragists to admit that there was a difference between a referendum on such a non-party issue and one on a party matter (such as Home Rule) and that 'advocacy of the one is no ground for a charge of illogicality or inconsistency in regard to the other'. Curzon was not enthusiastic about this notion. Churchill pressed the referendum idea on cabinet colleagues in December 1911, although Asquith was sceptical and John Morley had warned him months earlier that the Liberal Party at large would not stand for a referendum on the issue. At first, Churchill seemed to envisage two referendums before any legislative action: 'first to the women to know if they want it [the vote]; & then to the men to know if they will give it' (as he wrote to the government chief whip). Then it was to be a ballot of 'men or women or both – I do not care', as he put it to Sir Edward Grey. And then after meeting with Lloyd George and Grey (both strong suffragists) he wrote to Asquith with a compromise scheme whereby a referendum of 'the whole mass of women' would follow after a suffrage amendment to the Franchise Bill had been carried to 'decide whether they wd take up their responsibilities or not'. However, Churchill let slip his motive for favouring a referendum on this issue, saying to Asquith: 'it wd probably get smashed'.[43]

As Vernon Bogdanor shows, with the passage of the 1911 Parliament Act, which recognized the supremacy of the House of Commons in the constitutional system, the referendum ceased to be a major issue in constitutional debate in British politics until the 1970s (when it was revived in the context of the European issue). But it did surface on a number of occasions in the intervening years, and Churchill, far from denouncing referendums as constitutionally subversive (as in 1911), showed himself willing to back the idea if it suited his political needs or aims at the time. In 1925, as a member of the Baldwin government's House of Lords Reform Committee, he had supported the idea that differences between the second chamber and the House of Commons should be resolved by recourse to a referendum (insisting that that then made radical reform of the composition of the Lords imperative, which was his primary concern – see chapter 2). 'No one could impugn the democratic character of the referendum,' he told a meeting of the cabinet committee (overlooking the fact that he had done so at length fourteen years earlier), 'which had been found to work well in countries which had adopted it.' However, he did not develop this proposal into a general argument in favour of the regular or widespread use of referendums, and Lords reform ran into the ground. A few years later, in 1930, Churchill supported the pledge made by Baldwin (under pressure from Beaverbrook and Rothermere's 'Empire Crusade') for a referendum on protection and food taxes – transparently using the idea of a referendum as a lifeboat to get out of a tight spot, keep some room for manoeuvre, and neutralize a difficult and divisive issue. Later still, in 1945, as prime minister, Churchill rejected a call for a referendum on the establishment of a Scottish parliament (see chapter 3) but himself suggested that a referendum be held on the continuation of the wartime coalition government and the timing of a general election (Churchill would have preferred the government to stay in office until the war against Japan was won). The Labour and Liberal leaders turned him down, however, Attlee denouncing the referendum as a device 'alien to all our traditions' and pointedly telling Churchill that it had recently been 'the instrument of Nazism and Fascism'.[44] He hardly needed reminding of both these points. For Churchill, general elections, party politics and parliamentary government were the key motors and mechanisms of representative democracy in Britain. When he supported the referendum it was largely as a tactical device in a particular situation rather than as a serious general instrument of democratic reform.

FIVE

Churchill and the House of Commons

Churchill was, by any reckoning, one of the great parliamentarians. First elected to the House of Commons in October 1900, aged twenty-six, he served as a Member of Parliament (with a two–year gap when he lost his seat at Dundee in 1922) for a total of sixty-two years – longer than any other twentieth-century MP – finally standing down in 1964, only a few months before his death. He had become Father of the House in 1959, by that time being almost literally a figure from a different age as the only MP to have been first elected in the reign of Queen Victoria. 'Parliament always came first with Churchill,' argued Woodrow Wyatt, and the many statements he made of respect and reverence for the House of Commons over his career were undoubtedly genuine, sincere and deeply felt. 'I love, venerate and cherish the House of Commons from personal association as well as from general political conviction,' he declared in 1926. 'I am first of all a Parliamentarian and House of Commons man,' he told MPs in 1940. The British parliament, he insisted in 1931, was 'the oldest, the least unwise and the most democratic parliament in the world', the House of Commons being 'almost the only great real living popular chamber functioning in full power at the present time'. Parliament, and particularly the House of Commons, he said in his Romanes Lecture in 1930, was 'alone among the senates and chambers of the world a living and ruling entity; the swift vehicle of public opinion; the arena, perhaps fortunately the padded arena, of the inevitable class and social conflict; the college from which the ministers of state are chosen, and hitherto the solid and unfailing foundation of the executive power'. Parliamentary institutions, he believed, were 'precious to us almost beyond compare'.[1]

131

Churchill always deprecated any view of Parliament as simply a sort of routine legislative 'sausage factory'. He had an altogether more exalted view of the Mother of Parliaments and its role as 'the home and citadel of free government', as he put it in a 1911 speech. 'The worst chamber in the world is better than the best ante-chamber,' he quipped in 1926. The House of Commons, he said in 1950, was 'the enduring guarantee of British liberties and democratic progress'. In April 1917 he had argued that 'We have certainly not gone to war with Prussia [*sic*] in order to capture its Constitution', and in March of that year MacCallum Scott, then a fellow Liberal MP, recorded in his diary how, as they were leaving the Commons late one night, Churchill

> called me into the Chamber to take a last look round. All was darkness except a ring of faint light all around under the gallery. We could dimly see the table, but walls and roof were invisible. 'Look at it,' he said. 'This little place is what makes the difference between us and Germany. It is in virtue of this that we shall muddle through to success & for lack of this Germany's brilliant efficiency leads her to final disaster. This little room is the shrine of the world's liberties.'[2]

The Decline of Parliament

In *My Early Life*, Churchill – looking back to his first years in Parliament after 1900 – recalled his pride at being a member of 'this famous assembly which for centuries had guided England through numberless perils forward on the path of empire'. But within a few years he was arguing that the House of Commons was not what it used to be, and this was a theme to which he often returned. In July 1905 he moved a bill under the 'Ten Minutes Rule' to limit the duration of parliaments to five years instead of the seven that was then the legal rule, making a speech in which he outlined what he described as 'the increasing power of the Executive and the decline of Parliamentary authority'. The checks on government were growing weaker: 'We had borrowed from foreign nations almost every device which could weaken a representative institution; we had rejected almost every safeguard which could control the Executive Government.' In 1917 he spoke of his 'despair'

that the House of Commons was 'allowing power to slip from its hands and
. . . allowing itself to be made a useless addition to the Constitution'. 'Is
Parliament played out?' he asked, in an article in 1920. 'No one can pretend
that there has not been a decline in the personal distinction of the leading
parliamentary figures, and a deterioration in the quality of the debates in the
House of Commons.'

> The general average of ability and political knowledge is far higher probably
> than in the classic times of Pitt and Fox or the palmy days of Peel and
> Gladstone and Disraeli. But we cannot claim to have been able to fill what
> Lord Morley has called 'the vacant thrones' with House of Commons figures
> of the same commanding eminence. Still less can we rival their eloquence,
> their learning, or their mental force. Least of all can our debates compare with
> the earnestness and intensity of those famous discussions which riveted the
> attention of the Assembly through successions of grand continuous arguments
> lasting from dusk to dawn. More serious still is the present lack of new figures
> to rival and replace those who now hold sway. The vital strength of the House
> of Commons depends upon its power to renew from generation to generation
> its hold upon the public mind by drawing to itself a stream of men who, by
> their gifts, by their force, and by their virtues, are the true leaders of the
> nation.

Churchill told the Select Committee on Procedure in 1931 that 'the decline
in the power of the House of Commons to command national interest, to
rivet national attention' had been in progress all the time he had been an MP,
and that after the First World War there had been a very marked decline in
public esteem for Parliament, with the electorate taking less interest in
politics and 'a complete falling off' in press reporting of debates. To counter
this decline, he argued, parliamentary politics had to be made more interesting, and Churchill saw as key to this 'the resuscitation of the fierce and
tense threshing out of great public questions which is not going on now to
any large extent'.[3]

Two additional factors had contributed to the decline of parliamentary
authority and to what Churchill called 'the great maltreatment' of the House
of Commons since the late nineteenth century. First, Parliament was now

'swamped by a flow of minor business'. Under every government, he asserted, Parliament had been 'encumbered with an enormous mass of day-to-day detail which it can only partially understand and cannot possibly control'. (Hence his support for devolution, to reduce overload at Westminster – see chapter 3.) Second, the rise of obstruction as a political weapon by the Irish Nationalists in the late nineteenth century had 'destroyed the true procedure of the House, and we have never got out of the rut'. 'It still remains a serious element in public life,' argued Churchill in 1926, 'that the will of the majority can be obstructed other than by weapons of argument and debate.' The tactic of obstruction leads to 'physical exhaustion, dull and brutish methods on both sides, and in the end the party which is stronger numerically invariably exerts its will'. 'No one should undervalue the sprightliness, eloquence and wit which the Irish Nationalists brought to the House of Commons,' Churchill wrote in 1935. 'Nevertheless, the presence of this avowedly foreign body in the heart of a characteristically English Assembly cost us dear. It cost the House of Commons a large part of the old freedom of debate which was its glory and its strength.' The consequence had been that Parliament had been 'fettered and trammelled by every kind of arbitrary restriction; not indeed as to the freedom of opinion – for that has always been preserved – but upon what, when, and how it should debate'. Churchill told the Procedure Committee in 1931 that now the Irish Nationalists had gone and 'Parliament consists entirely of British people from this single island', there was a much greater possibility of returning to what he saw as the old procedure of the House of Commons, with greater flexibility to debate the burning issues of the day – which he saw as the real, vital function of Parliament.[4]

Rebuilding Parliament

It was inevitable that, when the old House of Commons chamber was destroyed by German bombing in May 1941, Churchill would want passionately to restore it much as it was in its Victorian heyday. 'There I learnt my craft, and there it is now, a heap of rubble,' he said to Lord Moran. 'I am glad that it is in my power, when it is rebuilt, to keep it as it was.' Ten years earlier, in 1931, Churchill had declared himself 'entirely opposed to any

134

alteration in the architectural lay-out of the Chamber'. After the Commons had been blitzed, a small number of MPs would have preferred a brand new parliamentary building on a new site, but most were behind Churchill in wanting to retain the essential features of the old House. For a while the Commons met in nearby Church House and then moved into the chamber of the House of Lords (occupying it for nearly ten years). It is not often realized that after his first year as prime minister, Churchill was not actually performing on what had been for forty years his central and defining political stage until MPs returned to the restored chamber in October 1950 (by which time, of course, he was leader of the opposition).[5]

'We shape our buildings and afterwards our buildings shape us,' Churchill told MPs in 1943, when plans for the rebuilding were discussed. He insisted on two key characteristics for the restored House of Commons. The first was that 'its shape should be oblong and not semi-circular':

> Here is a very potent factor in our political life. The semi-circular assembly, which appeals to political theorists, enables every individual or every group to move around the centre, adopting various shades of pink according as the weather changes. I am a convinced supporter of the party system in preference to the group system. I have seen many earnest and ardent Parliaments destroyed by the group system. The party system is much favoured by the oblong form of Chamber. It is easy for an individual to move through those insensible gradations from Left to Right but the art of crossing the Floor is one which requires serious consideration. I am well informed on this matter, for I have accomplished that difficult process, not only once but twice. Logic is a poor guide compared with custom. Logic which has created in so many countries semi-circular assemblies which have buildings which give to every Member, not only a seat to sit in but often a desk to write at, with a lid to bang, has proved fatal to Parliamentary Government as we know it here in its home and in the land of its birth.

The second vital characteristic was that the chamber 'should not be big enough to contain all its Members at once without over-crowding':

> The reasons for this has long been a puzzle to uninstructed outsiders . . . Yet it is not so difficult to understand if you look at it from a practical point of

view. If the House is big enough to contain all its Members, nine-tenths of its debates will be conducted in the depressing atmosphere of an almost empty or half-empty Chamber. The essence of good House of Commons speaking is the conversational style, the facility for quick, informal interruptions and inter-changes. Harangues from a rostrum would be a bad substitute for the conversational style in which so much of our business is done. But the conver-sational style requires a fairly small space, and there should be on great occasions a sense of crowd and urgency. There should be a sense of the impor-tance of much that is said and a sense that great matters are being decided, there and then, by the House.

He returned to this theme when he spoke on the opening of the restored chamber ('I am a child of the House of Commons . . . I was much upset when I was violently thrown out of my collective cradle'). It had been important to build a replica of the old chamber, seating at best two-thirds of MPs, because 'the intensity, passion, intimacy, informality and spontaneity of our debates constitute the personality of the House of Commons and endow it at once with its focus and its strength'. Fittingly, the entrance from the Members' Lobby, rebuilt with stones from the original structure, was at this time named the Churchill Arch.[6]

Churchill as Parliamentarian

It was sometimes argued that while Churchill was a great parliamentary figure, he was not a great parliamentarian. Attlee said in 1954 that 'he has never mastered the procedure of the House. He gives the impression that anyway the rules don't apply to him'. (Although, as John Ramsden suggests, he got away with it after 1945 because of the huge volume of accu-mulated respect he had built up.) 'Perhaps Churchill was not a master of the minutiae of procedure,' conceded Robert Rhodes James, '. . . But he had the lore of Parliament in his bones . . . [and] amazing knowledge of Parliamentary history. He had, after all, been a Member when many of the precedents had been created! And his researches for his biography of his father had given him a deep knowledge of the revised procedures of the House forced on it by the Irish Nationalists in the late 1870s and early

1880s.' The left-wing politician Aneurin Bevan thought that his weak spot was actually a limited 'feel' for the House of Commons: 'compared with Lloyd George, who had an amazing parliamentary mastery, Churchill was a poor manipulator of the House. He lacked subtlety and self-control, and was not quick to sense what the members, friends or adversaries, were thinking.' This was a perceptive criticism because Churchill was always perhaps more of a formidable parliamentary (and hustings) setpiece performer than a dexterous debater.[7]

The fact was that Churchill was not a master of the informal and conversational style of speaking that he said was best suited to the House of Commons (see above). He had not had the sort of debating apprenticeship that other leading politicians of his class and time received in the Oxford and Cambridge Unions. Far from being a natural impromptu speaker, his speeches were the product of long hours of careful preparation and drafting, and he would commit his texts to memory or speak from long and detailed notes (he once, traumatically, dried up in the Commons in mid-speech as a young backbencher when he lost the thread of his argument). As Arthur Balfour said, Churchill's speeches were not the 'unpremeditated effusions of a hasty moment'. His first major parliamentary speech (in 1901) took him six weeks to prepare and throughout his career he lavished time and intellectual energy on his speeches; as prime minister in the darkest days of the war, he devoted between twelve and fourteen hours to putting together a ten-thousand-word two-hour speech for a vital Commons confidence vote in 1942. But for all the force and brilliance of his formal orations, there were weaknesses in his style. He tended to speak *at* his audience, as Roy Jenkins put it, rather than get inside their minds and persuade them. In the 1930s he was often criticized for waltzing into the House of Commons to make his speech and then immediately leaving (acting 'as if God Almighty had spoken', complained a Labour MP) rather than staying to listen to the debate. For a while, during the lengthy debates on the India Bill in the 1930s, Churchill found himself able to make frequent short speeches and interventions – speaking three or four times a day, for five, ten or fifteen minutes, sometimes for half an hour – in a more casual, off-the-cuff style without notes ('talk[ing] to the House of Commons with garrulous unpremeditated flow', as he described it to his wife), but apparently he soon reverted to type.

The meticulous preparations could produce an inflexibility in debates, though in the 1940s and 1950s his wiliness in provoking interruptions and delivering devastating ripostes and put-downs was notable. And with his long ministerial experience, he could be 'remarkably ready and quick when answering Questions', noted Robert Rhodes James.[8]

The Role of Parliament

Churchill's 'belief in Parliamentary democracy was deeply held', says his biographer Martin Gilbert. 'He was convinced that all policy decisions, however controversial, could be explained fully to Parliament, fought for in Parliament, and carried out with Parliamentary approval.' He ranked the House of Commons (which, to put the Lords in their place, he maintained was 'the centre of the life of Parliament') as 'the most powerful Assembly in the whole world' but also asserted that 'There has never been an Assembly of such great powers, which has shown so much restraint in the using of them'. This was because there was a well-understood and 'wise division of power'. 'The House of Commons has recognized, to a large extent, its own limitations,' he explained to readers of the *News of the World* in 1938. 'It does not try to govern the country. The Cabinet governs the country. The House of Commons supervises the Cabinet; it controls the Cabinet. If necessary, it changes it. It is a college in which Ministers are trained, and from which they are selected.' In a speech in 1926 he had noted that the Commons 'rigidly abstains from any inroad upon the direct functions of the Executive'. The function of the House of Commons, he described in an article for the *Daily Mail*, was to 'supervise, criticize, correct, sustain, or change the Government, and to lead the thoughts of the nation upon the politics of the day'. There was a broader, stabilizing political function too, which Churchill believed was important. Parliament, 'properly viewed and properly guided, is the greatest instrument for associating an ever-widening class of citizens with [the] actual life and policy of the State', he argued in 1926. With the growing strength of the 'Socialist [i.e., Labour] Party', Churchill was (in 1935) therefore thankful that 'The amazing quality of the House of Commons is its power to digest, assimilate, conciliate and tame all kinds of new elements'.[9]

The pre-eminent role of the House of Commons, in Churchill's view, was to provide a national political focus as a forum for general debate. To leave the floor of the House of Commons free for dramatic general debates, he was in favour of sending more detailed business 'upstairs' to be scrutinized by committees, as he made clear when giving evidence to the Procedure Committee in 1931. In investigating and reporting on public expenditure in particular, he saw a role for a specialized parliamentary select committee. As far back as 1902 he had been voicing concern about the problems of parliamentary control over government expenditure, badgering the prime minister, Balfour, with calls for a parliamentary inquiry and sitting on the National Expenditure Committee (1902-1903) which was appointed to study the issues. He wrote a carefully argued memorandum giving his views about improving parliamentary control (returning to the problem in a speech in 1905). Questions about expenditure *policy* (objectives and aims of spending) were for the cabinet to decide (subject to parliamentary ratification), he argued. The machinery for the *audit* of accounts (i.e., post mortem review and control of spending) was 'very good and powerful', involving the comptroller and auditor-general, backed up by a specialist audit staff, expert evidence and the cross-examination of officials by the Public Accounts Committee (PAC), producing reports of 'unique value'. But there was a 'lacuna' in the 'middle ground', Churchill argued, relating to investigation of the *merit* of expenditure, or the 'value for money' aspects of departmental spending plans. Here, he said, the existing parliamentary examination through the 'Supply Days' debates were 'a series of farces from beginning to end'. He proposed the creation of an Estimates Committee, supported by trained expert officers, as the PAC was, and holding hearings to question witnesses, to provide for the 'systematic and scientific examination' of departmental estimates, feeding in reports so that MPs could hold 'Supply' debates on the basis of accurate and independent information.[10]

The House of Commons Estimates Committee, established in 1912, going into abeyance in 1914 and being recreated in 1921, did not measure up well against these imaginative proposals of Churchill's and there was widespread criticism of Parliament's financial procedures and its control over public expenditure in subsequent decades. Giving evidence to the Procedure Committee in 1931, Churchill repeated his call for a committee to mount 'searching and effective' reviews of the estimates, focusing points of criticism and highlighting issues for MPs before the estimates came before the full House (and he made the same proposal again in a speech in 1945). Churchill maintained that as chancellor of the exchequer he would have welcomed such informed and expert parliamentary examination and criticism of government expenditure and that, as a spending minister, 'I would always be ready to go before a Committee and explain fully to them why things had cost so much or why we should not do it cheaper or whatever it was. I would be glad to be cross-examined by a Committee; I do not think any Minister ought to shrink from that.' But a key factor behind the continuing limitations of parliamentary expenditure control in this period was that successive governments did indeed shrink from the prospect of such exposure and criticism. Churchill himself acknowledged the stumbling block in this sense, and the realities of executive dominance and partisan politics: 'Everything must be covered by the Ministerial responsibility . . . [and] the Government will probably have a majority to support its Minister,' he conceded in 1931.[11]

'We must not regard this House as a mere treadmill,' Churchill warned in a debate on parliamentary procedure in August 1945. 'This House is not only a machine for legislation; perhaps it is not even mainly a machine for legislation, it is a great forum of debate.' The primary function of the House of Commons, he had similarly told the Procedure Committee in 1931, was to be 'the grand forum of debate'. He wanted it to reclaim its place as 'the centre of vital debates which everyone wanted to follow' by giving the House more control over its own business, lightening the routine work, and allowing it the flexibility to debate, as it had a hundred years previously, 'whatever it wanted to debate and whatever the country wanted it to debate pretty well when it liked'. 'Reviving the ancient practice of the House', was how he described it to MPs in 1940, 'which was that the Government of the day got through its necessary business with considerable expedition, and the House devoted itself to debating, usually on Petition, whatever were the topics of general public interest. . . . I believe, if this House is to keep its hold on the imagination and the interest of the public, that it is necessary that the great questions which appeal to the nation out of doors and occupy the Press should also be the questions subject to current discussion in this House. I very much deprecate the House falling into the debating of details and routine, and losing sight of its larger duty of giving guidance and encouragement to the nation and administering when required the necessary corrective to the Executive.'[12]

In many ways, Churchill's ideal was the House of Commons as he had first experienced it at the turn of the century. 'In those days,' he recalled in *My Early Life*, 'the proceedings in the House of Commons were fully reported in the Press and closely followed by the electors. Crucial questions were often argued with sustained animation in three-day debates. During their course all the principal orators contended, and at their close the parties took decisive trials of strength.' But nowadays, he complained in 1931, the business of Parliament 'dribbles out in a dreary stream during the . . . year. There is no feature: you cannot hold the attention of the more democratic electorate unless there is something definite done, something to be discussed at set times on great occasions'. An important contributory factor, he maintained, was that Parliament 'sits far too long in the year'. He proposed that except in times of war or great national emergency, Parliament should not sit more than five or six months each year, as had been the old practice: 'I think we kill Parliament by going on practically without intermission. I think we kill it.' By economizing on the time devoted to routine matters, he believed, 'Parliament can get through perfectly well all that has to be done.' 'The Ministers' business is to carry on in the interval, and if they know they have to meet Parliament and face it and will be called to account, I would give them good latitude,' he said – a revealing glimpse of Churchill the man of government as well as doughty parliamentarian. In the intervals between sessions, he said,

Ministers are able to study their task, discussions can take place on the platforms outside, a lot of foolish ideas are ventilated, passion is aroused, and so on; and then when Parliament meets again, everyone is delighted, and they say, 'It is high time Parliament met'; and there is keen attention in all parts of the country, everyone burning to have his grievance redressed, and so on.

Contracting the sessions of Parliament into half the year would thus enable 'a democratic chamber . . . to fortify its hold upon public opinion'.

Churchill's devolution ideas fit in here too, of course, contributing to the freeing-up of the Westminster timetable, but the trend was in the other direction, with the parliamentary session lengthening from an average of 129 sitting days before 1914 to 163 after 1945 – an increase of 25 per cent.[13]

It is interesting to note in this context that Churchill did not, in 1931 at any rate, appear to share the concern about the growth of ministerial orders and delegated legislation famously criticized as *The New Despotism* in Lord Hewart's 1929 book of that title. Shorter sessions of Parliament would still allow abuses to be checked, he argued, and in any case 'It does no harm for a few grievances to accumulate; they come with a good head of steam.'[14]

'Parliament is not a mere apparatus for passing Bills,' Churchill insisted in 1934. Parliament had many important functions apart from its legislative function, he believed, and 'in its legislative aspect', he told the 1931 Procedure Committee, 'Parliament is as much concerned with preventing legislation as with passing legislation.' 'I never knew there was any difficulty in passing Bills,' he argued. 'I think the trouble that we suffer from is rather the facility with which Bills are passed.' He was not opposed in principle to timetables on Bills, he explained: 'the Government must have power effectively to legislate and to pass important measures into law.' But he was adamant that 'The practice of Parliament must be judged, not by quantity, but by quality', as he put in 1934. 'You cannot judge the passing of Bills by Parliament as you would judge the output of an efficient Chicago bacon factory.' 'It seems to me to be absolutely essential that people should not try to shape our procedure as if perfection would be attained when legislation was most easy,' he argued.

> Most Bills, I believe, cost money, lose votes, create officials, and worry the public, and certainly Parliament has to stand between the great mass of the public and the strong pressure of organized sectional interests, or organized party interests, which from time to time endeavour to imprint their special wishes, or convictions, or fads, upon our Statute Book.

If not able to stop bad bills passing, Parliament's function was at least 'mitigating their effects', he said in 1945, recognizing that a majority government will carry through its programme. It was in the interests not just of the public but also of the government 'that their Bills should be really tested and sifted in Parliament, because, otherwise, all kinds of things slip through, which give needless offence when put into operation, and involve the Government in needless discredit'. 'It would be a great mistake,' Churchill maintained, 'to think that all you have to do to improve the procedure of the House of Commons is to make it able to turn out the largest number of Bills in the shortest amount of time.' Nor was he anxious to help private members' bills, commenting in 1931 that 'I have seen a great many of them brought forward, and in most cases it was a very good thing that they did not pass. I think there ought to be be a very effective procedure for making it difficult for all sorts of happy thoughts to be carried on to the Statute Book'.[15]

Economic Sub-Parliament

One such 'happy thought' that did not make headway, and was indeed soon dropped by its author, was Churchill's plan for an 'Economic Sub-Parliament'. When the Fabian socialist theorists Sidney and Beatrice Webb had set out a plan for separate 'Social' and 'Political' parliaments, Churchill had dismissed their ideas as 'ludicrous'. However, that did not stop him putting forward a rather impracticable reform scheme of his own, at a time when, across the political spectrum, people were casting around for ways of responding to mass unemployment and economic depression in the late 1920s and 1930s. Proposals for an 'Economic General Staff', a 'Parliament of Industry', a 'National Economic Council', an 'Economic Planning Ministry', or similar bodies, abounded in this period, reflecting a wide-spread feeling that established institutions were on trial and could not deal properly with these pressing and seemingly intractable problems. Seen in this context, Churchill's contribution to the debate was not particularly original or well thought-out, as Trevor Smith notes, but it was important as coming from such a senior Conservative politician. His presentation of his thinking in his Romanes Lecture, given in Oxford in June 1930, attracted most attention but he had earlier tried out his argument in a speech in Wanstead in his constituency in March 1930. The starting point of Churchill's analysis was his belief that 'The House of Commons is well suited to deal with ordinary party issues such as had occupied us before the War', but that 'It is a feeble instrument to handle the grim economic realities on which the livelihood of millions and the prosperity of the nation depend'. Ministers were 'overweighted and overworked' and 'hampered . . . by party exigencies'. The civil service was 'faithful and competent to the last degree, [but] cannot supply constructive inspiration'. The political process itself was part of the problem: 'I am sure that our troubles in trade and unemployment will not be cured by party politicians trying to score off each other and manoeuvring for position and winning an election. They will be cured only when expert, disinterested, free, and non-party proposals are shaped by persons specially competent in industry, business and finance . . .' Hence the need for 'an additional organ in the Constitution – a kind of sub–parliament to deal with economic issues and to present conclusions to the Government of the day and to the House of Commons after full, open, brutal and candid discussion of all the most difficult, delicate and harassing topics'.[16]

'Political brawling' was not the way out of the contemporary economic and financial crisis, asserted Churchill in his Romanes Lecture: 'it is evidently a matter requiring high, cold, technical, and dispassionate or disinterested decision' and 'treatment . . . on national and non-party lines'. His solution was an 'Economic sub-Parliament', subordinate to the House of Commons and about one-fifth of its size, its membership chosen by the 'political Parliament' in proportion to its party groupings and composed of persons of 'high technical and business qualifications'. This new, expert body would examine and debate financial, trade and economic questions 'with fearless detachment from public opinion' and 'without caring a halfpenny who won the General Election'. A year later, in a memorandum to the Procedure Committee in June 1931, Churchill provided a few more details. He now envisaged an assembly consisting of 120 members serving three-year terms, of whom forty would be MPs experienced in economic and commercial matters, and eighty businessmen, union representatives and economists; among those chosen there would be not less than twenty members of the House of Lords. Again, the whole body would be chosen by party leaders and reflect the party balance in the Commons. It would have the power to initiate inquiries and discussions on economic questions, summon witnesses, and consider all bills dealing with trade and industry after they had received their second reading in the main parliament. The House of Commons could accept or reject the sub-parliament's recommendations as it wished, Churchill argued, thus preserving the formal supremacy of the Commons and the responsibility of the executive.[17]

Churchill soon dropped the idea for an Economic sub-Parliament as he became preoccupied with other issues, particularly India (though it cropped up briefly once more in a 1934 magazine article of his). Members of the Procedure Committee had given him a hard time when he appeared to give evidence on it, and they had raised awkward questions about its composition, scope and powers. The plan raised constitutional issues of far-reaching importance, as *The Economist* had noted at the time, and Churchill's 'rather vague' scheme really raised more questions than it answered. It was difficult to see how a non-partisan atmosphere could be reconciled with selection by party leaders, for instance. How would friction or deadlock between the two parliaments be handled? Where did the consumer, as opposed to the producer, interest fit in? Would a parliament of 'experts' be able to escape the limitations of the contemporary conventional wisdom on economic policy? The more the scheme was examined, the more unrealistic it seemed (although it should be said that the Conservative politician and thinker Leo Amery later argued that a 'House of Industry' could have a useful advisory role). Some critics – the Labour MP Emrys Hughes in the 1960s, and Clive Ponting in the 1990s – claimed that what Churchill was really advocating was the grafting on to the British system of a Mussolini-style, semi-Fascist, corporate state institution. This is an exaggeration, though Churchill's Economic sub-Parliament idea did reflect his wider dissatisfaction with and doubts about modern mass democracy in the early 1930s (see chapter 1). Churchill wanted an advisory, expert and subordinate body, but does not seem to have realized that the role he envisaged was better filled not by a quasi-legislative institution but by something internal to the executive or by a purely consultative body (as with later 'tripartite' institutions bringing together unions, business and government, like the National Economic Development Council set up by Harold Macmillan in 1961).[18]

The Role of the MP

As the 1930s went on, Churchill became less interested in reshaping the institution of Parliament than in defending the rights and powers of its members. To give some background, it is worth noting that in his early career he had been a classic 'carpet-bagger' MP without local connections, moving from sitting for Oldham (1900-1906), to North-West Manchester (1906-1908), and then Dundee when – newly appointed cabinet ministers in those days being obliged to submit for re-election – he lost his Manchester seat in 1908. Dundee turned out not to be the 'seat for life' Churchill had thought it to be: remote from London, his visits were infrequent and he lost badly in 1922 (to a Prohibitionist and to a Labour candidate, this was the occasion when he memorably wrote that 'I found myself without an office, without a seat, without a party, and without an appendix'). Even as an Essex MP, though (sitting for Epping from 1924 and later Woodford – seats conveniently close to central London and Chartwell), he generally confined himself to biennial visits for whistle-stop tours around the constituency, summer fêtes and the party annual general meeting. Sir James Hawkey, a leading figure in the local party and on the district council, handled much constituency business as a 'sort of surrogate MP', although Churchill apparently had a strict rule that he would answer every letter from the constituency. It was, however, a far cry from the regular 'surgeries' and constituency visits of modern MPs.[19]

From the start of his career, his main focus had in any case been national and international, rather than local, issues, and he had a Burkean view of the role of the MP in relation to his constituents, local activists and local interest groups. One of the dangers of tariff reform, he had argued, was that MPs would be pressurized into becoming advocates for the special interests of local industry rather than the general interests of the nation as a whole: 'every member will be a trade member'. Churchill acknowledged that 'the House of Commons is founded on the party system, and, in the main, very much in preponderance upon the two-party system'. But his belief in parliamentary democracy, as Martin Gilbert puts it, 'was also a belief in the value of opinions outside the Party mould, and of Members of Parliament willing to express the unpopular view'. 'I claim and practise a wide measure of independent judgement upon public questions,' Churchill told his local party in 1935. In the 1930s – out of sympathy with the National Government and clashing with his own party leadership over India and rearmament – he also criticized 'the growing power of party . . . machinery' and complained that the independent backbench MP was regarded as 'a public nuisance', going on to praise the 'more intractable people . . . [with] their awkward way of thinking things out for themselves'. Back in 1906 he had mused about the 'small scope for the supporters of a Government': 'The Whips do not want speeches, but votes. The Ministers regard an oration in their praise or defence as only one degree less tiresome than an attack. The earnest party man becomes a silent drudge, tramping at intervals through lobbies to record his vote and wondering why he came to Westminster at all.' In the 1930s, he argued, the scene was even more dismal:

> The House of Commons declined in liveliness and debating power. The bulk of its members became functionaries to register the will, or lack of will, of the party leaders. The large Conservative majorities did not require to be sustained by eloquence or dialectic. There was plenty of party spirit, but without that clash of more or less equal forces which gives to Parliamentary life its light and colour. A high level of docile, disciplined mediocrity has been attained.

'The vitality and life of the House of Commons is one of the real interests of those who wish to see constitutional government maintained,' Churchill argued, in a speech in 1934. 'To crush out the liberty of the House of Commons and make it an organized voting machine will detract from its influence in the country.' In the row over his referral to the Committee of Privileges in 1934 of allegations that ministers had leaned on and improperly influenced witnesses to a select committee, his short-term political motives (over India) were mixed with concerns for Parliament's standards and authority: 'These are not the days, alas, when Parliament can afford to be too lax and easy going in the assertion of its rights and responsibilities.'[20]

Churchill's dissent over Munich brought out into the open opponents in his local party who, in late 1938 and the first few months of 1939, seem to have been acting in league with Conservative Central Office, trying to undermine him in his constituency and possibly oust him. Some branch meetings were swamped by newly signed-up members who outvoted local stalwarts and Churchill loyalists, but Churchill successfully fought back against the revolt, at one point threatening to resign and 'appeal to the electors' if he was not backed up. 'What is the use of Parliament if it is not the place where true statements can be brought before the people?' he argued, in a powerful speech in his constituency in March 1939. 'What is the use of sending Members to the House of Commons who say just the popular things of the moment, and merely endeavour to give satisfaction to the Government Whips by cheering loudly every Ministerial platitude, and by walking through the [voting] Lobbies oblivious of the criticisms they hear? People talk about our Parliamentary institutions and Parliamentary democracy; but if these are to survive, it will not be because the Constituencies return tame, docile, subservient Members, and try to stamp out every form of independent judgement.'[21]

Parliament in Wartime

With this background and these views, it is not surprising that, as prime minister, Churchill took the House of Commons seriously during the Second World War, paying it more attention and showing it more respect than Lloyd George had done in the First World War. Speaking as a backbench MP in April 1917, Churchill had voiced concern at the failure of the House of Commons 'to watch with severe attention the course and management of the war', and the danger of it 'losing all means of controlling or influencing or warning the Government' because of it 'relaxing its vigilance'. The 'abdication of Parliament' had 'given an altogether disproportionate power to the Press, which, working in its proper balance in the Constitution, would discharge only beneficial functions'. Even at this dangerous point in the war, he wanted 'to express. . . a firm belief in Parliamentary institutions and in Ministries responsible to representative assemblies', and he called for a secret session debate so that the prime minister and MPs could speak fully and frankly on war policy. 'On every side you see the power and influence of this House menaced,' he had argued in March 1917. 'The House of Commons would be to blame and failing in its duty if upon all these great questions connected with man-power, the supply of men, and our military policy, they do not insist upon some serious discussion in which the Ministers could take part, and in which hon. Members could really address themselves to questions in which the life and fortunes of the country depend.'[22]

There were more than sixty secret sessions of the Commons while Churchill was prime minister in the Second World War, although around half of them concerned only arrangements for parliamentary sittings. Churchill 'never forgot the over-riding authority of Parliament', recalled Lord Bridges, his cabinet secretary. 'When any really important event took place, he was always insistent that "the Parl." should be told at once. And if, as often happened in the early days of the war, the news was bad news, he would take the greatest care to keep nothing back.' Watching Churchill from his vantage point in the Number 10 private office, Sir John Martin also felt that 'At no time was Parliament's right of criticism restricted, and, if anything, he seemed over-sensitive to parliamentary opinion, insisting on debates and votes of confidence even when it was clear that he enjoyed the support of the over-whelming majority'. He never forgot that it was a parliamentary revolt that had made him prime minister in 1940 and that, as he told the US Congress in December 1941, 'on any day, if they thought the people wanted it, the House of Commons could by a simple vote remove me from my office'. In addition, Churchill was actually the last prime minister to act as leader of the house, a post he held until February 1942 (when Stafford Cripps was given the job) and he did deal with some routine business in that capacity (for example, debates on times of sittings and the move to Church House), though dele-gating most of the work to Attlee, the Labour Party leader and *de facto* deputy prime minister. Geoffrey Best puts it well:

> Because of his deep-rooted constitutionalism, and because the House of Commons was the altar of his mystic communion with the British people, he took pains to keep Members informed of the major events and developments of the war, grim ones no less than grand . . . He could not do anything the House of Commons would surely disapprove of, he always laid before it matters that might cause it concern, and he had to do a lot of explaining to it at times when the war seemed to be going inexplicably badly.

On the other hand, there is something in the argument of Woodrow Wyatt that 'Churchill did not often take the opinion of the House into considera-tion when executing policy. He paid the House of Commons elaborate respect but little attention. His aim was usually either to control the House for his purposes or to use it as a vehicle for appealing to the nation and the world'. Wyatt quotes a story about Churchill and Stafford Cripps. 'Two things I put above everything in my life,' Churchill is supposed to have said. 'God and the House of Commons.' 'Well,' replied Cripps, 'I hope you treat God better than you do the House of Commons.'[23]

At the end of the war, there was a great deal of parliamentary self-congratulation with Churchill declaring that 'the House had proved itself the strongest foundation for waging war that has ever been seen in the whole of our long history'. It had not, of course, been parliamentary 'business as usual'. With the coalition there had been an electoral truce: the Conservative and Labour whips had worked together in a joint whips' office to manage the Commons; there were fewer sittings and shorter sessions (normally a three-day parliamentary week); the amount of legislation introduced was drastically cut; space in the timetable for private members' legislation was removed; Churchill insisted on acquiring the power to waive the normal rules relating to MPs holding 'offices of profit' (by 1941 about 200 MPs held some form of official position and another 116 were in uniform, fuelling concern about the large number of 'place men'). Above all, there was no organized alternative government-in-waiting. Scrutiny and criticism came from a sort of 'second eleven' opposition of Labour and some Conservative MPs, with the most telling attacks coming from a few maverick figures, of whom Aneurin Bevan became probably the most prominent. Complaining of the tameness of the Commons, Bevan claimed in 1941 that Churchill had 'not been sufficiently kicked in this House', and perhaps it was a measure of his effectiveness as a gadfly and critic that Churchill in 1945 described him as having been 'a squalid nuisance' during the war. There was no love lost between the two later, when Bevan became a radical and controversial minister of health in Attlee's Labour government. But in keeping the traditions of parliamentary government alive during the war, Bevan's role and contribution were as important as Churchill's – however much the latter disliked the experience, and maybe because he did.[24]

When the tables were turned after 1945, Churchill did not exactly distinguish himself in what has been called the worst job in British politics – that of leader of the opposition. His attendance in the House was irregular, and he frequently left Anthony Eden in charge of the Conservative Party in the

Commons as well as chairing the regular business meetings of the shadow cabinet in Churchill's absence, though the fortnightly lunches for the Tory high command at the Savoy were more to his liking. Churchill's appetite for the detail and drudgery of effective parliamentary opposition politics was limited, and he spent more time working on his war memoirs and playing the role of world statesman. Although some Conservatives specialized in partic-ular areas of policy (for instance, Eden on foreign affairs, Oliver Stanley on financial policy), Churchill's philosophy was 'out of office let them wander free and unencumbered'. There was no formalized and announced allocation of responsibilities to a long list of 'shadow ministers' and a rigidly organized opposition team, such as has become the rule since 1955. Nor did Churchill get very involved in opposition policy-making in this period, leaving most of the running to Rab Butler, put in charge of the Conservative Research Department, and others (for example, the party's Industrial Policy Committee). Churchill was of the view that 'when an Opposition spells out its policy in detail . . . the Government becomes the Opposition and attacks the Opposition which becomes the Government. So, having failed to win the sweets of office, it fails equally to enjoy the benefits of being out of office'. The main task of the opposition, he emphasized in 1950, was 'criticizing and correcting, so far as they can, any errors and shortcomings [in government measures]'. He argued that 'the Opposition are not responsible for proposing integrated and complicated measures of policy. Sometimes we do, but it is not our obligation'. 'The job of the leader of the Opposition,' Churchill told Lord Moran in 1947, was 'to attack the Government – that and no more.' It was an approach to opposition very different from that adopted by a later Conservative leader like Edward Heath (in 1965-1970), for instance.[25]

Conclusion

Parliament, and particularly the House of Commons, was central to Churchill's conception of democracy as 'government by talking'. 'The object of Parliament is to substitute argument for fisticuffs,' as he once put it. The House of Commons was 'the workshop of democracy', he declared in a speech in 1950. 'It is the champion of the people against executive oppression . . . The House of Commons has ever been the controller and, if need be, the changer of the rulers of the day and of the Ministers appointed by the Crown. It stands forever against oligarchy and one-man power.' He also saw it, along with the monarchy (see chapter 8), in the grand sweep of British history and political development:

> Its structure has stood the strain of the most violent contentions. Its long tradition, its collective personality, its flexible procedure, its social life, its unwritten inviolable conventions have made an organism more effective for the purpose of assimilation than any of which there is record. Every new extension of the franchise has altered the character, outlook, and worldly wealth of its members. The Whig and Tory squires of the eighteenth century and the gifted nominees or sprigs of the nobility have given place to the mercantile and middle classes, and these in turn receive into their midst hundreds of working men. Yet though the human element has undergone these substantial changes, the nature and spirit of the assembly is the same. We may be sure that Fox or Burke, that Disraeli or Gladstone, if they returned today [in 1930], would in a few months feel quite at home and speedily reclaim their rightful place. Indeed, they might find it an all-too-easy conquest.

This positive and Whiggish view of the importance and vitality of Parliament was, however, combined with a feeling, which came to a head in the early 1930s, that it was an institution in decline. 'The House of Commons a generation ago was honoured, a generation ago it was regarded almost as ideal for its purpose. Now it is a threatened institution and even a despised institution,' he warned in 1931. 'The House of Commons as a vehicle of the popular will has gradually become the repository of almost all the power in the State, yet at the same time it has steadily declined in public repute and shows itself increasingly inadequate to deal with the real topics of public interest.' Churchill was not alone in expressing such views, which in part were based on nostalgia for a lost pre-1914 'golden age' of parliamentary government, and in part on a sense of a system under stress and failing to cope with the demands on it in the new political and economic environment of post-1918. The 'pessimistic picture of a Parliament in decline must be taken with a pinch of salt', cautions Stuart Ball, 'but the anxieties expressed after 1918 were the product of real fears of constitutional breakdown'.[26]

With the growing menace from the dictators, Churchill became more concerned to trumpet the virtues of and rally support for the House of Commons. As he wrote in a somewhat purple passage in 1935:

> There is no greater guarantee of our liberties than the House of Commons. Go at Question Time and listen to all the highest Ministers of State being questioned and cross-questioned on every conceivable subject, and entering into the whole process with respect and with good will. Where else in the world can you see the representatives of democracy able to address the leading personages of a powerful Government with this freedom? How the foreigners gape at this performance when they visit the Gallery! What a sign it is that here the people own the Government, and not the Government the people. In the vitality of the House of Commons, in its scenes, in its sensations, in its turbulences, in its generosity, and above all, in its native tolerance and decency, it is the august symbol and instrument of all that liberates and dignifies our island.

There is a real point being made here about the role of Parliament in holding government to account, but that Churchill's view may be over-romanticized is apparent when one considers what a senior interwar civil servant, H. E. Dale, had to say about the perfect answer to a parliamentary question being 'one that is brief, appears to answer the question completely, if challenged can be proved to be accurate in every word, gives no openings for awkward "supplementaries", and discloses really nothing' – a remark that captures exactly the executive mindset. It is arguable that with his emphasis on the drama and theatre of parliamentary debate, Churchill was too sanguine and complacent about the power and strength of the House of Commons as a check on the executive and its growing power in the twentieth century.[27]

Long before he died, Churchill had become 'a part of the legend of Parliament', as a newspaper headline put it in 1965. He had indeed been 'a lifelong and deliberate supporter of the British parliamentary system'. Parliament had been the scene of some of his greatest triumphs and some of his greatest rebuffs, but the latter had never made him waver in his affection for or pride in the House of Commons. 'Powerful institutions rich in tradition mark the people who serve them,' notes the German writer on

Churchill, Christian Graf von Krockow, 'and the British House of Commons shaped Churchill into becoming the great parliamentarian he was . . . It made him into a parliamentarian of conviction', someone who not only saw Parliament as a useful and practically indispensable institution but who also had a deep emotional tie to the institution. When audiences heard him declare 'our Parliament is the best in the world' (1930), they knew he really meant it.[28]

SIX

Churchill and Whitehall

Serving in seven different departments over the course of his long career and as prime minister twice, Churchill had nearly thirty years' ministerial experience of Whitehall and the civil service at close quarters, both departmentally and at the centre of the government machine. In one sense he was a civil servant's ideal minister: decisive, self-confident, industrious and battling hard for his policies at cabinet level. But he was also impulsive, erratic, capricious, argumentative and domineering – he was never an easy minister to work for and at times could be pretty impossible. According to John Colville (his Downing Street private secretary), 'having been in a position to give orders all his life, and seldom obliged to execute them, he had no conception of the practical difficulties of communication and of administrative arrangements'.[1] Unlike a couple of his successors in Number 10 – namely Harold Wilson and Edward Heath – Churchill could never be imagined as a permanent secretary *manqué*.

Churchill and the Civil Service before 1914

In his biography of his father, published in 1906, Churchill had set out an orthodox conception of the constitutional position of the civil service, but in rather overblown language: 'Concealed from the public eye among the deeper recesses of Whitehall, seeking no fame, clad with the special knowledge of lifelong study, armed with the secrets of a dozen cabinets, the slaves of the Lamp or of the Ring render faithful and obedient service to whomsoever holds the talisman. Whatever task be set, wise or foolish, virtuous or evil, as they are commanded, so they do.' Lord Randolph

Churchill had been chancellor of the exchequer for six intense months in 1886 and old Treasury hands like Sir Francis Mowatt, Sir Edward Hamilton and Algernon West helped Winston Churchill with their recollections and reminiscences. 'Over all public departments the department of finance is supreme,' Churchill wrote. 'Erected upon the vital springs of national prosperity, wielding the mysterious power of the purse, the final arbiter in the disputes of every other office, a good fairy or a perverse devil, as "My Lords" may choose, to every imaginative Secretary of State, the Treasury occupies in the polity of the United Kingdom a central and superior position.' The Treasury upheld 'the great traditions of Gladstonian and Peelite finance' and subjected new ministers to 'a baptism of economic truth'. 'Reckless Ministers are protected against themselves, violent Ministers are tamed, timid Ministers are supported and nursed. Few, if any, are insensible to the influences by which they are surrounded.' In Churchill's account, Lord Randolph was 'a Minister of that type that Civil Servants appreciate. He ruled as well as reigned. He had a quick mind, and made it up; a policy and enforced it. He was quick in acquiring information, quick in seizing the real point, quick in understanding what [officials] wished to convey to him . . . ready and willing to hear what [officials] had to say, whether it accorded with his own views or not.'[2]

What Churchill could only admit years later, however, was the way in which Sir Francis Mowatt and other Treasury officials had supplied him as a young and ambitious backbencher with information and briefings on controversial economic and financial matters. In the first two or three years of the 1900 parliament, Churchill made something of a name for himself as a strong supporter of economy, limited public spending (criticizing plans for army expansion) and low taxation; like the Treasury mandarins he was also a strong free-trader at a time when an intense political crisis over tariff reform was enveloping the Balfour government and the Conservative Party. 'Old Mowatt,' Churchill later recalled, 'then head of the Civil Service, said a word to me now and then and put me in touch with some younger officials, afterwards themselves eminent, with whom it was very helpful to talk . . .'. Churchill maintained that these Treasury civil servants did not divulge 'secrets' but rather briefed him with 'published facts set in their true proportion and with their proper emphasis' in order to help him 'take a prominent part in a national controversy'. It would not be the last time that a 'faithful servant of the Crown' was to establish behind-the-scenes contact with Churchill to arm him with 'facts and arguments' on issues of vital national importance. But an official acting in this way as part of a struggle against government policy was 'challenging the administration' and going 'beyond the ordinary limits' of the civil service, as Churchill recognized.[3]

Churchill was always an archetypal 'strong' minister: 'there was nothing of Mr Hacker being manipulated by Sir Humphrey . . . in his civil service relationships,' as Roy Jenkins put it. He was clear about what he wanted from his civil servants, instructing his permanent secretary at the Colonial Office in 1921, for instance, that he expected to receive minutes with either 'a definite recommendation for action or two alternative courses submitted for decision', to which he could simply add his initials if he agreed. But he insisted on writing (or, rather, dictating) major state papers, speeches, cabinet memoranda and important letters himself. At the Board of Trade (1908-10), he worked with some of the most dynamic and innovative senior officials of the day, such as Sir Hubert Llewellyn Smith and William Beveridge. Churchill relied greatly on their advice but he was more than just a 'mouthpiece or puppet of the civil service' insists Paul Addison: 'without him his officials would have been powerless.' He made a notable impression on policy-making and on administrative detail with his landmark social reforms in that department (labour exchanges and unemployment insurance). As home secretary (1910-11), in charge of a more traditional, formal and rigid ministry, there were tensions in his relationship with his civil servants. 'The old hands in the department were rather dismayed by the temerity with which he challenged principles and practices which had remained sacrosanct for many years,' recalled one official. According to Sir Edward Troup, the permanent secretary, 'Once a week or oftener Mr Churchill came to the office bringing with him some adventurous or impossible projects; but after half an hour's discussion something was evolved which was still adventurous but not impossible.'[4]

Churchill was not averse to bending or overriding the normal civil service rules and practices when it suited his purposes. He insisted, for instance, on Edward Marsh, his first private secretary and long-time friend from his time as a junior minister at the Colonial Office (1906-08), being transferred from department to department to be his private secretary in every ministerial office he held until 1929. When planning a high-profile two-week campaigning tour in Lancashire before the January 1910 general election, he ordered his civil servants to draw up an inch-thick file of statistics and analysis to be used in his speeches from Liberal Party platforms about free trade. Civil servants, as he knew well, are supposed to be strictly neutral in party-political terms. 'But just as Treasury officials had briefed Churchill against Tariff Reform in 1903,' notes Paul Addison, 'so now the officials of the Board of Trade were happy to brief him for the same purpose in 1909.'[5] Churchill was anxious to bring outsiders with special expertise or experience into Whitehall, opening up the closed ranks of the established civil service. He brought William Beveridge into the Board of Trade as an outside expert at a salary of £600 – more than that paid to similar staff. Churchill also insisted that the new labour exchanges should be staffed by businessmen, trade unionists, social reformers and other outsiders recruited via a special appointments committee, bypassing the normal civil service 'open competition' procedure – this arrangement was later criticized before the 1912 Royal Commission on the Civil Service as 'jobbery' and 'patronage', and the system was abandoned. Years later, as prime minister in the 1950s, Churchill thought nothing of ordering his private secretary to check Conservative Party canvassing returns when he wanted a prediction for the result of a forthcoming by-election. That same (diplomatic service) official, seconded to act as Churchill's private secretary after his retirement from the premiership, wrote political speeches for the old man and accompanied his wife, Clementine, to constituency functions.[6]

One or two of Churchill's ideas at this time chimed with the analysis and arguments of the so-called 'National Efficiency' campaigners, but fundamentally he did not share the Webb–Milner dissatisfaction with the nature and capabilities of the British state and its institutions or their interest in a more 'scientific' model of government. In 1909 he sketched out in a memorandum to Lloyd George some ideas for new co-ordinating and planning machinery to deal with poverty and unemployment, analogous to the Committee of Imperial Defence on the military side. The Board of Trade should become something like the 'Intelligence Department' of government, accumulating information, preparing plans and making forecasts of trade and unemployment to be fed into a 'Committee of National Organization', an inter-departmental committee of ministers and top officials, chaired by the chancellor of the exchequer, which would orchestrate the government's response, co-ordinating spending, relief schemes and development projects. Although nothing came of this idea, it was in some ways a far-seeing proposal for what today would be called 'joined-up government', Churchill talking of 'clamping together' central and municipal (local government) plans for counteracting trade depressions, better co-ordinating 'the study of these problems' with speedy action by the various departments concerned, 'preventing over-lapping, waste, friction and omission, and . . . securing a continuous policy'.[7]

Reforming the Ministry of Munitions

Churchill's ministerial drive and administrative skills were seen to good effect during his time as a minister under Lloyd George, 1917-22. Martin Gilbert writes:

> At the Ministry of Munitions in 1917, and as head of the Middle East Department in 1921, Churchill set up entirely new administrative machinery to deal with previously unco-ordinated problems. To each Department of which he was head, he brought in officials with a wide range of expertise, encouraged them to use their initiative, scrutinized what they did, stirred them to action by constant questioning and supported their policies when they went forward to the Cabinet for decision.

'There is no more capable chief of a department than he is,' Christopher Addison, his cabinet colleague, thought. As minister of munitions, he insisted on changing the cumbersome internal organization of the ministry, which by the time he took it over had grown like Topsy and was made up of fifty departments each operating semi-independently and reporting directly to the minister, who was swamped by 'heaps of bulky files' and 'numberless minor decisions', as well as having to deal with 'most intricate and inter-related problems'. Churchill overhauled this creaking structure by grouping the fifty departments into ten large units each run by a head who was responsible to the minister, and by forming these top officials into a Munitions Council, normally chaired by the minister, which met daily to co-ordinate policy and was underpinned by a number of specialist sub-committees. The senior staff of the ministry were, in Churchill's words, a mixture of '"big business men" . . . assisted by a strong cadre of Civil Servants . . . Thus we had at once the initiative, drive, force and practical experience of the open competitive world coupled with those high standards of experience, of official routine, and of method, which are the qualifications of the Civil Service.' As well as the inevitable Eddie Marsh, Churchill also brought in some senior officials he had previously worked closely with at the Admiralty (Sir William Graham Greene and James Masterton-Smith – the latter had been Churchill's private secretary at the Admiralty and later became his permanent secretary at the Colonial Office). Churchill described himself as free now to take an overall view, concentrating on determining priorities and taking special initiatives. He practically always approved a Council committee report exactly as it was submitted. 'Instead of struggling through the jungle on foot,' he wrote, 'I rode comfortably on an elephant whose trunk could pick up a pin or uproot a tree with equal ease, and from whose back a wide scene lay open.' He was less successful in his aim of reducing the size of the munitions ministry headquarters staff which stood at 12,000 when he arrived in 1917, and which had doubled to 25,000 by the end of the war, occupying comman-deered hotels near Trafalgar Square.[8]

Churchill and the Treasury

In contrast to his earlier achievements and successful dealings with Whitehall, the usual image of Churchill the minister being a 'powerhouse of original ideas' who 'refused to be browbeaten by civil servants' is, in many accounts, rather dented by his experience as chancellor of the exchequer, 1924-9, when he is often portrayed as having been 'bounced' and misled by the experts and as having caved in to the weight of official opinion supporting the ill-fated decision to return to the gold standard in 1925. The idea of Churchill as 'an unwilling dupe of the authorities . . . [who] used their technical expertise to foist their own opinions upon an untutored Chancellor, whose acquiescence was nominal, reluctant, and rueful' can be traced back to J. M. Keynes's polemic *The Economic Consequences of Mr Churchill.* By 1928 Churchill was complaining to his private secretary about 'the complacency of the Treasury and the Bank [of England]' and almost disavowing ministerial responsibility by saying that '*they* have caused an immense amount of misery and impoverishment by *their* . . . handling of the problem' (emphasis added) and he later came to regard the decision as his greatest blunder. In *Great Contemporaries*, published in 1937, he pointedly commented that 'All British Chancellors of the Exchequer have yielded themselves, some spontaneously, some unconsciously, some reluctantly to [the] compulsive intellectual atmosphere' of the Treasury. In a newspaper article, he described how Treasury officials' 'high abilities and immense knowledge of matters very difficult to be understood, requiring a lifetime to master, give them a real power, which they use sometimes rightly, sometimes wrongly', but he conceded that they used this power 'always honestly, selflessly, and in what they sincerely believe to be the public interest'.[9]

The 'doctrine of bad advice', as Robert Rhodes James called it, does seem applicable in this case. Churchill was not in a strong political position in the Conservative Party at that time, and Treasury, Bank of England and 'Establishment' opinion and advice were virtually unanimous and compelling. But Churchill was not a weak minister or putty in his advisers' hands. The overall picture painted by his private secretary, P. J. Grigg, is of a minister strongly pressing his own views during his tenure of the Treasury, with a 'rough' process of 'heated and even violent arguments' needed before officials could convince him that his bright ideas and projects were flawed or unworkable. The decision to return to gold was not rushed or ill thought through: it came after two months of intensive discussion and argument during which Churchill took advice widely, including from outside experts like Keynes and former chancellor Reginald McKenna, who were sceptical on the issue. But although an experienced minister, and with some background in economic and trade issues from earlier in his career, he did not have the depth of technical knowledge and understanding of complex financial and exchange rate issues to do more than express some uneasiness and vague doubts about the consequences of the decision. Churchill did, in any event, share the general orthodox free trade and 'sound finance' convictions of his Treasury advisers, even if his appetite for rumbustious disputation and constant starting of hares unsettled the more conventional mandarins. He had envisaged a strong Treasury (and chancellor) having an active policy role on a wide front across government, including the social policy field, although the Treasury's traditional role in holding down public expenditure and taxation limited what could be done in this respect – indeed, he once likened Treasury officials to 'inverted Micawbers, waiting for something to turn down'. This did not, however, stop Churchill rebuking Sir Warren Fisher, the Treasury's permanent secretary, in 1925 for submitting a memorandum about the alleged 'impossibility of any reduction in the emoluments or numbers of the Civil Service', or from noting with satisfaction in his 1928 Budget speech that 7,000 civil-service posts had been cut in the first three years of the Conservative governments elected in 1924, while announcing plans to cut a further 11,000 over the next five years.[10]

Churchill did not get on too well with Warren Fisher, who annoyed him by spending most of his time working to the prime minister as head of the civil service rather than advising the chancellor – and he criticized Fisher for acting as though he had some sort of independent authority in that role, which was, in Churchill's words, 'obviously unconstitutional' (a view shared by some Conservative MPs, though Baldwin brushed aside the criticisms). (How Churchill would have reacted if he had known that Fisher was privately complaining to Neville Chamberlain, then minister of health, that the chancellor was 'a lunatic, an irresponsible child, not a grown man' can only be guessed at.)[11]

A Constitutional Bulwark?

On a wider front, Churchill had a keen sense in the 1920s of the important constitutional role played by the civil service, 'that most unjustly and ignorantly abused class'. 'Powerful, uncorruptible, anonymous, the Civil Service discharges a function in this country which is invaluable, and without which immediate disaster would overtake any Administration which attempts to carry on the business of the State,' he said in 1922. 'What a vital thing it is to have some instrument which is thinking not in days or months or in

Parliaments, but is thinking of the affairs of the British Empire in terms of a whole lifetime.' A 1928 speech is worth quoting at length:

> The Civil Service is quite incompetent to run the country by itself just as the politicians are quite impotent to run it by themselves. It is a question of combined effort. It is a case of the reciprocal struggle of discordant forces which draws out the harmony of the whole. United we stand; divided we fall. Whether you own the humble crystal set, or whether, as at the Treasury, you possess an eight-valve outfit, the results and experience are the same. The moment you put too much current on the machine it howls and shrieks at you. . . You have to key it down to a more moderate tone, and that, I believe, will be the experience of every Government which takes office in this country. They will find an instrument of marvellous complexity – and perfection – and as long as they use it, it will respond to every lawful, earnest effort and wish that they may express, but the moment they go too far, and lay violent hands upon the machine and put too much current upon it, then it will be incapable of rendering a proper response to their desire.[12]

The notion of the civil service as a constitutional bulwark was shared by other leading Conservatives at this time, Balfour arguing that the civil service 'mitigate[d] the stresses and strains inseparable from party warfare' and Baldwin describing it as a 'stabilizer' and a 'shock absorber'. The implication was that it was an institution that would loyally serve but also constrain, educate and tame a Labour government. Churchill had insisted in 1919 that 'The suggestion that a Labour Government would not find the means of carrying on the administration of the affairs of the British Empire at home and abroad is utterly unworthy of the spirit of the British public life. Admirals, Generals, Diplomatists, Civil Servants would be bound to lend their aid, and their loyal aid within the limits of the Constitution. The King's Government must be carried on'. In 1922 he anticipated 'an era of kaleidoscopic politics' in which governments would 'rise and fall and succeed each other with baffling rapidity', with ministers – and he clearly meant socialist ministers – 'entirely inexperienced, untutored, undisillusioned, and with no true measure of the difference between what could be said and what could be done' entering office. 'If that were so,' he went on, 'a still greater function than that which the Civil Servants are now discharging would descend upon them, and on them would come the full, dead, massive weight of responsibility in maintaining the continuity of government of this great Empire.' The civil service, he maintained, had to be kept free from party politics. To this end, he opposed an American-style 'spoils system' in which a government would import its nominees and partisans into Whitehall and, while welcoming the 'legitimate development of trade unionism in the Civil Service' and the Whitley Council system (staff nego-tiating machinery), he maintained after the General Strike of 1926 that civil-service trade unionism should not have a political character (legislation was passed banning civil-service unions from affiliating to the Labour Party). Civil servants' 'obligations to the State' were paramount.[13]

In these constitutional terms, however, Churchill and his various inform-ants were skating on very thin ice in the mid-1930s, when he was in receipt of 'leaks' from inside Whitehall of confidential official information about German and British military preparations, which he then used to press the government in the House of Commons over rearmament and the threat from Nazi Germany. Churchill's sources were well placed and senior figures inside the intelligence community, the Foreign Office, the Air Ministry and the air force, including Desmond Morton, head of the Industrial Intelligence Centre (created by the Committee of Imperial Defence to monitor arms manufacturing in Europe and German rearmament); Ralph Wigram, head of the Foreign Office's Central Department, with special responsibility for Germany; Sir Robert Vansittart, the Germanophobe permanent under-secretary of the Foreign Office; and Squadron Leader Charles Torr Anderson, director of training in the RAF. They and others ensured that Churchill was regularly supplied with secret reports, copies of despatches from the British embassy in Berlin, and the latest intelligence figures on the scale and pace of German arms production and Luftwaffe and RAF rearmament. 'Chartwell [Churchill's country house] became a virtual private intelligence centre,' in David Stafford's words, and 'out of office [Churchill] may have been, but he was frequently better informed about both British and Nazi rearmament than many Cabinet ministers.'[14]

The government clearly knew something of what was going on or suspected it: Wigram was threatened with a distant overseas posting if he did not stop seeing Churchill (in fact he died in 1936) and the cabinet secretary, Sir Maurice Hankey, strongly rebuked Churchill for receiving secret information from serving military officers. Desmond Morton's claim that he had been given special authority to keep Churchill informed by Ramsay MacDonald and his successors in Number 10 (Baldwin and Neville Chamberlain) is uncorroborated and unlikely; years later, when John Colville asked Churchill whether this was indeed the case, all he would say was, 'Have another drop of brandy.' That Churchill's informants had patriotic motives, were alarmed by Nazi intentions, and concerned about Britain's lack of military preparedness and the general stance of British policy towards Germany, does not make their actions legitimate ones for government servants, as they and Churchill surely knew. It is beside the point that Churchill was a senior member of the Privy Council and that there is no evidence that secret sources were compromised. The unauthorized release – and receipt – of any official information was a criminal offence under the 1911 Official Secrets Act, a measure with which Churchill had been closely associated as home secretary before the First World War. As David Stafford points out: 'Churchill, not to mention other informants, blatantly defied the Official Secrets Act throughout the 1930s. Convinced of the rightness of his course, he tried to reassure his informants about the propriety of their acts. When Torr Anderson passed on one highly secret document, he confessed that he had never been so frightened in his life. Churchill's response that loyalty to the state overrode loyalty to the RAF would have cut no ice in law.'[15] The activities of Churchill and his Whitehall 'moles' at this time were, in strict terms, illegal, improper and contrary to civil-service constitutional ethics – that they were vindicated by history is another matter altogether.

Wartime Whitehall

The senior civil-service mandarins were in general dismayed by Churchill's accession to the premiership in 1940 – they had mostly worked well with, and respected, Neville Chamberlain, and some certainly hoped that Halifax would succeed him. For his part, Churchill seems to have distrusted at least some top civil servants and to have been suspicious or had a low opinion of some government departments (the War Office, for example, he believed was 'hidebound, devoid of imagination, extravagant of manpower and slow'). Whatever his public 'bulldog' reputation, his judgement, personality and style as a minister had given him a poor reputation among 'insiders', as John Colville recalled in his memoirs:

> In May 1940 the mere thought of Churchill as Prime Minister sent a cold chill down the spines of the staff at 10 Downing Street, where I was working as Assistant Private Secretary to Mr Neville Chamberlain. Churchill's impetuosity had, we thought, contributed to the Norwegian fiasco, and General Ismay had told us in despairing terms of the confusion caused by his enthusiastic irruptions into the peaceful and orderly deliberations of the Military Co-ordination Committee and the Chiefs of Staff. His verbosity and restlessness made unnecessary work, prevented real planning and caused friction. Indeed we felt that Chamberlain had been weak in allowing the First Lord of the Admiralty to assume responsibilities far in excess of his Departmental concerns, and if we had known he was conducting his own telegraphic correspondence with President Roosevelt we should have been still more horrified by such presumption. Our feelings at 10 Downing Street were widely shared in the Cabinet Offices, the Treasury and throughout Whitehall.

'Seldom can a Prime Minister have taken office with "the Establishment", as it would now be called, so dubious of the choice and so prepared to find its doubts justified,' wrote Colville. But 'within a fortnight all was changed. I doubt if there has ever been such a rapid transformation of opinion within Whitehall and of the tempo at which business was conducted'. This was not least because of the impact of Churchill's more positive and inspirational qualities – his energy and zeal, his injection of a sense of purpose and urgency. 'Churchill arrived on the scene like a jet-propelled rocket,' recalled Colville:

> The pace became frantic and totally unfamiliar methods had to be adopted . . .
> The hours expanded from early morning till long after midnight. Telephones of various hues were installed in every nook and cranny . . . There was no longer a shallow black box [used by Chamberlain to hold his overnight paperwork and ministerial briefs], but at least two large, thick and bulging ones.

166

Labels marked 'Action This Day' or 'Report in Three Days' were attached to the ceaseless flow of minutes, dictated straight on to a typewriter, which poured out of the Prime Minister's bedroom, the Cabinet room or even the Bath Room. The Chiefs of Staff, the Secretary to the Cabinet, Ministers of all kinds and dozens of almost unidentifiable characters came and went with bewildering speed. Replies were expected within minutes of questions being asked, staid officials actually took to running and bells rang continuously. Whitehall was galvanized and the office at No.10 was pandemonium. We realised that we were at war.[16]

A year before war broke out, Churchill had expressed the view that, whatever might be the case with the quality of contemporary political leaders compared with the pre–1914 statesmen, there had been no decline in the civil service, which continued to attract 'a perennial stream of the finest brains in the nation' and which in the top ranks provided ministers with 'official advisers whose qualities have never been surpassed' – and he cited Sir Robert Vansittart and (presumably tongue-in-cheek) Sir Horace Wilson as examples. Wilson was Chamberlain's *éminence grise*, a key adviser on all matters, including foreign policy, and was dragged into prominence as an arch-appeaser who was denounced as one of the 'Guilty Men' in the famous pamphlet of that title published in 1940. The 'Churchillians' in reality despised Horace Wilson. Chamberlain had made him permanent secretary to the Treasury and head of the civil service early in 1939. As prime minister, Churchill was intensely suspicious of Wilson and effectively banished him from the centre of power – he was unceremoniously evicted from his office next to the Cabinet Room on Churchill's first day as PM (his things thrown into the corridor during the lunch-hour) and was thereafter confined to running the Treasury (as a department, rather under a cloud during the war) and routine civil-service functions, and was not allowed to call at Number 10. That the Labour Party had its own reasons for demanding Wilson's removal from any influence in Number 10 as a condition for them joining the wartime coalition government could only have strengthened Churchill's determination to oust him. But (perhaps because Churchill's position against the Chamberlainites in his own party was initially not strong) Wilson was not sacked and was allowed to continue in his post until he reached the normal retirement age in July 1942, when his advice about his successor was ignored and Churchill instead appointed Sir Richard Hopkins, with whom he had worked as chancellor in the 1920s.[17]

Churchill liked to work with and through a small group of people he would see frequently, who would be at his beck and call at all hours, who were absolutely discreet, and who could adjust to and accept his distinctive, even sometimes quite peculiar, working methods including his habit of holding meetings into the small hours (Churchill kept going with an hour's nap in the afternoon) and his insistence that submissions put to him should cover no more than one side of typescript. There was an informality about his style which meant that his key advisers were often drawn into his social circle at Chartwell or Chequers: his favourite private secretaries were treated as part of the family, and meals would be enlivened by 'the Prof' (Professor F. A. Lindemann, later Lord Cherwell) calculating with his sliderule the volume of champagne consumed by Churchill throughout his life. Serviced on a day-to-day, round-the-clock basis by his private secretaries, what Churchill called his 'Secret Circle' included senior official advisers, notably Sir Edward Bridges and General Sir Hastings Ismay, and three personal counsellors, friends and aides: 'the Prof', Brendan Bracken and Desmond Morton. This was the key group, whom he trusted and whose abilities he respected, connecting him to the Whitehall machine and enabling him to operate the levers of power. But Churchill was never in any of his advisers' pockets. 'He was open to persuasion, although it often needed courage to press the point,' recalled John Colville:

> He did need restraining and one of his virtues was that pertinaciously though he might contest an issue, tirelessly though he might probe, he did not reject restraint once he had convinced himself that the arguments for caution were neither craven nor bureaucratic. Unless he was so convinced, he was not susceptible to influence even by his closest friends and advisers . . . Nevertheless . . . however much Churchill was determined to make up his mind, he seldom refused to listen and he was always prepared to weigh a good argument from whatever source it came.

Churchill needed civil servants around him 'to steady him and keep him on the rails', Lord Moran later noted.[18]

Civil service 'insiders' feared that 'the Prof', Bracken and Morton, the three intimates, advisers and henchmen who accompanied Churchill into Number 10 in May 1940 – dubbed the 'crazy gang' by one civil service private secretary – would be the nucleus of a Lloyd George-type 'Garden Suburb' or 'Kitchen Cabinet', a personal apparatus bypassing the normal institutions and procedures at the centre of Whitehall. Though Churchill was often attracted and enthused by the idea of special teams or units (unofficial 'private armies') outside the normal bureaucratic hierarchies, he did not in fact undermine the regular, tried-and-tested mechanisms of Number 10 and the Cabinet Secretariat. Morton, who had kept Churchill supplied with leaked secret intelligence information in the 1930s and had been attached to Churchill's staff at the Admiralty (1939-40), was a link with the security and intelligence services and a liaison person with allied governments in exile in London, but within a year his influence had faded and he moved to the outer fringes of the Churchill regime. Bracken had been Churchill's parliamentary private secretary at the Admiralty, and in Number 10 seems to have taken on the role of an all-purpose 'fixer' and prime-ministerial confidant, one of the men closest to Churchill, sitting up late at night with him, supplying political intelligence and parliamentary gossip, and advising on appointments and on patronage decisions. But after 1941, when he became minister of information, he ceased to have the same continual direct access and influence with the prime minister. 'The Prof' was a constant presence in Churchill's entourage (having become an indispensable Churchill acolyte in the 1920s and 1930s) and was supported by the Prime Minister's Statistical Section (the 'S' branch: comprising six or seven staff, mostly economists), which functioned as something like Churchill's personal think tank. Churchill was concerned that Whitehall did not give scientific advice and advisers a high enough priority, and so appointed 'the Prof' as his personal scientific adviser (first at the Admiralty, then at Number 10) to provide a high-level *entrée* (a 'doormat for inventors', Bracken once said) and to act as an 'interpreter' for the PM on complex technical issues. But 'the Prof' was more than this and would today be described as an influential Downing Street special adviser and prime-ministerial 'guru'. He received all the cabinet papers and those of high-level committees, and also took on a wide-ranging role as a provider of information, analysis and advice direct to the PM on logistical and production questions, economic policy, post-war reconstruction, and other issues – producing graphs, charts and arresting statistics that Churchill used to good effect to probe and prod his ministers and the bureaucracy. After December 1942, when he was made paymaster general, Cherwell was able to attend ministerial meetings in his own right while continuing his role as a personal and independent adviser to the prime minister, as an irritant to departments and a counter-force to any Whitehall consensus.[19]

The main connecting links between Churchill and the rest of government in the wartime years ran through the official channels of the PM's private office in Number 10 and the War Cabinet Secretariat. It was in fact Churchill who introduced the term 'private office' to Number 10 from the Admiralty. Under Chamberlain there had been four private secretaries, assisted by a few typists; under Churchill the private office had to expand to cope with the greater volume of work and prime-ministerial activity, to include six or seven private secretaries and over twenty support staff and typists. The private secretaries played a key role as gatekeepers, filtering the mass of paperwork pouring into Number 10 and deciding which items needed Churchill's personal attention, and juggling his diary to fit in his meetings and ration the access of the many people who wanted to see him. Churchill expected his private secretaries to note his decisions and pass them on to those who needed to act upon them – he did not expect or want them to be policy advisers or to exercise a delegated power (perhaps a reaction, it has been suggested, to his experience with P. J. Grigg, his tough-minded, sharp and assertive private secretary at the Treasury 1924-9; Eric Seal, who did at times try to 'steer' Churchill, was promoted out of the Number 10 private office in May 1941). There was a 'personalization' of the private office in the sense that it was very important to Churchill that the staff in it were 'on his wavelength' – he did not 'take' to some recruits, who had to be moved out of it – and he became close to some officials, particularly John Colville and Leslie Rowan.[20]

It was exposure to what the War Cabinet Secretariat, and particularly General ('Pug') Ismay, could do for him as PM that was crucial in convincing Churchill to abandon any idea of building up a full-scale prime ministerial ('Garden Suburb') staff of his own, centred around his personal acolytes. The War Cabinet Secretariat, with mixed civil-service and military staff and greatly strengthened during the war, was the bureaucratic nerve centre of the wartime Churchill government. Ismay ran the military side of the Secretariat and was chief staff officer to Churchill in his capacity as minister of defence, being made, at the PM's insistence, a member in his own right of the Chiefs of Staff Committee. He played a vital role as an intermediary and buffer between Churchill and the chiefs of staff, interpreting the one to the other, sorting out problems and following up on decisions. Highly respected by the military and in Whitehall, he had a shrewd understanding of Churchill, describing him as 'superb in a Test Match but no good at all at village cricket', and could be relied on, if necessary, to talk Churchill out of his more 'dangerous' or impractical ideas. Sir Edward Bridges, secretary to the cabinet since 1938, did not have the same sort of close personal rapport with the PM as that between Churchill and Ismay but forged a highly effective working partnership, dealing with home-front issues, processing decisions, liaising with civil departments, and advising on the handling of cabinet business and on machinery-of-government issues (oiling the workings of the cabinet committee system). As with Ismay, Churchill came to place great reliance on Bridges' advice and judgement and, always unhappy about changes in the faces around him, in early 1945 insisted that he must continue as cabinet secretary while also taking on the post of permanent secretary to the Treasury and head of the civil service (an unwieldy arrangement that continued formally until the end of 1946). The great and indispensable contribution of Bridges, Ismay and their staffs was in quietly harnessing Churchill's unique individual political force and creativity to an effective administrative mechanism (which did function occasionally as a brake or a 'clamping machine') almost without him realizing it.[21]

As wartime prime minister, Churchill presided over a Whitehall bureaucracy that was inevitably greatly increased in size (expanding from 347,000 staff in 1939 to 1.1 million in 1945) and in the range of its activities compared to pre-war days. New departments sprang up, while existing ones expanded and took on new functions. The civil service was a crucial instrument in producing the most effective mobilization of national resources of any country in the war. However, Britain's military setbacks up to the end of

1942 stimulated extensive criticism in the press and Parliament, and from all parts of the political spectrum, of the government machine and the civil service over the organization of the war effort; and the looming problems of post-war reconstruction also provoked concern about the administrative capabilities of the British system of government. Sir Stafford Cripps, then lord privy seal, appears to have seen this public discontent as a lever that he could use in a bid to replace Churchill as prime minister and pressed in 1942 for an outside inquiry into civil service efficiency and the management of the government machine. Politically, Cripps was soon outmanoeuvred and seen off, but Churchill was in any case distinctly unenthusiastic about such an exercise, pooh-poohing 'academic and philosophical speculations which ought in these times to be the province of persons of leisure', and he was sceptical too of the desire to achieve 'unnatural symmetry' in the pattern of cabinet and departmental organization. Senior mandarins were predictably determined on an 'inside job' and the process of 'MG' inquiry and review was pushed down into a network of Whitehall committees presided over by Sir John Anderson, a former permanent secretary and a key wartime minister (a state servant of awesome and chilly efficiency, dubbed the 'automatic pilot' by Churchill), which ensured that the result was cautious adaptation in line with civil-service thinking rather than root-and-branch change of the government machine. Some commentators, such as Peter Hennessy, believe that this was a great 'lost opportunity' but 'insiders' did not see it in those terms at the time and it is difficult to imagine any other reaction from Churchill, given the burdens he was carrying as wartime PM. At the Board of Trade and at the Ministry of Munitions in a different era he had toyed with ideas about, or set up, new machinery (see above), but it was understandable if he now regarded Whitehall reform as a distraction from more important matters. Plans for new 'house party' civil-service selection procedures, involving psychological tests, concerned him when he heard about them in early 1945 but he could not be expected to be seriously engaged with such detailed matters, for instance. He was not alone in his response and attitude: perhaps Attlee had more scope than Churchill to push through a radical overhaul of Whitehall after 1945 but it is notable that the post-war Labour government, too, shied away from fundamental reorganization of the civil service and machinery of government. The civil service had had a 'good war', on the whole, and both Churchill and Attlee felt that the Whitehall machine was basically sound and in the capable hands of men they liked and trusted and had worked with closely and successfully. There was thus no 1940s equivalent of the Lloyd George 'administrative revolution' that had transformed much of Whitehall and reorganized the civil service in the 1916–21 period.[22]

Return to Power

The allegedly excessive size of the civil service, 'bureaucracy' and controls were obvious targets for Churchill and the Conservatives in the late 1940s, against a background of 'austerity', shortages and continued rationing under the post-war Labour government. Churchill's controversial 'Gestapo' speech in 1945 had included a swipe at the 'vast bureaucracies' that would be created in a socialist state, composed of civil servants 'no longer servants and no longer civil'. The excessive number of civil servants, he complained at different times in 1947 and 1948, was a 'scandal', the administrative machine was overburdened, and the extent of controls and red tape threatened to make the country 'one vast Wormwood Scrubbery'. But he insisted that he had the 'highest regard for our civil servants . . . It is no fault of theirs if they are now made too numerous; it is the fault of this [Labour] Government'. The 1951 Conservative manifesto pledged to 'simplify the administrative machine' and reduce 'waste and extravagance' in government, and as prime minister Churchill was soon upbraiding his minister of food for not reducing quickly enough the number of ministry 'snoopers' (enforcement officers). Prompted by Lord Cherwell, he queried the enlarged size of the Admiralty – 33,500 in 1953 compared to 13,000 in 1939 – asking why there was one civil servant to every ten sailors in 1939, but one to every four and a half now. Although moving to abolish controls and rationing, the Churchill government, however, found it difficult to bring about a significant reduction in the size of the civil service: by 1955 it had fallen by around 30,000 out of the three-quarters of a million who had been in place when the Tories took office in November 1951. Further cuts were made – with difficulty – throughout the second half of the 1950s, but the number of civil servants started to increase again under Macmillan in the early 1960s. It was never going to be easy to cut the size of the Whitehall bureaucracy when, rather than adopting a thoroughgoing economic liberal platform, the Conservatives under Churchill and his successors were basically presenting themselves as better at running the Keynesian welfare state than the Labour Party.[23]

Churchill and other Conservatives had returned to power in 1951 with some suspicions of the political leanings of the civil service, concerned that it was institutionally pro-Labour and pro-state controls. Harold Macmillan, for instance, believed that 'the "Trade Union" of officials is back in power. The Treasury planners are supreme. Ministers are treated very politely, but with firmness, as temporary nuisances'. Churchill is said to have balefully inspected the Number 10 private secretaries he inherited from Attlee before remarking – unfairly and inaccurately – that they were 'drenched with socialism'. But on the other hand, for him to regard the two leading officials of the day, Sir Edward Bridges and Sir Norman Brook, as his 'chums' among the higher civil service and for him loftily to say to Macmillan that 'the "boys" would know' how to set about the government's housing drive suggests a more trusting, if complacent, attitude. That trust went only so far, however. He continued to regard the Treasury with a wary eye – 'a lot of mean swine' – and set up a ministerial advisory committee (which soon disappeared) to watch over his chancellor, Rab Butler, and as a check on Treasury advice; the revival of Cherwell's Statistical Section (1951–3) to some extent served the same end. And Churchill had absolutely no love for the Foreign Office (although he held some individual diplomats, such as his private secretary John Colville, in high regard). 'A lot of scuttling rabbits' was a typical complaint. 'He suspected them of pursuing their own policy, irrespective of what the Government might wish,' wrote Colville, 'and he mistrusted their judgement.' The FO was 'an excellent institution for explaining us to other countries, but when its head is weak it seems to spend its time seeking agreements abroad at our expense', he moaned to Lord Moran in 1953. 'The Foreign Office is probably the best educated of the Departments and in many ways the most agreeable,' Anthony Montague Browne recorded him as saying. But the taint of appeasement still stuck to it: 'They are adept at analysing a foreign power's views and explaining why we should fall in with them. They are not nearly so good at the reverse process . . . Our diplomacy tends to turn the other cheek to the wrong people, and sometimes it turns all four.'[24]

Now aged seventy-seven, Churchill more than ever wanted familiar people around him and insisted on unpicking Whitehall's carefully worked-out dispositions (although he normally rubber-stamped the recommendations for top-level departmental appointments made by the head of the civil service.) In October 1951, he did not want to take the new Number 10 principal private secretary (David Pitblado) appointed only three months before by Attlee. Sir Edward Bridges had to talk him out of demanding the return of Leslie Rowan (by that time a senior Treasury official) who had been in his wartime private office, but Churchill then pressed for the appointment of John Colville, who was, properly speaking, too junior for the post but with whom Churchill had had a close and trusting relationship during the war, who left his post in the Lisbon embassy and served in joint harness with Pitblado. Widely known to enjoy Churchill's special confidence, Colville was in an influential position between 1951 and 1955. At the same time, Churchill vetoed the planned move of Sir Norman Brook from his post as secretary of the cabinet to the Treasury. Brook had been deputy secretary of the war cabinet, 1942-3, and had remained in touch between 1945 and 1951, visiting Chartwell quite often and helping Churchill with his war memoirs. Brook was a highly politically attuned operator (who went on to become the most powerful of Harold Macmillan's advisers after 1957), who always greatly admired Churchill and became exceptionally close to him in the 1951-5 government, seeing him virtually every day, sitting alongside him in cabinet and cabinet committee meetings, accompanying him on his trips to confer with the Americans, and advising him on every possible subject, including ministerial appointments and reshuffles. Churchill trusted and relied more on him than on anyone else – minister or official. Brook was a steadying influence: 'He was wise in his advice,' noted John Colville, 'and while appearing to fall in, at an early stage, with ideas that he privately thought wrong or extravagant, he presented the counter-arguments so skilfully and so tactfully that they were nearly always approved.' Such was Churchill's esteem for Brook that he had him made a privy councillor in 1953, a very rare honour for a civil servant (he took some persuading to recommend Edward Bridges too). Churchill's flagging energy and failing health made Brook all the more indispensable, and that Churchill was able to continue in office for as long as he did owed a great deal to Brook's loyal service and the active role he played as cabinet secretary. Indeed, for several months after Churchill's stroke in June 1953, Brook, Colville and Churchill's parliamentary private secretary (and son-in-law) Christopher Soames kept Number 10 on the road, in some cases taking decisions in the prime minister's name but without his specific authority.[25]

Civil service reorganization did not attract a lot of Conservative attention in opposition in the late 1940s, though fairly conventional 'reformist' ideas (similar in fact to those canvassed by Fabian and Labour Party writers at the time) were aired by some Tories, including better use of scientists and other experts, improved recruitment and training practices, and ending Treasury control of the civil service. However, on Churchill's return to office in 1951, no political weight was put behind these proposals. Lord Woolton complained in 1954 that the cabinet had never discussed the reform of the machinery of government. Top civil servants were cautious and defensive, leading ministers took little interest in the issue and Churchill had his own ideas, wanting to reduce the power of the Treasury, cut back the interde-partmental committee system and introduce his 'overlords' idea (see chapter 7). But after spending some time with Sir Norman Brook early on in the government discussing 'MG' issues, he soon lost any enthusiasm for reform. A Royal Commission on the Civil Service (the Priestley Commission) was appointed in 1953 (reporting in November 1955, after Churchill had retired), but illustrating the unwillingness to open up a wide-ranging debate about civil service and Whitehall reform to meet the changing needs of a larger, more interventionist state, its remit was a narrow one, confined to pay and conditions of service issues. (On which front the Churchill government had finally agreed to the introduction of equal pay for women in the civil service in January 1955.)[26]

The impression of the civil service well into the 1950s is of an enduring, self-confident and complacent institution developing and adapting at its own pace. By that stage Churchill was too tired, too old and too grand to take a great deal of interest in administrative questions. Later Conservative prime ministers – Macmillan in the early 1960s, Heath in the 1970s, Thatcher in the 1980s, and Major in the 1990s – were, in contrast, in their own ways radical and impatient administrative reformers, and in the 1990s Conservative ministers talked of (and pushed through) a managerial 'revolution' in Whitehall. For all his rhetoric about the excessive size of the civil service, the firing off of personal minutes about bureaucratic problems or abuses catching his attention, his grumbles about the Foreign Office, his inveterate 'personalization' of those parts of the machine serving him, and so on, Churchill regarded the civil service as an estate of the realm with its own proud traditions and performing a vital role in the constitutional order. 'With his devotion to Parliament,' said Colville, 'Churchill thought that even junior ministers were always on a higher level than officials.' (He certainly always acted himself on that principle: at the start of his career, as junior minister in the Colonial Office, the permanent secretary had complained to Churchill's ministerial boss that the young-politician-in-a-hurry was 'most tiresome to deal with'.) But while asserting the priority of politicians/ministers in the government system, Churchill also believed that the civil service had a legitimate role as ministerial advisers and as the agency through which government policies were implemented. The Thatcher-Major Conservatism of a later era was obsessed with 'business efficiency' in the civil service and 'taking on' the mandarins. Churchill was certainly not starry-eyed about the civil service but, characteristically, was always more conscious of constitutional fundamentals and the sweep of history. As he said in 1928: 'In the Civil Service there resides a great responsibility for keeping the life of Britain – her greatness, her fame, her future alive through all the variations of party chiefs and party majorities and giving to them the means of realizing at any given moment the best that is in the country.'[27]

SEVEN

Churchill, the Cabinet and the Premiership

The man who first became a member of the cabinet aged thirty-three as president of the Board of Trade in 1908 sat in the central seat at the cabinet table – the very same cabinet table – nearly half a century later in his second stint as prime minister while in his late seventies.[1] By that time, he had more first-hand knowledge and experience of the ways of government and Downing Street than any other man alive. Before becoming prime minister for the first time in May 1940, Churchill had served in the cabinet for a total of around seventeen years under four previous premiers (Asquith, Lloyd George, Baldwin and Chamberlain), and had been a thrusting junior minister in the government of a fifth prime minister, Sir Henry Campbell-Bannerman. The veteran Lord Salisbury and then Arthur Balfour had been prime minister during his time as a young backbencher after 1900, and in this period Churchill had also become a friend of Lord Rosebery, Liberal prime minister 1894–5. He was out of Parliament during Bonar Law's short premiership (October 1922 to May 1923) but was a close observer of Ramsay MacDonald as Labour (1924, 1929–31) and then 'National Government' (1931–5) prime minister. With all this experience and these contacts – combined with his clear understanding of how politics really worked in the Victorian period – he naturally had a keen awareness of the burdens, the potential and the limitations of the prime ministership in the British parliamentary and cabinet system.

Churchill on Cabinet Government and on Prime Ministers

'The Prime Minister is in theory only primus inter pares among his other Cabinet colleagues and his actual power varies with the political circumstances of the time,' Churchill had noted in October 1934 when he was asked by his American friend, the financier Bernard Baruch, to outline the working of the British cabinet and the powers of the prime minister. His description of the system was couched in terms made familiar by the classic works of F. W. Maitland and John Morley, and was summed up by Churchill as: '(1) The conduct of the executive government by the persons who control the House of Commons. (2) Their collective responsibility. (3) Their dependence from day to day on the confidence of the House of Commons.' 'You will see how different this is from the American constitution,' he told Baruch, 'where the executive is divided from the legislature, where the ministers are really the personal assistants of the President and do not actually guide and manage the assemblies.' 'The essence of the British system,' Churchill explained, 'is that the Cabinet is formed from influential members of the legislature who are then appointed to the executive offices and form a committee of the Privy Council with collective responsibility. The King sends for whomever he considers most likely to command a majority in the House of Commons, almost invariably though not necessarily a party leader. This gentleman being made Prime Minister chooses about twenty leading politicians who are willing to act with him and who together he considers will hold the confidence of the majority in the elective chamber.' The House of Commons by a simple confidence vote can overturn the cabinet but 'it is usually dominated by the powerful personalities and politicians in that body and its majority is held together by the party organization' – the prime minister normally heading the party and controlling both 'the caucus in the country' and the government whips in Parliament. 'The Cabinet as such finds no place in the English constitution, yet it has become incomparably the most important body functioning today,' argued Churchill. Quoting Pitt's comment that 'I did not come here to count noses', Churchill said that it was contrary to the spirit of cabinet government to settle important matters by a vote of the ministers. The cabinet's procedure was in fact 'entirely flexible and not too formal'. The prime minister sums up the discussion and states what he considers to be the opinion of the cabinet, to which ministers are then bound by the doctrine of collective responsibility. 'Usually,' he noted, '. . . there grows up an inner group of four or five of the principal office-holders or most powerful members which in fact guides the policy.'[2]

The crucial link between the cabinet and Parliament was the party system, Churchill recognized. Back in 1911 he had rejected any suggestion of cabinet dictatorship over the House of Commons. 'The Cabinet is the creature of the House of Commons. It springs from the House of Commons and dwells in the House of Commons. It is checked and corrected by the House of Commons, and by the shrug of the shoulder of the Private Members of the House the Cabinet can be scattered.' The system worked not because of 'machinery for flouting and dragooning the House placed at the disposal of the Prime Minister', he insisted, but because of the 'process of intelligent anticipation' by which ministers ascertained and conformed to the general wishes and opinions of the majority of the House in formulating and putting forward their proposals. Behind the strength and force of the cabinet in the House of Commons was the influence and power of MPs of the governing party and their constituencies.[3]

Whatever the 'primus inter pares' theory he had described to Bernard Baruch, Churchill knew that in practice the prime minister was more powerful than that. 'No one but a Prime Minister can guide and shape the policy of a British Government,' he had said in 1923. 'The office of Prime Minister in modern times towers up over any and all other Ministerial posts.' 'You cannot run the British Cabinet system without an effective Prime Minister,' Churchill maintained: a 'head and commanding mind ranging over the whole field of public affairs'. On the other hand, in a 1935 magazine article he asserted that he did not believe that 'it is any part of a Premier's duty to immerse himself in a mass of petty details or to spend hour after hour poring over documents. If he is not able safely to delegate responsibility, he has chosen the wrong men as his colleagues and subordinates' – words that must have provoked a hollow laugh from those insiders who knew about his own hyperactivism in office and his appetite for interfering in other ministers' areas of responsibility.[4]

Writing about Asquith in his (1937) book *Great Contemporaries*, Churchill suggested that a prime minister needed some additional qualities. Asquith had an orderly and disciplined mind but gave the impression of approaching politics too rigidly, with a fixed set of opinions, convictions and standards. 'In some respects this was a limitation . . .' wrote Churchill. 'Conditions are so variable, episodes so unexpected, experiences so conflicting, that flexibility of judgement and a willingness to assume a somewhat humbler attitude towards external phenomena may well play their part in the equipment of a modern Prime Minister.' Asquith, however, did have 'that ruthless side without which great matters cannot be handled'. (Churchill also noted, with approval, Balfour's 'cool ruthlessness where public affairs were concerned . . . Had his life been cast amid the labyrinthine intrigues of the Italian Renaissance, he would not have required to study the works of Machiavelli'.) In 1908 Asquith had repeated to Churchill Mr Gladstone's celebrated adage that 'the first essential for a Prime Minister is to be a good butcher', and Churchill recalled that 'Loyal as he was to his colleagues, he never shrank, when the time came and public need required it, from putting them aside – once and for all. Personal friendship might survive if it would. Political association was finished. But how else can States be governed?' (Churchill himself would seem to have failed this particular test in the 1950s, telling Lord Moran about the 1954 government reshuffle: 'Reconstructing the Cabinet is like solving a kaleidoscopic jig-saw puzzle. It was all so personal, and you know how much I hate hurting people's feelings.' Sir Norman Brook, the cabinet secretary, commented that Churchill disliked telling people they were no longer wanted: 'He gets out of it whenever he can. All the juniors, for instance, who were discharged had to be seen by the Chief Whip.' He got Lord Salisbury to tell the Lord Chancellor [Simonds] that he must step down.)[5]

Churchill's judgements of some of the prime ministers he had worked with or seen in action were damning. MacDonald he once dismissed as 'the boneless wonder', writing to Clementine in 1935 that 'The wretched Ramsay is almost a mental case – "he'd be far better off in a Home"'. Baldwin – whom he underrated, frequently to his own cost – was 'crafty, patient and also amazingly lazy, sterile and inefficient where public business is concerned'. In 1947 he sounded off to Lord Moran about the 'incompetence' of the inter-war Conservative businessmen prime ministers – Bonar Law, Baldwin and Chamberlain: they 'had not been a success'. Andrew Bonar Law he described as 'a narrow, doctrinaire Glasgow profiteer'. But on a later occasion (1952), he mused suggestively that 'Baldwin was a remarkable man. I like to make people do what I wish. Baldwin liked to do what they wanted. But he was a great party organizer'. In *Great Contemporaries* he had noted Baldwin's 'phlegmatic capacity of putting up with a score of unpleasant and even humbling situations, in order to be master of something very big at the end of a blue moon' – the prime minister as a great survivor, compromising and playing the long game. In contrast to Baldwin, who liked a quiet life, he recognized that Chamberlain 'sought to exercise a masterful control in many Departments' – and did so, not least in relation to foreign affairs.[6]

Balfour had once argued that 'democracy threatens to kill its servants by the work it requires of them', and Lord Robert Cecil talked of 'the Prime Minister's disease' in 1932, arguing (with MacDonald and Baldwin clearly in mind) that the pressure of government business was affecting the health of leading ministers, leading to indecisiveness and inefficiency. Churchill would have none of it: 'Frankly, I do not believe in this legend of the intolerable strain of the Premiership.' He pointed out that Gladstone was able to sustain the role into his eighties. It is difficult not to read his comments (in a 1934 article) without reflecting on the events of 1940:

> if the tenancy of No. 10 Downing Street carries with it great responsibilities, these should be a spur to effort, and not a burden under which one staggers and falls. There is an old saying that God gives men strength as they need it. In my own experience there is something in the challenge of a crisis, in knowing that vital issues depend upon him, that draws upon hidden reserves in a man's nature and makes him rise to the height of a great occasion.

'Examining the careers of . . . great Prime Ministers, we find little support for this theory of high office as something which, in the course of a few years, will reduce a strong man to a valetudinarian wreck,' Churchill robustly argued.[7]

The premiership was, he acknowledged, a unique post. 'In any sphere of action,' he wrote, 'there can be no comparison between the positions of number one and numbers two, three or four. . . The loyalties which centre upon number one are enormous. If he trips he must be sustained. If he makes mistakes they must be covered. If he sleeps he must not be wantonly disturbed. If he is no good he must be pole-axed.' Individual PMs comported themselves in their lonely eminence in different ways, he once told Lord Riddell:

Premiers have to give so many important decisions and are pressed for so many concessions, that they have to protect themselves by some sort of shield. Campbell-Bannerman's was a kindly manner which caused the applicant to go away feeling that his request would if possible be granted, and that if it was refused the Premier would regret the refusal more than anyone else. Arthur Balfour's was a method of statement which left the applicant quite uncertain whether his request had been granted or not, or whether A. J. B. agreed with him or not, and in the case of Asquith it is a gruff, impenetrable reserve which crushes the visitor's enthusiasm.[8]

Churchill's argument (in 1902) that Lord Rosebery possessed 'the three requirements an English Prime Minister should have', namely 'a great position in Parliament, popularity in the country . . . [and] rank and prestige', suggested, as Roy Jenkins noted, 'somewhat romantic criteria for leadership'. His comments on some of the other great nineteenth-century leaders are also revealing. 'It is sometimes necessary at the summit of authority to bear with the intrigues of disloyal colleagues, to remain calm when others panic, and to withstand misguided popular outcries,' he wrote of US President Abraham Lincoln, but the argument clearly had a wider relevance. Sir Robert Peel, he wrote in his *History of the English-Speaking Peoples*, 'had absolute control of his Cabinet, himself introduced the Government's more important Budgets, and supervised the work of all departments'. Churchill clearly admired this 'dominating force and personality . . . [who] towered above the scene'. His comment that 'Peel maintained that his duty to the nation was higher than his duty to his party . . . It is true that he split his party, but there are greater crimes than that' was telling. He quoted with obvious enthusiasm and approval Peel's remark that 'The fact is, people like a certain degree of obstinacy and presumption in a Minister. They abuse him for dictation and arrogance, but they like being governed'. The successes of Gladstone's first government (1868-74) he attributed to the prime minister's 'boundless energy', reinforced by 'a determined Cabinet and a united party'. In the 1880s, however, although Gladstone still 'towered above his colleagues', the divisions between Whigs and Radicals inside the Liberal Party were becoming unbridgeable and the PM himself clashed with his colleagues on the main issues of the day. The lesson was that

'A Cabinet with such deep cleavages was unlikely to prove an effective instrument of government'.[9]

Churchill served for seven years in Asquith's cabinet and while describing him as 'probably one of the greatest peacetime Prime Ministers we have ever had', argued that he lacked 'those qualities of resource and energy, of prevision and assiduous management' required in a wartime leader, and which Lloyd George provided after 1916. Asquith's style was effective but certainly unChurchillian: 'In Cabinet he was markedly silent. Indeed he never spoke a word in Council if he could get his way without it. He sat, like the great Judge he was, hearing with trained patience the case deployed on every side, now and then interjecting a question or brief comment, searching or pregnant, which gave matters a turn towards the goal he wished to reach.' Along with this air of detachment and authority, he used 'the potent instrument of Time with frequent advantage in domestic affairs', postponing decisions if the moment was not ripe or he needed to steer round some internal cabinet argument and find a compromise or avoid a resignation. 'In times of Peace, dealing with frothy, superficial party and personal bickerings, this was often successful.' But the stresses of world war demand 'a frenzied energy at the summit', Churchill argued, and 'an effort to compel events rather than to adjudicate wisely and deliberately upon them'. Though published in 1937, these remarks − like others quoted above − are suggestive in the light of Churchill's activist conception of the premiership between 1940 and 1945.[10]

Wartime Prime Minister

Churchill finally reached the summit himself and became prime minister on 10 May 1940. He was sixty-five and only two other twentieth-century PMs were older on first entering that office: Campbell-Bannerman and Neville Chamberlain. It had been a long parliamentary apprenticeship too: nearly forty years as an MP before first becoming PM − a longer period than any other premier except Palmerston (forty-eight years; Gladstone and Campbell-Bannerman coming closest with thirty-six and thirty-seven years respectively in the Commons before first entering Number 10 as prime minister). Like Lloyd George in 1916 and Ramsay MacDonald in 1931,

Churchill was not the leader of the majority party in the House of Commons when appointed prime minister – though obviously no PM would be able to accept or continue in office without the support or acquiescence of that party. He was not the King's preferred candidate as prime minister, or that of the ruling 'Establishment' circles, and while Conservative Party MPs had no direct say in his selection as PM, it is clear that if they had been allowed to vote (as happened only from 1965) then he would not have been chosen. He became prime minister essentially because of the collapse of confidence in Chamberlain's government (the Tory majority of 213 falling to 81 in the great debate of 7-8 May) and Chamberlain recognizing that he could not continue as PM, together with Lord Halifax then lacking the stomach to seize the ultimate prize (which was within his grasp, notwithstanding his position as a peer). Churchill had been a political 'outsider' for much of his career, and never a 'safe' party man, and he saw himself as the head of a 'national' government formed on a wide basis, telling Chamberlain on 16 May that he did not want to be Conservative Party leader. Such was the weakness of his party-political position in the first few months that he took great trouble over his relations with Chamberlain (it was significant that Conservative backbenchers cheered wildly when Chamberlain entered the chamber of the House of Commons on 13 May, but they virtually cold-shouldered Churchill for two months). Only when Chamberlain resigned due to ill-health did Churchill take on the Conservative Party leadership, in October 1940, and even then many Tories were still deeply suspicious of him.[11]

The four other members of Churchill's original war cabinet of five were the top party leaders from each side: Chamberlain and Halifax for the Conservatives, Attlee and Arthur Greenwood for Labour. The party balance of his coalition government was always a concern – 'I well appreciate the necessity of preserving the piebald complexion of my pony,' he once remarked. The three service ministries were parcelled out between the Conservative (War Office), Labour (Admiralty) and Liberal (Air Ministry) parties; the appointment of Labour's Ernest Bevin (minister of labour) to the War Cabinet in October 1940 was balanced by that of the Conservative Kingsley Wood (chancellor of the exchequer); and there were similar calculations operating right down the hierarchy of junior ministers. Labour originally held sixteen posts in Churchill's government against the Conservatives' fifty-two (and three for the Liberals). By March 1942, the Labour ministerial contingent had increased to eight ministerial and fourteen junior minister posts, and by April 1945 to ten ministerial and seventeen junior posts. Labour ministers became particularly influential on the cabinet committees dealing with home front economic, social and recon- struction issues. But non-party technocrats, businessmen and administrators were given important ministerial assignments too (Chamberlain had also made some appointments of this kind). From the business world, Lord Leathers became minister of war transport in 1941, Oliver Lyttelton became minister of production and Lord Woolton was put into the cabinet as minister of reconstruction in 1943; P. J. Grigg – formerly Churchill's private secretary at the Treasury in the 1920s – was in 1942 transformed overnight from being permanent secretary of the War Office to being that department's ministerial chief; and the former civil servant and imperial pro-consul, Sir John Anderson, brought into Parliament and Chamberlain's government in 1938, came to play a vital role as first lord president of the Council and then chancellor of the exchequer. (In 1945 Churchill secretly advised the King that if both he and Eden were to die, then Anderson should become prime minister.) The more orthodox and 'reliable' Conservatives (largely 'Chamberlainites') were inevitably appalled by the appointments given to Churchill's cronies and courtiers – men like Lord Beaverbrook, Brendan Bracken, Lord Cherwell and Duncan Sandys (Churchill's son-in-law) – but they were far from putting 'the gangsters . . . in complete control' (to use Halifax's language).[12]

As prime minister, Churchill had clear and strong views about the basis on which his war cabinet should be organized, rejecting the Lloyd George model from the First World War of a war cabinet composed of five or six ministers free from departmental duties. As minister of munitions from 1917, Churchill had complained about himself and the service ministers being excluded from membership of the war cabinet and precluded from exercising influence over general policy, although in practice departmental ministers like them often attended its meetings when relevant issues were being discussed. (At the end of the war, Churchill and others had also pressed for an immediate restoration of the normal peacetime size of cabinet instead of a 'narrow and unrepresentative body', but that did not formally happen until November 1919.) Twenty years later, it looked at one point as though Neville Chamberlain might have formed a non-departmental war cabinet in September 1939, perhaps offering Churchill a post as a minister without portfolio, but in the event he decided to form a war cabinet of nine, which included only three non-departmental ministers and Churchill came in as first lord of the Admiralty, joining the other two service ministers around the cabinet table. Churchill was very glad, he later wrote, to have a definite executive responsibility and not the general advisory role of a non-departmental minister given the job of 'exalted brooding over the work done by others'. One of the unhappiest times of Churchill's career had been his removal from the Admiralty and his few months in the sinecure cabinet post of chancellor of the Duchy of Lancaster in 1915, when he had felt like a 'spectator' – one who 'knew everything' but 'could do nothing'. He had resigned and rejoined the army, preferring life in the trenches to the frustrations of a powerless 'advisory' role.[13]

Pressure for a small non-departmental war cabinet – calls for such a body coming at different times from the press, from outside critics like William Beveridge, and from Lord Beaverbrook and, more insistently, Stafford Cripps inside the government in 1942 – was resisted by Churchill. 'A group of detached statesmen, however high their nominal authority, are at a serious disadvantage in dealing with the Ministers at the head of the great Departments vitally concerned . . .', Churchill later wrote in his war memoirs. 'The War Cabinet personages can have no direct responsibility for day-to-day events. . . They may advise in general terms beforehand or criticize afterwards . . . They therefore tend to become more and more theoretical supervisors and commentators . . . Often they can do little more than arbitrate or find a compromise in inter-departmental disputes.' War cabinet members, he argued, 'should also be the holders of responsible offices and not mere advisers at large with nothing to do but think and talk and take decisions by compromise or majority'. 'I did not like having unharnessed Ministers around me,' he admitted. 'I preferred to deal with chiefs of organizations rather than counsellors.'[14]

John Grigg argued that Churchill wanted a war cabinet most of whose members also had heavy departmental or other administrative duties because 'he thought it would strengthen his own position to have colleagues who were too busy to compete with him in overall contemplation of war policy and grand strategy', claiming that 'In fact, it tended to leave him isolated and weakened his position vis-à-vis the chiefs of staff'. (On Churchill and the service chiefs, see pages 191–3) One could perhaps read such small-*p* political and personal motives between the lines, as it were, of Churchill's comment that 'Everyone should do a good day's work and be accountable for some definite task, and then they do not make trouble for trouble's sake or to cut a figure'. But there were perfectly good administrative arguments for Churchill's system, not least the need to integrate departments into cabinet policy-making, rather than separating the responsibilities for making plans and carrying them out. 'You must have machinery which carries to the Cabinet with the least possible friction the consent and allegiance of these great Departments,' Churchill insisted. The power of Whitehall departments must not be underestimated, he told MPs in 1941. It was 'in many cases irresistible because it is based on knowledge and on systematized and organized currents of opinion'. 'There are great difficulties in dealing with Departments of State,' Churchill argued, 'unless the key Departments are brought into the discussion in the early stages and . . . take part in the original formation and initiation of our designs.'

> It is better that there should be in the responsible directing centres of Government [i.e., the Cabinet] some, at any rate of the key Ministers . . . It is better to work in that way than to have five Ministers entirely divorced from [the] Departments, because that means that when a discussion has taken place in the Cabinet, the leaders of these Departments have to be summoned, and then the whole business has to be gone over again in order to learn what it is they think they can do and to persuade them and convince them that it is necessary to do what has been decided upon.[15]

Churchill's war cabinet generally therefore included a number of ministers heading key departments. Admittedly his first cabinet, formed in May 1940, was made up of only five ministers, including himself as PM and minister of defence, three non-departmental ministers (Chamberlain, Attlee and Arthur Greenwood) and only one departmental minister (the foreign secretary, Halifax). But by October 1940, the ministers of aircraft production and of labour, and the chancellor of the exchequer were all members. In later years, membership was seven or eight, and departments such as the Ministry of Production, the Home Office, and the Ministry of Reconstruction were represented, with the Ministry of Supply and the Dominions Office represented in the war cabinet at different times, and the chancellor and Treasury left outside the cabinet from February 1942 until September 1943.

Churchill told MPs that 'general policy' was 'determined by the War Cabinet' with the prime minister and 'in the last resort' the cabinet settling and adjusting the most serious interdepartmental differences. It was vital, he stressed, that 'the Cabinet itself shall not be overburdened with business'. As he graphically put it: 'Ministers [in the war cabinet] must be free when they will to stand away from the intricate machinery of government and the routine of daily work and together survey the stormy skies.' He believed that 'the advantages of free discussion . . . without any formality and without any record being kept, are very great'. 'Formal sessions' did not always deal effectively with 'the large issues', he had argued to Chamberlain in 1939, proposing occasional meetings of the war cabinet without the Secretariat or military staff being present – and as prime minister himself he held many informal ministerial meetings, often at Chequers. Indeed, Sir Edward Bridges thought that even in 1939 Churchill had some lingering doubts as to the constitutional propriety of the very existence of the Cabinet Secretariat, but he recognized its practical value and relied greatly on its senior staff (though complaining that the minutes were too long and detailed – Bridges was virtually 'running a magazine', he once said). He was, however, scrupulous in insisting that all directions and orders coming from him as PM should be made or immediately confirmed in writing.[16]

The government in effect operated through a series of cabinet committees, with some ministers playing important roles on and through these as co-ordinating ministers. Churchill deprecated the sort of 'consultative and advisory committee . . . attended by representatives of many branches and Departments . . . [that tries] to agree upon forms of words for a report, and then, too often, they are inclined to pass the buck to some other futile body, equally respectable'. But he was prepared to admit that cabinet committees had some advantages if 'based upon the Ministers, the co-ordination of whose Departments is essential to the solution of the problem . . . and if they do agree, they can make their Departments carry out their decisions . . . with alacrity and good will'. He was concerned, however, that the proliferation of committees in Whitehall (ministerial and civil-service committees) was wasting time and frustrating decision-making. Whitehall was in danger of being overrun by committees, as Australia was with rabbits, he complained on one occasion. 'There are far too many committees of one kind or another which Ministers have to attend and which do not yield a sufficient result,' he had minuted the cabinet secretary in May 1940. 'The committee system has been allowed to run riot,' he insisted in a cabinet note in March 1941, criticizing the 'inordinate and unchecked growth of committees' (saying that there were then 800 in central government alone) and demanding a 'purge' and reduction in their number by 25 per cent. Despite this prime-ministerial concern, the growth of a complex and extended system of cabinet (and official-level) committees was key to the successful operation of the machinery of wartime government. (Developed further by the Attlee Labour administration, this system was to be the backbone of the post-war British government machine too.)[17]

From the start, Churchill was clear that as prime minister he was going to concentrate on running the war, with Neville Chamberlain as lord president of the Council the key figure for domestic policy – 'I was 'relying on him to look after the Home Front for me,' he admitted in November 1940.[18] The Lord President's Committee, subsequently chaired by Sir John Anderson (1940-43) and then by Attlee (1943-5), was the central committee – functioning as a virtual 'sub-cabinet' – for the broad range of home-front matters including economic policy. Other committees – a changing pattern, including at different times economic policy, food policy, home policy, civil defence and so on, and various *ad hoc* groups – were in effect a subordinate tier and often fed into this powerful committee. There were interdepartmental and personality conflicts in the area of war production/industrial priorities, with the Ministry of Supply, the Ministry of Aircraft Production, the Ministry of Labour and powerful figures like Beaverbrook and Bevin fighting it out. The creation in early 1941 of an 'Import Executive' and a 'Production Executive' to try to co-ordinate policy did not succeed in reducing the friction, and the result was the appointment of a new minister of production in 1943, as a war cabinet minister, to co-ordinate policy and set production priorities, with the other 'supply' ministers (except Bevin at the Ministry of Labour) outside the cabinet (but with an announced right of appeal to the War Cabinet or the PM, and with their responsibility to Parliament for the administration of their departments supposedly unaltered). Planning for post-war reconstruction was another important area of policy, neglected by Churchill personally, where the key decisions were taken through co-ordinating cabinet committees (the Reconstruction Priorities Committee set up in January 1943 to handle the Beveridge Report being a particularly high-level and high-powered body), and then in November 1943 a Ministry of Reconstruction was set up under Lord Woolton, who took the chair of a new cabinet committee on reconstruction. Much of this 'government by committee' was remote from Churchill himself. From time to time, major policy issues or conflicts would filter up to him and/or the cabinet, but he sat only on the defence committee (and, as minister of defence, co-ordinated military policy).

No British prime minister has been so involved in supervising military strategy and defence decision-making as was Churchill during the Second World War. (Equally, he is the only one to have worn military uniform(s) in office, as innumerable wartime photographs show.) Lloyd George had toyed with the idea of becoming his own minister for war as well as PM in 1918, but the King had objected. Churchill had witnessed Lloyd George's failure to control the generals during the First World War, and he was determined to gather the reins of control into his own hands and establish civilian control over the military. He was adamant that as prime minister he should also be minister of defence. 'This was a new post unknown to the British constitution,' as Robert Blake noted, and Churchill 'did not seek any statutory authority for its creation and . . . was careful to avoid defining its scope and powers'. (There had been a minister for the co-ordination of defence from 1936 to 1940 whose role and power were, however, very limited.) The three service ministers were excluded from membership of his war cabinet (though the chiefs of staff attended cabinet meetings) and their position became a subordinate and largely administrative one. The chiefs of staff reported directly to Churchill who operated in the defence sphere through a small personal defence secretariat (akin to a *cabinet militaire*), in which the key figure was General Hastings Ismay (see also chapter 6).[19]

Churchill in effect handled the military side of the war – strategy, operations and major supply/resource issues – through the chiefs of staff and the Defence Committee rather than through the war cabinet; though the cabinet was kept informed, as the war progressed more and more matters were left to the PM, the Defence Committee and the service chiefs. The Defence Committee had two forms: Supply and Operations. Chaired by Churchill, and including the deputy prime minister (Attlee) and the foreign secretary, the service ministers and the chiefs of staff, it met very frequently in 1940 (forty times) and 1941 (seventy-six times) but thereafter less often (twenty meetings in 1942, falling to ten in 1944). Churchill increasingly called informal meetings – which he called 'staff conferences' – with ministers with relevant responsibilities and service chiefs, and he spent much time closeted alone with the chiefs of staff. These arrangements meant, as P. J. Grigg put it, that Churchill 'could know everything that was going on in the operational sphere and at the same time could be in a position to give immediate decisions at any hour of the day or night'. He maintained that he would not have wanted to remain prime minister for an hour if he had been deprived of the office of minister of defence and denied 'full power of war-direction':

> More difficulty and toil are often incurred in overcoming opposition and adjusting divergent and conflicting views than by having the right to give decisions oneself. It is most important that at the summit there should be one mind playing over the whole field, faithfully aided and corrected, but not divided in its integrity.

When the war was going badly in 1942, critics called for the appointment of a separate minister of defence or (in the case of Stafford Cripps) for a reorganization of the chiefs of staff machinery to form an independent 'war planning directorate'. But Churchill would not accept that as PM he should carry responsibility without the power of effective action. Neither a 'generalissimo' figure (as Kitchener had been in the First World War) relegating the prime minister to a secondary position (confined to making 'the necessary explanations, excuses, and apologies to Parliament when things go wrong'), nor the creation of a 'disembodied Brains Trust to browse among our secrets and add to the already immense volume of committees and reports', were considered acceptable or workable by Churchill.[20]

These arrangements allowed Churchill to bring powerfully to bear an experience of war and military issues unrivalled by any other possible PM or defence minister; they brought him into the preparation of military plans from the early stages, avoiding the presentation to ministers of a single 'take it or leave it' military plan and no alternative; and they also avoided the damaging 'top brass' versus 'frock coats' military-politician splits of the First World War. Of course, all was not sweetness and light in the relations between Churchill and the chiefs of staff: there were rough arguments and strong feelings on both sides. He 'never sought to circumvent them when he did not like their advice, but he was always impatient of restraint and of the orthodox view, and suspicious of obstruction', as Sir Ian Jacob saw from his position in Churchill's military secretariat. He never overruled the service chiefs on a purely military matter. ('They nearly always got their way on strategic issues, if at the cost of endless midnight palavers and debilitating loss of sleep,' comments John Grigg.) But he constantly chivvied, harried, prodded and meddled with (and, if necessary, sacked) generals and field commanders – with mixed results, it must be said. From 1942 onwards, Churchill's personal influence undoubtedly weakened, however, with the appointment of the strong-minded General Sir Alan Brooke as chairman of the chiefs of staff and, following the US entry into the war, with the creation of the combined chiefs of staff in Washington both increasing the influence of the military experts.[21]

Churchill's wartime regime was never the 'one-man show' that critics and some outside observers believed it to be. Churchill was a powerful, resolute and dominating prime minister but not a dictator. Harry Hopkins (Roosevelt's emissary) once said that 'the provisions of the British Constitution and the powers of the War Cabinet are just whatever Winston Churchill wants them to be at any given moment', but Churchill (rightly) denied this suggestion. He always sought to maintain the principle and the reality of collective responsibility. While there were very few large issues on which he was overruled by his colleagues, he said, he had to remind

Roosevelt and Stalin that he was the only one of the 'Big Three' who could at any moment be dismissed from power by a vote in Parliament and who was controlled from day to day by the opinion of a cabinet representing all parties in the state. He always had to carry his ministerial colleagues with him: 'they [Roosevelt and Stalin] could order; I had to convince and persuade.' This is not to deny that he used to the full the powers and resources at any prime minister's disposal. To the institutional resources of his office were added the force of his personality and character, and his strong popular position in the country (reflected in staggeringly high opinion poll ratings for him personally as PM – consistently over 80 per cent average approval ratings throughout the war, although admittedly politicians took little, if any, notice of polls at that time). He had also taken care to become Conservative Party leader in October 1940 after Chamberlain's resignation from the government (he died the following month), giving him control over the party machine and the whips (he wanted to avoid a Lloyd George-like position at the end of the war by securing a strong party base). But the Canadian politician Mackenzie King exaggerated when he likened the members of Churchill's war cabinet to 'a lot of schoolboys frightened by the headmaster'.[22]

Churchill's amazing energy, driving power and dynamism as wartime prime minister, together with his idiosyncratic work timetable, are well known: the afternoon naps, the meetings carried on late at night and into the small hours. He (in wartime, at any rate) and Margaret Thatcher were probably the hardest-working twentieth-century prime ministers. Close aides have testified to his strong personal control at the centre of government. 'His general method of work,' recalled Sir Norman Brook, 'was to concentrate his personal attention on the two or three things that mattered most at any given moment . . . He was thus able to control the use of his own time, and to prevent its being eaten into by the demands of colleagues wishing to have his help in solving their problems.' At the same time, however, says Sir Ian Jacob, 'He constantly took a keen interest in details and demanded information on all kinds of activities that no normal Prime Minister would have paid any attention to.' He fired off a constant stream of personal memoranda on all manner of subjects, great and small, that had come to his attention (often via Professor Lindemann/Lord Cherwell, his one-man Downing Street think tank): the famous 'Action This Day' messages, dubbed 'prayers' by Whitehall (as they frequently began with the word, 'pray . . .'). Ministers and their departmental officials often resented what they felt was unwarranted meddling in trifling details, but this roving 'searchlight beam' technique kept them up to the mark, and was in that sense a rational technique of prime-ministerial power. Churchill was also always fertile in ideas – some good, some bad – and he needed people around him ready to argue him out of the bad ones, as Attlee said, recalling that Lloyd George had once told him: 'There's Winston, he has half a dozen solutions to it and one of them is right, but the trouble is he does not know which it is.'[23]

'All I wanted was compliance with my wishes after reasonable discussion,' Churchill famously wrote in his memoirs. 'He pressed his own proposals hard, and was reluctant to abandon them,' was Sir Norman Brook's tactful summary of what could seem more like a knock-them-down-and-drag-them-out process of argument and disputation. 'A Cabinet as conducted by Mr Churchill could be a splendid and unique experience,' recalled Anthony Eden. 'It might be a monologue, it was never a dictatorship.' However, he noted waspishly, 'The disadvantage, to those with specific duties to perform or departments to run, was the time consumed.' Sir Ian Jacob gave a vivid account of Churchill's style at his peak, noting that he was not the cold, efficient, orderly chairman of a meeting (unlike his predecessor Chamberlain and his successor Attlee):

Churchill talked a great deal, and, though he could listen when he wanted to, he could also debate, browbeat, badger and cajole those who were opposed to him, or whose work was under discussion. He had a most devastating method of argument. He would start by stating his case strongly. Often what he said could only be described as a half-truth. The strong emphasis would be on one particular sore point, and many of the surrounding factors would be disregarded or distorted. The result of this method of attack was that the person addressed didn't quite know whether to defend the particular point seized upon by the Prime Minister, or to deal with the distortions in order to try and get the emphasis restored. Churchill would continue the attack, and the unfortunate victim often ended in confused silence. The only hope was a vigorous reply, even a counter-attack, and a clear and accurate statement of the case. Those who were capable of this had no difficulty in holding their own, and earned his respect. He might continue the attack, but he listened to the reply. Those who were naturally tongue-tied found the situation most difficult, and found him most unreasonable. Churchill, too, failed to appreciate them.

The comparison with Margaret Thatcher's style and her way of running her cabinet, forty years later, is irresistible and striking! 'Churchill's method,' Jacob considered, 'was the result of his innate pugnacity mixed with his somewhat cross-grained and unorthodox nature, and of many years of partisan debate in Parliament. It wasted a great deal of time, and created a good deal of misunderstanding and heart-burning, but it made people take great pains to be sure of their ground.'[24]

With his long experience of cabinet-level politics, Churchill knew all about the tactics of delay and how to keep options open:

The Prime Minister, curiously enough, was never keen on making decisions on matters that did not demand immediate action. Unless one had to be made he liked to discuss the pros and cons at length, and would then adjourn the meeting for further thought, particularly if the decision was likely to be one which went against the grain. There would then be a period of private discussion, further documents . . . and perhaps of more meetings . . . At all times, however, the situation was quite different when he had made up his own mind and was bent on driving on with what he wanted to bring about. There was no delay then, and no lack of decision. Everybody and everything was pressed into service with the sole object of getting his project under way. The long discussion, the procrastination, the 'putting on the hob', were all methods that came into play when others were urging action, or propounding a suggested policy, which he did not at first agree with. These methods were designed to test the case of the authors of the proposal under consideration, and they gave him opportunities of trying to demolish it, or modify it to bring it nearer his own ideas.

There is evidence of growing ministerial and official discontent, towards the end of the war, with this sort of behaviour and with Churchill's conduct of government. Complaints were made about long, rambling and indecisive meetings ('Someone has only to start any new hare and W. [Winston] cannot resist chasing it himself across many fields by which time it is pretty difficult to pull up others,' Eden noted in his diary in 1944); about Churchill not bothering to read his papers so that time was wasted in having to explain issues to him; and about his supposed reliance on cronies like Lord Beaverbrook, Brendan Bracken and Lord Cherwell to second-guess recommendations from departments and from cabinet committees. The deputy prime minister, Attlee, had the pluck to write a long and frank letter to Churchill about all this in January 1945 – and the PM's entourage and wife all agreed with Attlee's rebuke – but nothing really changed. In the end, insiders knew that Churchill was the indispensable war leader, and that his strengths mattered more than his faults.[25]

Prime Minister, Cabinet and Foreign Policy

'No Prime Minister can be denied control over foreign policy,' Churchill maintained. Throughout both his premierships he played an active role in foreign policy-making. He had bitterly fought Neville Chamberlain's appeasement policy in the late 1930s but, in an article published in 1939, noting how the PM 'began increasingly to take the Foreign Office into his personal control' from 1937, conceded that 'He had a perfect right to do this'. Chamberlain had forced out Anthony Eden in 1938 and replaced him with Lord Halifax, who shared his views, and Churchill was clear that the PM was 'absolutely within his rights to have a foreign secretary of his own choice'. In that context, it did not even matter that the foreign secretary was in the Lords, Churchill argued, because MPs could get at the prime minister in the Commons. 'What is the point of crying out for the moon,' he said, rather sarcastically, 'when you have the sun and you have that bright orb of day from whose effulgent beams the lesser luminaries derive their radiance?' In the first volume of his Second World War memoirs, Churchill made the same argument. In contrast to the quiescent Baldwin, Chamberlain had had strong views on foreign policy and an 'undoubted right' to assert them. He noted that 'the Foreign Secretary has a special position in a British Cabinet':

He is treated with marked respect in his high and responsible office, but he usually conducts his affairs under the continuous scrutiny, if not of the whole Cabinet, at least of its principal members. He is under an obligation to keep them informed. He circulates to his colleagues, as a matter of custom and routine, all his executive telegrams, the reports from our Embassies abroad, the records of his interviews with foreign Ambassadors or other notables . . . This supervision is of course especially maintained by the Prime Minister, who personally or through his Cabinet is responsible for controlling, and has the power to control, the main course of foreign policy.

From the prime minister, Churchill said, 'there must be no secrets'. 'No Foreign Secretary can do his work unless he is supported constantly by his Chief. To make things go smoothly, there must not only be agreement between them on fundamentals, but also a harmony of outlook and even to some extent of temperament.'[26]

For all except the period May to December 1940, when Halifax continued in post (before being sent as ambassador to the USA), Churchill's foreign secretary during his time as prime minister (1940-45 and 1951-5) was Anthony Eden. Their relationship from 1940 to 1955 was crucial both to the conduct of foreign policy and also to the Conservative Party, with Churchill promising Eden the succession in late 1940. During the war, as John Colville saw from inside Number 10, 'There was no question of Churchill leaving Eden an entirely free hand, for he conducted relations with America person-ally and he interfered as and when he chose with any aspect of foreign policy that took his fancy.' (Churchill and Roosevelt exchanged nearly two thousand letters and telegrams during the war, and Churchill laid great – perhaps exaggerated – emphasis on his personal diplomacy with FDR and with Stalin.) However, for the duration of the war, said Colville, Eden 'with only occasional grumbles, was content to be Churchill's lieutenant'. Perhaps fortunately for their relationship, the foreign secretary never got wind of Churchill's idea (in March 1944) of becoming foreign secretary himself, while remaining PM and minister of defence. Churchill mistrusted the diplomatic machine, and believed that he could put some backbone into it, and he regretted that one of the few high offices of state he had never held was that of foreign secretary. But this combination of posts in wartime would have been a bigger portfolio than even that of Lord Salisbury back in Queen Victoria's reign (MacDonald also combining the premiership and the Foreign Office in the first, short-lived Labour government of 1924), and any attempt to realize it would surely have provoked a cabinet backlash.[27]

As prime minister after 1951, Churchill was adamant that he had 'got to keep an eye on foreign affairs at any time', as he told Moran. The 'special relationship' and dealings with the super powers were his main interests. A great believer in prime-ministerial personal diplomacy, he visited the USA for high-level talks with Presidents Truman and then Eisenhower on three occasions and, accompanied by Eden, attended the Western Summit (the US, Britain and France) at Bermuda in December 1953 (preferring to read C. S. Forester's novel of the Napoleonic Wars, *Death to the French*, on the flight out rather than Foreign Office briefing papers, he declared that he only really wanted to meet Eisenhower – handling the 'bloody Frogs' was the foreign secretary's job!).[28]

The relations between the prime minister, the Foreign Office and the foreign secretary in the 1951-5 Churchill government were strained. Eden and his advisers resented what they felt was constant interference and the prime minister 'butting in all the time', often on trivial matters; and Eden was increasingly frustrated at Churchill delaying his retirement. Large swathes of foreign policy, where Churchill was simply not interested, were left to Eden, of course, and Churchill's flagging powers were another limitation on his scope. It was noticeable that when Churchill took over the Foreign Office while Eden was away ill he was highly selective in the issues and papers he would deal with and did not try to play a day-to-day 'hands-on' role ('I have lived seventy-eight years without hearing of bloody places like Cambodia,' he sounded off to Moran). For his part, Churchill talked of Eden as having become 'Foreign Officissimus' and thought 'All might be well if they [the diplomats] were imbued and led by a strong guiding spirit, but this is not so' Churchill-Eden relations 'were never to regain the instinctive understanding and warmth of the War years', comments the then Number 10 foreign affairs private secretary, Anthony Montague Browne. There were suspicions that the Foreign Office was withholding secret intelligence from the prime minister (perhaps aiming to forestall 'interference') and on one occasion an irate foreign secretary told Browne: 'You are not doing your duty. Your job is to further Foreign Office policy with the Prime Minister, not to oppose it.' In cabinet and in public they tried to maintain an image of unity, Churchill saying in a 1954 speech that if a foreign-policy question was put to them separately, the odds were four or five to one that their answers would be the same. But there were, in fact, real policy differences between them, particularly on the Middle East and over Churchill's desire for a summit with the Russians. Not surprisingly, outside observers talked of there appearing at times to be two different foreign policies: that of the prime minister, and that of the foreign secretary and the Foreign Office (which was often more in line with the Americans).[29]

As is usual in British governments, the full cabinet had, for the most part, only a limited foreign-policy role. Ministers were kept informed but few had the knowledge or experience to question or challenge Eden's policies, and the cabinet was scarcely used as a forum for discussion on foreign affairs, argues Anthony Seldon (prompting Kilmuir to complain later of 'an abrogation of the role of Cabinet'). There was no cabinet foreign policy committee and the Defence Committee (which under Attlee and Bevin had frequently discussed broad foreign-policy issues), chaired by Churchill himself, was 'under-utilized', says John Young. None of this necessarily upset the foreign secretary and his diplomats, of course, but the way in which the prime minister acted as an 'old man in a hurry', anxious to go down in history as an international peacemaker, appalled them. In pursuit of his personal aim of a summit meeting with the post-Stalin Russian leadership (aiming to reduce Cold War tensions), Churchill was ruthlessly and unscrupulously willing to circumvent normal procedures to outwit the Foreign Office and 'bounce' or bypass the cabinet. He proposed an East-West leaders' summit meeting in a Commons speech in May 1953 without consulting the cabinet, while also keeping most of the Foreign Office in the dark about his plans. A year later, he came to grief when his actions in despatching a telegram to Moscow proposing an informal top-level meeting with Malenkov, the Russian leader, while aboard the *Queen Elizabeth* returning from talks in the USA – manipulating procedures effectively to pre-empt cabinet comments – provoked an astonishing cabinet crisis in July 1954, with a number of stormy meetings (the exchanges were so explosive that the Secretariat drafted specially restricted 'confidential annexes' to the cabinet minutes), challenges to Churchill and his policy, and resignation threats freely bandied about (both from Churchill and from some of his critics). The Russian counter-move – a proposal for a general conference of European states (prompting Churchill's caustic comment: 'Foreign Secretaries of the world unite; you have nothing to lose but your jobs') – got the government off the hook and ended the cabinet crisis. But Churchill was badly damaged by this high-stakes row, cabinet ministers like Macmillan now considering him incapable of continuing as PM and questioning his judgement. Within a year, he had resigned.[30]

Prime Minister and Cabinet, 1951-5

'It would not be possible in time of peace to construct Governments with the same freedom as in war,' Churchill had told the cabinet secretary, Sir Edward Bridges, back in 1942. 'A Cabinet of from fifteen to twenty men has been found by long experience to be necessary to swing a Parliamentary majority in the House of Commons. Four or five super Ministers, each directing groups of Departments would be a pretty easy target for opponents and rivals.' Churchill evidently believed that the sort of scheme championed by the veteran Conservative statesman Leo Amery, among others, for a small 'policy Cabinet' made up of six or seven ministers free from departmental responsibilities but each co-ordinating clusters of ministers outside the cabinet was politically unrealistic in normal peacetime conditions. The 'Whitehall view', as articulated by Sir John Anderson's wartime Machinery of Government Committee, and upheld by the top officials of the day, like Sir Norman Brook, was also against a system of 'supervising ministers' (favouring co-ordination through standing cabinet committees instead). All the same, on returning to power in October 1951 Churchill wanted a smallish cabinet, the total of cabinet ministers being sixteen (including the PM) at the start of his government – one fewer than in Attlee's outgoing Labour Cabinet – creeping up to nineteen in September 1953 and eighteen from November 1953 onwards. (The peacetime cabinets of Asquith, Lloyd George, Baldwin and Chamberlain had all been bigger than this, as were the Conservative and Labour cabinets after 1955, only Heath getting numbers down to eighteen for a while in 1970.) This was possible because formally kept outside the cabinet in 1951 were thirteen ministers in charge of some pretty important departments (including the ministries of Education, Transport, Pensions, National Insurance, Agriculture, Fuel and Power, and the three service departments, together with Health after May 1952 – whose ministers would, however, attend cabinet meetings if their departmental business was on the agenda and who were members of relevant cabinet committees) and by the appointment of a number of co-ordinating or supervising ministerial 'Overlords', as they came to be known.[31]

The 'Overlords' experiment, 1951–3, was controversial and short-lived.[32] It was Churchill's own idea, which he insisted upon in the face of opposition from senior civil servants (Brook tried hard to dissuade him), from some top ministers, from the officials and ministers in the departments supervised by the 'Overlords' (soon dubbed 'Underlings'), and from the Labour opposition. Churchill's innovation did not represent 'new thinking about the requirements of cabinet government in modern conditions', as Peter Hennessy notes, but was driven by his preference for a small cabinet, recreating some features of his war cabinet system, and by his desire to gather around him trusted and familiar figures from his 1940–45 administration – the 'Old Guard' as *The Economist* called them, the PM's 'hangers-on', according to Labour's Herbert Morrison. There was indeed an 'Auld Lang Syne' feel to it all, as John Colville (recalled to the Number 10 private office) put it.[33] Eden went back to the Foreign Office, Lord Ismay, Churchill's link with the chiefs of staff during the war, was made Commonwealth relations secretary, and his favourite general Field Marshal Lord Alexander of Tunis was appointed minister of defence (from March 1952; Churchill himself taking that post for the first four months of the government) – neither Ismay nor Alexander was a successful minister, which casts doubt on Churchill's judgement in appointing them. The 'Overlords' were Lords Woolton (who had been minister of food and then minister of reconstruction during the war, before becoming Conservative Party chairman), Leathers (minister of war transport 1940–45) and Cherwell (see chapter 6). Woolton was made lord president of the Council and given responsibility for co-ordinating the policies of the Ministry of Agriculture and Fisheries and the Ministry of Food. Leathers was appointed secretary of state for the co-ordination of transport, fuel and power. Cherwell did not co-ordinate or supervise specific departments in the same way but became paymaster general again, dealing with scientific and particularly atomic energy/weapons issues, and acting as a general prime ministerial *éminence grise* and adviser. Churchill had wanted to appoint John Anderson, Viscount Waverley, as a fourth economic 'Overlord', to preside over the Treasury, Board of Trade and Ministry of Supply, but Anderson refused the assignment and told Churchill that the 'Overlords' system was unworkable.

'I had no experience of being Prime Minister in time of peace,' Churchill told MPs in November 1953, explaining that he had looked for 'the grouping of Departments' so that as PM he would be 'able to deal with a comparatively smaller number of heads than actually exists in peacetime'. Churchill's main interests as prime minister after 1951 were foreign and defence policy; he took little detailed interest in the broad field of domestic policy, and was 'perplexed' by economic policy issues, according to his chancellor of the exchequer Rab Butler. 'Government . . . had become more complicated than it used to be,' he grumbled to Lord Moran in 1953. 'We have to consider intricate matters . . . which never came before the Cabinets I can remember.' In this context, as Paul Addison argues, the 'Overlords' can be seen as 'an interesting experiment, in trying to co-ordinate areas of policy in which he perhaps didn't feel entirely confident himself'.[34]

The problem was that the exact functions and role of the 'Overlords' were never made clear, and the constitutional implications for the theory and practice of ministerial responsibility and parliamentary accountability proved to be major stumbling blocks. Labour complained that the 'Overlords' system blurred ministerial responsibility and got particularly steamed up about the fact that the supervising ministers all sat in the House of Lords and thus could not be directly questioned and held accountable by MPs and the House of Commons. Churchill's cabinet had in fact twice as many peers as the outgoing Labour one: six, increasing to seven with Lord Alexander's appointment in 1952 (with eighteen peers overall in the government, compared to Labour's sixteen), leading to exaggerated talk of a throwback to nineteenth-century or even eighteenth-century practice. Government explanations of the 'Overlords' system simply muddied the waters, Rab Butler stating that departmental ministers remained directly responsible to Parliament for all powers imposed on them by statute, and Woolton arguing that the work of the 'Overlords' involved not a responsibility to Parliament but a responsibility to the cabinet. 'I hate the word "co-ordination",' Churchill had remarked in an unscripted parliamentary outburst in November 1951. His carefully worded formal statement in May 1952 was rather defensive in tone, but confirmed that the 'Overlords' were far from being powerful 'super-ministers'. 'The co-ordinating Ministers have no statutory powers,' he explained. 'They have in particular no power to give orders or directions to a Departmental Minister.' Departmental ministers always had access to the cabinet where the normal rules of collective responsibility applied: if overruled there, they had to accept the cabinet's decision or resign. The 'Overlords', he said, performed no formal acts and had no statutory powers; they were not 'non-responsible', however, for they shared in the government's collective responsibility. As he blandly put it: they 'invited' departmental ministers to 'adjust' their policies to accord with the 'wider interests of the Government as a whole'. 'Thus the existence and activities of these co-ordinating Ministers do not impair or diminish the responsibility to Parliament of the Departmental Ministers whose policies they co-ordinate,' he concluded.[35]

Churchill also claimed that the role of the 'Overlords' was 'a natural evolution in the process of conducting the collective business of Government'. 'In former days,' he argued, 'all reconciliation of Departmental policies was done in the Cabinet, of which all Departmental Ministers were members, or by the Prime Minister himself.' But with the growing scale and complexity of modern government that task was too great for them, and in addition the Cabinet no longer included all ministers in charge of departments. In the past, he noted, special co-ordinating responsibilities had been given to non-departmental ministers such as the lord president and the lord privy seal, who had been linchpins of the system of standing cabinet committees that had developed during the war and under Attlee's Labour government. The new system, he argued, simply took all this a stage further by publicly announcing the specific areas of co-ordination assigned to Lords Woolton and Leathers. It was, however, disingenuous for Churchill to present the 'Overlords' as a mere variant of the cabinet committee system for the signs are that at the start of the government he had intended them to function to some extent as an alternative to co-ordination through such committees, which he disliked and wanted to cut back.[36]

Churchill had in fact come into office in 1951 concerned that the Whitehall and cabinet committee system had got out of hand under Attlee and saying that he wanted to 'slaughter . . . a great number of second- and third-grade committees which now, I am assured, cumber the ground'. The cabinet secretary, Sir Norman Brook, had fought back, arguing in favour of the committee system as relieving the burden on cabinet, permitting a smaller cabinet (which he knew the prime minister wanted), and being consistent with the doctrine of collective responsibility. Churchill took Brook's advice on the main shape of the committee system, setting up an economic policy committee (which the chancellor of the exchequer, Butler, chaired rather than the PM, in contrast to the position under Labour), and committees for home affairs, defence and legislation. On Churchill's orders, Brook then produced a list of committees seventeen pages long, but recommended the axing of only nine, leading Churchill to explode that 'you seem to have got very few birds out of this enormous covey'. Several more were then also abolished, but Cabinet Office figures subsequently showed no real reduction in the number of meetings of the main cabinet committees (or the numbers of papers they generated) in 1952 and 1953, though significantly fewer *ad hoc* committees were set up under Churchill than under Attlee. The cabinet committee system was never in any real danger from the 'Overlords' experiment.[37]

It is clear, as Peter Hennessy says, that Churchill 'never grasped the detail of how his peacetime "overlords" actually performed within the realities of early-1950s Whitehall'. They were left to interpret their role in their own way and get on with the job as best they could, working with limited back-up from their small private office staffs. Inevitably, the results were limited and patchy. Woolton attempted only light-touch supervision of Food and Agriculture and Fisheries, not attempting to control detailed operations, as he told Churchill, and in practice seems to have had little direct influence on the main policies of the two departments (which were merged in 1954). Serious illness in 1952 further limited his effectiveness, and the departmental ministers he was supposedly co-ordinating increasingly bypassed him. Leathers tried to be more interventionist but got bogged down in details; was faced with a rather incoherent portfolio in which he was more at home dealing with transport than with fuel and power issues; clashed with the ministers he was supervising; and was a poor performer in the House of Lords. After only a year in office, by October 1952, he was telling Churchill that he wanted to resign – 'I only kept him by calling him a deserter,' Churchill told Moran. It was obvious that the 'Overlords' system was breaking down some time before it was formally terminated in September 1953, when Leathers resigned and Woolton was switched to become minister of materials (Cherwell too soon leaving the government to return to Oxford). The ministers for food and for agriculture were promoted to the cabinet (along with the minister for education, Florence Horsbrugh – Churchill thus appointing the first female Conservative cabinet minister). Churchill told MPs that he had decided to 'hush it all up and manage it in the Cabinet', in other words to rely on the normal cabinet and cabinet committee processes of decision-making and co-ordination.[38]

Churchill had partly appointed the 'Overlords' as a convenient way of bringing into the cabinet trusted figures from his wartime team without imposing on them heavy administrative and departmental tasks they did not want. In principle it was a valid approach to dealing with a genuine problem in the machinery of government, as some other senior Tories – including Harold Macmillan, Churchill's successor-but-one in Number 10 – also believed. (Macmillan had, in fact, advocated the creation of an 'inner Cabinet' of four or five powerful ministerial lieutenants, exercising the PM's delegated authority and co-ordinating specific fields of policy, in his 1938 book *The Middle Way*.) The problems of co-ordinating and giving coherence and direction to the policies of different departments were becoming acute, but the forces of 'departmentalism' in the Conservative government of the 1950s were strong. 'In peacetime Departmental Ministers, particularly on the home front, assume much more importance than in wartime,' Sir John Anderson had warned in February 1945 – and perhaps Churchill was slow to realize that when he returned to Downing Street. The constitutional and accountability aspects had not been properly thought through, Churchill himself telling MPs that he did not think it possible to lay down detailed rules and dismissing 'metaphysical questions' about how the arrangements worked. The 'Overlords' were never a fully developed intermediate level in the system of government, covering only a few policy areas, and the experiment was further unbalanced by drawing the co-ordinating ministers from the House of Lords, something that was bound to frustrate MPs as well as ambitious younger Conservative ministers. Churchill's attempt at cabinet co-ordination through 'Overlords' was ultimately a half-hearted and ineffective experiment.[39]

It would be wrong to write off Churchill himself as an ineffective prime minister, second time round, 1951-55, contrary to the caricature view of him being 'gaga', self-obsessed, unfit for office and useless as a director of government. He was certainly not a 'presidential' figure in style or ambition, and indeed thought that that would be unconstitutional. 'You must remember that the office of Prime Minister is not a dictatorship, certainly not in peacetime,' he told Anthony Montague Browne. As he explained to Lord Moran: 'Most people feel that the Prime Minister is always responsible; he should insist on getting his own way. That is not my idea. I don't think he should be an autocrat. I never was, even in the war. Of course I had great powers, my relations with Roosevelt and things like that ensured this. But the Cabinet ought to have their say.' (Although he added: 'There are a few occasions, of course, when the Prime Minister must have his own way or resign.')[40]

Churchill clearly had less energy than at his peak during the war, he was very selective in the policy areas and the issues in which he got involved, and he was easily bored by details. As Leslie Rowan (a wartime Number 10 private secretary and in the 1950s a senior Treasury official) noticed in 1952, 'he has lost his tenacity; he no longer pushes a thing through. He has lost, too, his power of fitting in all the problems to one another.' Up until his serious stroke in the summer of 1953 (which was kept secret in a way unimaginable today) he was more or less holding his own, but, as a practitioner of traditional cabinet government, operating (except in the areas of foreign policy and defence) very much as a 'hands-off' prime minister, leaving his departmental ministers to get on with the job of running their departments. Some ministers actually felt that he gave them too little attention and guidance, Woolton writing in his memoirs that 'Mr Churchill rarely sent for ministers of cabinet rank who were not in the War Cabinet or, in post-war days, the inner Cabinet, for a general conversation about what they were doing'. His Number 10 staff and Sir Norman Brook played a vital behind-the-scenes role in keeping the prime minister 'on the road', as it were, but despite that support, insiders could see that Churchill's performance was seriously deteriorating through the second half of 1954. He clung on, to the growing consternation and frustration of many ministers – not least his anointed successor, Eden – and finally left office in April 1955.[41]

Serving under Churchill, Harold Macmillan once said, was 'like constantly having tea with Dr Johnson'. Woolton claimed that 'not infrequently the entire time of the meeting had gone before he arrived at the first item on the agenda', but the complaints about long prime-ministerial monologues and rambling and indecisive cabinet meetings have to be kept in perspective. What was perceived as 'lack of grip' could actually be 'skilful manoeuvring', as Macmillan shrewdly recognized (and he was later to practise such tactics himself), giving the example of a theatrical Churchill 'filibuster' at one meeting in October 1952 when the Old Man wanted to pre-empt Eden and the Foreign Office and deliberately eat up time to avoid discussion of an unwanted item about the continuing presence of British troops in Egypt.[42]

'I am a great believer in bringing things before the Cabinet,' Churchill told Moran in April 1953. 'If a Minister has got anything on his mind and he has the sense to get it argued by the Cabinet he will have the machine behind him.' Uniquely, he broke with his own wartime practice, and with the practice of Attlee, by bringing nuclear weapons decision-making before the full cabinet in July 1954 with the decision on whether Britain should proceed with making a H-bomb. The war cabinet had not been informed or consulted about the manufacture and use of the atomic bomb, and after 1945 Attlee had kept these matters within a very small circle in secret *ad hoc* committees. Admittedly the decision had been largely pre-cooked beforehand by the defence committee and an *ad hoc* group – GEN 464 – of six senior ministers chaired by Churchill, but when the issue reached the full cabinet, it took three meetings before the ministers around the table finally (and inevitably) agreed, with the implications being discussed in detail. The whole story bears out the remark by Anthony Seldon, historian of the 1951-5 government, that Churchill 'regarded the Cabinet as extremely important, even sacrosanct, and would only rarely ride roughshod over it to get his way'.[43]

Conclusion

Rooted in and respectful of the traditional institutions and constitutional practices of British parliamentary and cabinet politics, Churchill was clearly one of the 'old school' prime ministers. The modern 'presidential' prime ministers – pre-eminently Margaret Thatcher and Tony Blair – cut very different figures: focused on television presentation and media packaging of personality and policies; distant from the House of Commons; downgrading the cabinet and centralizing power in Number 10 Downing Street.[44] The notion of the prime minister and Number 10 'managing media relations' or developing a 'media strategy' would have been incomprehensible to him, though he did have close personal relations with key 'press barons'. Churchill initially refused even to have a prime-ministerial public relations/press adviser when he became PM in 1951 (he had not had one during the war, although the Attlee government had had a Labour-supporting journalist in that role) and took some persuading before he consented to the appointment of a press aide, who – symbolically – did not have an office in Number 10. He never gave a television interview at all while prime minister and was highly suspicious of this new medium. Deliberate ministerial 'leaks' of information were still comparatively rare in the early 1950s.[45] A veteran MP himself, Churchill believed that prime ministers should be attentive to and accountable to MPs in the House of Commons, and even during the Second World War he regularly gave major speeches there, took part in debates and answered questions (PQs) – in contrast to Lloyd George, who had largely ignored Parliament while PM during the First World War. In 1953, after his illness, the concession was made to him that the PM should answer PQs on only two days a week (Tuesdays and Thursdays) rather than being in the firing line on four days each week (including Mondays and Wednesdays) as had been the case up until then. But on all the measures of parliamentary activity, the contrast between Churchill and Thatcher or Blair is striking.[46] Churchill's personal ascendancy within the government during the war cannot be doubted, but he took the cabinet and the norms of collective responsibility seriously both during the war and after 1951. In the 1950s he would normally hold two cabinet meetings each week (there were 108 in 1952, falling to 81 in 1953 and 92 in 1954). Mrs Thatcher rarely held more than one meeting each week – half as many as Churchill – and also drastically cut back on the cabinet committee apparatus and reduced the number of cabinet papers and memoranda circulated.[47] Under the even more 'presidential' Tony Blair, the cabinet has further atrophied, with some cabinet meetings being particularly short and perfunctory, and there has been an unparalleled build-up of Number 10 staff and policy advisers working directly to the PM – a virtual 'prime minister's department'.

As Dennis Kavanagh has pointed out, there was no permanent redefinition of the office of prime minister as a result of Churchill's tenure. Churchill's own institutional changes – while important for the conduct of the war – were specific and limited: the smaller war cabinet, the appointment of a number of his own friends and cronies to ministerial or adviser posts, the innovation of appointing himself minister of defence in order to deal direct with the chiefs of staff (but he did not overrule the military chiefs). Lloyd George's innovations after 1916 had been far more radical: the 'Garden Suburb' staff of prime-ministerial advisers, the non-departmental war cabinet, the cavalier and 'presidential' style of the premier, the virtual usurpation of the position of the foreign secretary and the Foreign Office. And Lloyd George's creation of the Cabinet Secretariat was an enduring and important institutional innovation.[48] The development of an extended cabinet committee system, and of the Whitehall interdepartmental committee labyrinth, during and after the Second World War was something Churchill was worried about, as we have seen, rather than viewing it as a positive thing. His 'Overlords' experiment soon foundered and, in any case, did not represent a fully thought-out and thoroughgoing reform of the cabinet system. Churchill's personal style and methods in office might have been unusual and idiosyncratic, but in institutional terms he was pretty traditionalist as regards the prime ministership and the cabinet, and not a radical reformer.

As with other central institutions of the British state (the monarchy, the House of Commons), Churchill was a great romantic about the cabinet system. He was indeed 'a great Cabinet-government man', as Peter Hennessy says, referring to Churchill's 'reverence for Cabinet government'. 'Did you enjoy Cabinets?' Churchill once asked Lord Cherwell. 'Sometimes,' 'the Prof' said, in a noncommittal way. 'I loved every minute of them,' Churchill replied.[49] It was a revealing exchange. Churchill wanted to be at the centre of things and to take part in the play of power and politics. He was interested in the substance of power, not its shadow. He wanted to be prime minister and to exercise power, but he did not conceive of that office in a dictatorial way. For him, the cabinet was definitely not one of the 'dignified' elements of the British constitution.

EIGHT

Churchill and the Constitutional Monarchy

'Parliament and the Monarchy were to him sacred things,' Desmond
Morton once ruminated about Churchill.

> He did literally worship the authority of Parliament, and of the British
> Monarch, even if the latter had really ceased to exercise much authority . . .
> He would never hear a word of criticism against either, though his worship of
> Monarchy and his worship of Parliament were slightly different mental
> reactions. He had fear for the authority of Parliament – real fear, and not only
> from what Parliament might do to him, or how it could affect his fortunes. It
> was a real mystical fear, not wholly susceptible to reason, and going far beyond
> respect. He had no fear of the British Monarch, but a respect which also was
> somewhat mystical, transcending the person who wore the crown. Yet he had
> little or no respect for foreign monarchs, above ordinary politeness. Presidents
> and other Prime Ministers he treated as equals with himself, only he was
> rather more equal than others. The 'others' were respected according to the
> degree of power they actually wielded.

Churchill had, emphasized Morton, 'immense mystical respect for the
British Monarch, and for the *British* Monarch alone'.[1]

The Monarchy and the Political System

Morton knew Churchill well and had, shrewdly, put his finger on an
important point: he had a deep, intense and profound belief in the British
monarchy. But Churchill's attitude towards the monarchy (and towards the

monarchs he served) was complex and has to be analysed and understood on several different levels.[2] There was, to be sure, something of a quasi-religious or reverential angle. 'King and country, in that order, that's about all the religion Winston has,' Lord Moran noted. Clementine Churchill once told John Colville that she thought her husband was the last surviving believer in the Divine Right of Kings (she felt reasonably sure that King George VI was not another), and Colville commented that Churchill's 'respect for the monarchy amounted almost to idolatry'. In a particularly speculative mood, Churchill one day 'could not help wondering whether the government above might not be a constitutional monarchy', reported Colville, 'in which case there was always a possibility that the Almighty might have occasion to "send for him"'. On occasion his public remarks were couched in mystical or spiritual terms too: thus the Crown, he once said, was 'the symbol which gathers together and expresses those deep emotions and stirrings of the human heart', and it 'has become the mysterious link – indeed, I may say, the magic link – which unites our loosely bound but strongly interwoven Commonwealth of nations, states and races'. Monarchs 'personify the spirit of the State', he once wrote. Pimlott's description of Churchill as 'the secular high priest' of the Queen's coronation in 1953 also captures something of this dimension of his attitude to the mystique of monarchy.[3]

'I like the glitter of the past,' Churchill once admitted. He had a strong sense of the drama, spectacle, romance and pageantry of the monarchy. In 1897, as a young subaltern, he had been proud to serve Queen Victoria as Empress of India: 'I must array myself with those who "love high-sounding titles", since no title that is not high-sounding is worth having.' 'You are Monarchical No. 1,' Clementine Churchill told him, 'and value tradition, form and ceremony.' He could speak with complete sincerity of the coronation of George V in 1911 as an occasion for 'National rejoicing and Imperial Unity'. 'Crowning a King is the supreme festival of the British Constitution,' he declared in a radio broadcast before George VI's coronation in May 1937. 'From ancient times all classes have shared in it with rejoicing . . . The British Constitutional monarchy embodies the traditions of a thousand years. The King will be crowned tomorrow not only under a ritual which has come down from the Plantagenets and Tudors, but which revives forms and customs of Anglo-Saxon times.' In straight Bagehotian terms he argued in March 1937 that 'If you are not to have the glitter and the splendour of ceremonial pageant, I do not really know how the great mass of the people would be associated with the main facts of the State'. The glamour, ritual, ceremony and symbolism associated with the Crown was 'of high practical importance to the masses of the people', and all the more so after the abdication crisis. Would the public really approve of 'the abolition of the coaches of State'? 'Of course, the Sovereign might come in a motor-car to the House of Commons, the House of Lords being abolished, and might take the Oath in our presence, and then return in a motor-car to his habituation, but I am not at all sure that the public would view such a change with satisfaction.' 'The pomp and circumstance,' insisted Churchill, '. . . which have been hitherto associated with the English [*sic*] Monarchy should not be pared away from it in these modern days.'[4]

He took a detailed interest in the preparations for the Queen's coronation, the timing of which in June 1953 gave him scope to delay still more his own retirement from the premiership. 'He had set his heart on seeing the young Queen crowned before he gave up office,' Moran noted, and indeed he took a mischievous (and paternalistic) delight in 'laying down the law about the Coronation arrangements'. Moran recalled the scene:

'I'm doing some scratching and clawing. They were going to charge everyone in the Abbey – three thousand of them, the elect from all over the place – sixteen shillings for sandwiches. I stepped in and stopped that. The people in the stands at Hyde Park Corner, by Byron's statue, will be there from seven in the morning till five in the evening. They were seeing to their sanitary needs, but doing nothing for them in food and drink.'

A great grin prepared me for a sally:

'Looking after their exports while neglecting their imports. And why?'

A look of withering scorn crossed his face.

'Because alcohol had not been drunk in the royal parks for a hundred years, they were to have nothing to drink. I altered all that. Even the people not in the stands will have booths.'

'The Coronation was the apotheosis of WSC's love and reverence for the Crown,' says Anthony Montague Browne, his then private secretary.

'Dressed for the part, in the unique and bizarre uniform of the Lord Warden of the Cinque Ports, and with his Orders and medals, he was an unforgettable sight . . . Accompanied by CSC [his wife] he drove in the Royal procession in a horse-drawn carriage.'[5]

Churchill's public statements about the Crown and the monarchy were generally phrased in a rich and ornamental language calibrated to celebrate the centrality, importance and status of this most 'dignified' element of the constitution: 'an office of such extraordinary significance', he once called it. 'The British Monarchy has no interests divergent from those of the British people,' he declared in a 1909 speech. 'It enshrines only those ideas and causes upon which the whole British people are united. It is based upon the abiding and prevailing interests of the nation, and thus through all the swift changes of the last hundred years, through all the wide developments of a democratic State, the English Monarchy has become the most secure, as it is the most ancient and the most glorious Monarchy in the whole of Christendom.' The notion of the 'Royal and Imperial monarchy' and of the 'King-Emperor' had a strong hold on his imagination and he opposed the 1931 Statute of Westminster (which ended the sovereignty of the imperial parliament in London over the Dominions), but stressed the important role of the Crown as the unifying link in the new Commonwealth, talking proudly (in 1945) of a unique 'multiple Kingship': 'Governments so proud and independent that they would not brook the slightest sign of interference from [the House of Commons] vie with each other, and with us, in their respect for the ancient and glorious institution of the British Monarchy. It is the golden circle of the Crown which alone embraces the loyalties of so many States and races all over the world.' The accession of Elizabeth II prompted even more lavish rhetoric that nevertheless struck a chord with the 1950s public and 'chimed with the moment', as Pimlott notes. We 'will never see the Crown sparkle more gloriously than in these joyous days', Churchill said. The Queen was 'the gleaming figure whom Providence has brought to us' and 'a lady whom we respect because she is our Queen and whom we love because she is herself'. The Queen's (1954) Commonwealth tour was a 'gleaming episode', a 'royal pilgrimage'. The unifying role of the Crown was as important as ever: 'the central link in all our modern changing life, the one which above all others claims our allegiance to death'. And the institution of the monarchy had never been stronger: it was now 'far more broadly and securely based on the people's love and the nation's will than in the . . . days . . . when rank and privilege ruled society'.[6]

Like Disraeli, Churchill was 'a genuine romantic, even a sentimentalist, in his attitude to the throne' and tended to 'lay it on with a trowel'. When Disraeli flattered and wooed Queen Victoria he was, as Robert Blake notes, 'aware of the advantages to be gained from friendship with a sovereign whose constitutional powers, however diminished and ill-defined, were sufficient for her goodwill to make a difference'. By the time Churchill reached Number 10, there was no question of George VI exercising or seeking to exercise the sort of royal influence that his great-grandmother had. But it is striking and revealing that while Clement Attlee, for instance, as prime minister treated the royal family with what Pimlott describes as 'civility and respect', Churchill behaved with 'extravagant courtesy' and made 'exaggerated shows of deference'. Signing himself 'the vy. Old servant of Your Royal House . . . Your Majesty's faithful & devoted subject', Churchill's letters to the King painted an exalted picture of both their relationship and, in a wider sense, the integrating role of the monarchy in British society. In January 1941, for example, he wrote that 'this war has drawn the Throne & the people more closely together than was ever before recorded, & Yr Majesties are more beloved by all classes & conditions than any of the princes of the past'. In November 1942 he wrote to George VI paying tribute to 'the support and encouragement given by the Sovereign to his First Minister in good and dark days alike'. 'No Minister in modern times,' he went on, 'and I dare say in long past days, has received more help and comfort from the King . . . It is needless for me to assure Your Majesty of my devotion to Yourself and Family and to our ancient cherished Monarchy – the true bulwark of British freedom against tyrannies of every kind.'[7]

Inevitably, Churchill's understanding of, and relationship with, the monarchy reflected his strong sense of that institution's history. The language of 'the island Crown' and 'our ancient Throne' came naturally to him. 'The history of England, its romance and changing fortunes, is for Winston embodied in the Royal House,' commented Lord Moran – something seen clearly in the way in which he put together his multi-volume

History of the English-Speaking Peoples: history as a colourful and dramatic story of kings, queens and battles. Churchill's was a Whiggish 'wisdom of our ancestors' account of British constitutional development: 'We have known how to preserve the old and glorious traditions of hereditary monarchy while slowly building up a parliamentary system which has hitherto met the needs of a growing people and changing times. . .' he wrote in 1934. 'How proud we may be to have preserved the symbols and traditions of our glorious past, enshrined and perpetuated in an hereditary monarchy, and to have reconciled these treasures with a religious, civic and political freedom unexampled in any quarter of the globe!' 'Surely . . . we have the best of both worlds,' he argued in 1927. 'With a thoroughly modern and democratic practice we have managed, by characteristic British good sense, to preserve traditions and ceremonial which descend unbroken from an immemorial past, and robe the action of a modern State with forms derived from the Tudors and Plantagenets . . . It might be thought that the British people had achieved a perfect solution of one at least of the problems fundamental to all forms of human government.'[8]

Churchill had no time for republicanism, though he appreciated Bagehot's point about Britain being in effect a 'Crowned Republic', and he ranked Cromwell among the great men of English history; twice, in 1911 and 1912, he tried, unsuccessfully, to persuade George V to name a battleship after the great regicide and Lord Protector. (Churchill felt that Cromwell was patriotic, had saved Parliament's cause in the Civil War, and was one of the founders of the navy – but at the same time he disliked him, thought he was a bad man and had been a dictator.) Years later, a Labour MP was surely not far wrong when he speculated that if Britain had abolished the monarchy at the end of the Second World War, the 'great commoner' would probably have been elected President. But 'The joining together in a single person of the headship of the State and the headship of the government, or any approach thereto, open or veiled, has always been odious in Great Britain,' Churchill insisted. In 1937 he recalled that 'seventy or eighty years ago a lively section of the intelligentsia imagined that to move from a Constitutional Monarchy to a Republic would be a further step of progress. Hardly anyone in Britain or the British Empire, even the greatest simpleton, believes that today. The wage-earning masses realize that the Monarchy is the most practical obstacle to dictatorship or one-man power. No one can presume to set himself up as national representative against the hereditary rights of the King'. 'The old Republicanism of Dilke and Labby [Labouchere] is dead as mutton,' he explained to Lord Randolph, in his imaginary conversation with his father ('The Dream', 1947). 'The Labour men and the trade unions look upon the Monarchy not only as a national but a nationalised institution. They even go to the parties at Buckingham Palace. Those who have very extreme principles wear sweaters.' The idea that 'republics are more free and better governed than monarchies' was 'silly', he argued. He acknowledged (writing in 1920) that 'The twentieth century has been destructive of monarchs, and few now remain', but maintained that 'no proof has been given that the republican form of government produces better results for the mass of the people. On the contrary, there are many instances which show that the cost of government is greater under republics than under monarchies, that there is more corruption, less freedom and less progress, both physical and intellectual. There are, of course, exceptions . . . The fact remains, however, that it has been the experience of many nations to have dwelt more happily, more safely, more prosperously and more progressively under a monarchy than either an oligarchy or a republic'. He regretted the post-First World War 'holocaust of crowns' and the pulling down of 'the old kings' of the great European dynasties, arguing in the 1930s that Germany and Austria would have been better off under a restored version of the monarchical system – a stronger bulwark against dictatorship and tyranny than a republic.[9]

The ideal system, for Churchill, was the British 'political conception of a constitutional sovereign and a limited monarchy'. He was careful, in his attacks on the hereditary peers of the House of Lords in 1909, to argue that the principle of a hereditary constitutional monarchy was still valid: 'The experience of every country, and of all the ages, the practical reasonings of common sense, arguments of the highest theory, arguments of the most commonplace experience, all unite to show the profound wisdom which places the supreme leadership of the State beyond the reach of private ambition and above the shocks and changes of party strife.' But he emphasized that 'we live under a limited and constitutional monarchy. The Sovereign reigns, but does not govern. The powers of government are exercised upon the advice of Ministers responsible to Parliament'. What was axiomatic for him throughout his career was 'the supremacy of Parliament over the Crown [and] the duty of the Sovereign to act in accordance with the advice of his Ministers', as he put it in a speech in 1936. 'The Royal Prerogative is always exercised on the advice of ministers, and ministers and not the Crown are responsible,' he had explained to Clementine in 1909. In 1947, if the Crown was 'stronger than in the days of Queen Victoria', it was because 'they took the advice of the Ministers who had majorities in the House of Commons'.[10]

'When our kings are in conflict with our constitution, we change our kings,' Churchill bluntly told the Duke of Windsor (the former Edward VIII) in 1939. The survival and strength of the British monarchy as an institution, Churchill recognized, lay in monarchs accepting their role and place within the broader constitutional and political order as it had developed from the days of the Glorious Revolution of 1688 onwards. 'The Crown in England has not had for hundreds of years the power of making laws, and for two or three centuries has not had the power of stopping laws when they have been passed,' he explained to an election meeting in Burnley in December 1909. Writing about the reign of Queen Victoria, he noted that 'the development of popular Government based on popular elections was bound to diminish the personal power of the Crown'. Victoria had restored 'the dignity and repute of the monarchy', 'represented staunchness and continuity in British traditions' and had 'set a new standard for the conduct of monarchy which has ever since been honourably observed'. She gave to Britain and the Empire 'a sense of a great presiding personage'. 'In spite of her occasional leanings, [she] remained a constitutional monarch,' Churchill argued. King George V had played a crucial role, in Churchill's view, in upholding the constitution and helping to stabilize the political system in a period of 'great shocks and disturbances' that had been 'fatal to most of the empires, monarchies and political organizations of Europe and Asia' – his reign and example meant that the Crown 'far from falling into desuetude or decay' had 'breasted the torrent of events, and even derived new vigour from the stresses', a remarkable achievement, which was 'contrary to the whole tendency of the age'. 'Uplifted above class-strife and party-faction', the King's contribution had been to 'foster every tendency that makes for national unity'. 'The Constitution and the workings of Parliamentary Government were alike his guides and his instruments' and he was 'determined from the outset to show absolute impartiality in the Constitution to all parties, irrespective of their creed or doctrine, who could obtain a majority in the House of Commons'. By 'trust[ing] the people' and never fearing 'the British Democracy', the King had 'reconciled the new forces of Labour and Socialism to the Constitution and the Monarchy . . . assimilating and rallying the spokesmen of left-out millions . . . whose theories at any rate seemed to menace all existing institutions'.[11]

In a similar vein, George VI was praised for his 'thorough comprehension of our Parliamentary and democratic Constitution' and for his 'constitutional rectitude'. On the King's death in 1952, Churchill catalogued the functions and attributes of one whose 'conduct on the Throne may well be a model and a guide to constitutional sovereigns throughout the world today, and also in future generations'. Thus, King George VI was 'faithful in his study and discharge of State affairs, so strong in his devotion to the enduring honour of our country, so self-restrained in his judgments of men and affairs, so uplifted above the clash of party politics, yet so attentive to them; so wise and shrewd in judging between what matters and what does not . . . I made certain [during the war] he was kept informed of every secret matter; and the care and thoroughness with which he mastered the immense daily flow of State papers made a deep mark on my mind'.[12] What was absent from this list, of course, was any suggestion of royal influence over the policy or legislation of his government(s) – that was constitutionally and politically unthinkable.

Writing in 1920, Churchill had argued that had the Russian Tsar or the German Kaiser 'succeeded to their thrones under something like the British Constitution, and with the experienced political advisers at their side whom our constitutional system has always hitherto supplied, they might both be reigning peacefully at the present moment, and the world would have been spared the measureless calamities of the great war and the still unmeasured calamities which may follow from it'. That may seem a rather fanciful claim, but his analysis in that article of the British system of constitutional monarchy is worth quoting at length:

It seems probable that on the whole the best arrangement that can be made for the Government of a State is the kind of combination of Monarchy and Commonwealth which, by the patient and valiant efforts of so many centuries, we have achieved in Britain. We have the separation in our national life of what is permanent from what is temporary. We are able to divide what is the common inheritance of all from those matters which must necessarily be in dispute between classes and parties and factions. We have a Constitution which places the supreme position in the State beyond the reach of private ambition, but which at the same time assures to a political leader, in fulfilment of the wishes of the electors, a freedom and confidence of action unsurpassed in any land. Above all, we have that separation of pomp from power, which is perhaps one of the most important practical principles in the organization of a political system . . . With us the Sovereign reigns but does not govern. All the splendour and tradition of the realm belong to the Crown; but the difficult, doubtful, disputable, day-to-day business is transacted by plain men in black coats who can be turned out and replaced if they do not give satisfaction.

'The prerogatives of the Crown have become the privileges of the people,' is how he once summed up the position. The separation of 'permanent hereditary functions from actual executive responsibility' meant, he said, that 'when things go well the King is strengthened on his throne. If they go ill no reproach falls upon him – we find him better advisers. A great battle is lost – Parliament turns out the Government. A great battle is won – crowds cheer the King'.[13]

Churchill and His Monarchs

For all Churchill's great respect for and fine language about the institution of monarchy, and its important place in the country's history and constitution, in the day-to-day business of politics and administration he displayed some pretty robust attitudes when faced with what he regarded (in David Cannadine's words) as 'inappropriate royal interference in matters which were wholly within the realm of Parliament and government'. With his grand and historic ducal family background, Churchill had a Whiggish confidence in his personal dealings with monarchs and the Palace which could – particularly in the first part of his career – spill over into brashness. As Cannadine notes: 'he often saw individual monarchs as flawed personalities, political opponents and tiresome nuisances, with inflexible attitudes, reactionary opinions and obscurantist instincts, who deserved neither deference nor sympathy.' His time as a radical and crusading Liberal reformer and controversial first lord of the Admiralty up to 1915 was punctuated with complaints from Buckingham Palace courtiers and from Edward VII and George V about policies and actions of his that they disliked – in royal circles Churchill was seen and distrusted as bumptious, unprincipled and on the make ('Almost more of a cad in office than he was in opposition,' Edward VII once grumbled, and made a feeble joke about the initials W. C. being 'well named'). Churchill's criticisms of army 'brass hats [with] ornamental duties', his offensive remarks about the imperial pro-consul Lord Milner in 1906, his attack on the peers in 1909 as 'a miserable minority of titled persons', his speech in 1910 about 'the Crown and the Commons acting together against the encroachment of the Lords', and his comment in a letter to George V in 1911 about there being 'idlers and wastrels at both ends of the social scale' all provoked royal protests and rebukes. In return, Churchill could give as good as he got: 'The King talked more stupidly about the Navy than I have ever heard him before,' he complained to Clementine in 1912. 'Really it is disheartening to hear this cheap and silly drivel with which he lets himself be filled up.' Churchill was not alone in having a poor relationship with George V – other Liberal ministers also distrusted his political impartiality, doubted his competence, and found him difficult to deal with (Asquith likened a prime-ministerial audience with the King to having a tooth out, and Lloyd George and the King did not conceal their mutual dislike; even the Conservative Arthur Balfour once, maliciously, asked Lloyd George, 'Whatever would you do if you had a ruler with brains?'). The King had been delighted by Churchill's fall from office in 1915. In 1919, when Churchill was back as secretary for war, the King only reluctantly agreed to the award of war medals to Lloyd George when he learned that Churchill had, in a typically cavalier way, already promised them to the prime minister. Later, in the 1920s, their relations were 'scrupulously correct' rather than warm. George V praised the 'skill, patience and tact' that Churchill had shown in the negotiations for the Irish settlement.

And Churchill – after watching the Shah of Persia losing large amounts of his subjects' money at a casino – wrote archly to his wife that 'we are well out of it with our own gracious Monarch' (who was more interested, as he knew, in slaughtering pheasants and looking through his stamp albums).[14]

Churchill's role as a royal champion and supporter of Edward VIII during the 1936 abdication crisis has been widely discussed. Among the many misjudgements he made in that episode (which caused disastrous short-term damage to his political reputation and standing), it is striking that he does not seem to have realized the dangers involved for the system of consti-tutional monarchy he so fervently supported. The issue in that respect was not so much the nature of Edward's private life (about which Churchill was well informed, having been on friendly terms with him as Prince of Wales through the 1920s and 1930s), though Churchill had written in 1927 of the importance of the royal family's 'example of tireless public service', and of a royal 'domestic life' with which millions across the Empire could identify, in terms that might suggest questions about Edward's suitability for the throne. Churchill mistakenly thought that Edward's infatuation with Mrs Simpson was simply another passing attachment and he seems to have had little sense of the (largely shocked and hostile) reactions of ordinary people around the country to the King and his personal dilemma when the crisis broke in late 1936, although he certainly did not think that it was possible for Mrs Simpson to become Queen (for a while, he played with the idea of a morganatic marriage – but that was in reality a non-starter). Crucially, Churchill does not seem to have shared the growing doubts of Baldwin and other leading politicians – and, remarkably, the doubts of George V as well – as to (in Roy Jenkins' words) whether Edward's 'character and sense of public propriety made him . . . suitable for the demands of constitutional kingship'. He seems to have thought that Edward would actually make a good king. Churchill once admitted that Edward had 'very engaging, crowd-compelling qualities' but the problem came when he trespassed into political areas, and – when Prince of Wales – his airing of controversial opinions in public had earned rebukes from his father, George V. Much more dangerous, however, were Edward's reported pro-German opinions (as relayed back to Berlin by the German ambassador) and the disturbing admission that he wanted an active and overtly political role: 'nor did he hold his father's view that the King must blindly accept the Cabinet's decisions. On the contrary, he felt it to be his duty to intervene if the Cabinet were to plan a policy which in his view was detrimental to British interests.'[15]

Given that Edward was (as his brother described) 'dictatorial and obstinate if he could not get his own way', it is easy to imagine that he might have found it difficult to settle down to carry out in a responsible way the limited and constrained functions of a constitutional monarch. Churchill seems to have realized this only after the abdication (which, at the time, he thought avoidable and unnecessary). 'You were right,' he said to his wife at the coronation of George VI in May 1937. 'I now see that the "other one" wouldn't have done.' As Churchill told the King in November 1940, Edward's 'ideas and his pro-Nazi leanings would have been impossible during the crisis of the last three years'. In exile the Duke of Windsor was a wild-talking and dangerous liability ('pretty fifth column', according to one British diplomat), and the target of Nazi intrigue as a possible puppet or quisling king in the event of a successful invasion of Britain. 'Had Churchill succeeded in keeping Edward VIII upon the throne,' said Roy Jenkins, 'he might well have found it necessary in 1940-1 to depose and/or lock up his sovereign as the dangerously potential head of a Vichy-style state.' (After the war, Churchill wanted to protect the reputation of the monarchy and spare the royal family any embarrassment by urging that the captured German documents relating to their machinations around the Duke of Windsor should be destroyed, but they were eventually published in 1957.)[16]

Equally dangerous when considering the continued legitimacy of the monarchical system – and another Churchill blind spot at this time – was the way in which he seemed to come close to taking on the role of leader of a 'King's Party' during the abdication crisis. As Roy Jenkins put it:

> This could have had devastating constitutional consequences. It would have left those who took the other view in an 'anti-King's party' position, and the subsequent battle between the two parties would have totally compromised the political neutrality of the Sovereign, which is essential to constitutional monarchy. The danger was averted, not because of Churchill's wisdom, but because he found no basis of support. Both Parliament and country were over-whelmingly on Baldwin's side on this issue.

That Edward was prepared to go quickly and quietly when the crunch came, and not fight back against the advice of the government, also wrongfooted Churchill, who had been pressing the case for delay and trying to buy time in the hope that Mrs Simpson would disappear from the scene. Though Churchill did talk about the deep principles at stake ('the hereditary principle must not be left to the mercy of politicians trimming their doctrines "to the varying hour",' and 'The King was King, and could only be unmade if he gravely offended against the state'), the idea that in practice he was exploiting the crisis and was manoeuvring to lead a 'royalist' government if Baldwin resigned because Edward would not take ministerial advice over the question of marriage to Mrs Simpson was the subject of considerable political speculation at the time. The Labour and Liberal party leaders had assured Baldwin that they would not form an alternative government in those circumstances, but many insiders mistrusted Churchill and he did not help matters by releasing a long public statement in which he implied that ministers were acting unconstitutionally by pressurizing the King into abdication and argued that it was wrong for them to issue 'an ultimatum' in the form of a threat to resign if their advice was refused, while at the same time blocking the possibility of him sending for the leader of the opposition via the assurances just mentioned. One Churchill supporter did write to him arguing that if the King asked him to form a government, then the backing of forty or fifty MPs could keep an interim administration in power until Parliament could be dissolved and he could go to the country (it is not clear how seriously he took this advice, and it is open to question how well any 'King's Party' would have fared against the combined Conservative, Labour and Liberal leaderships and their party machines).[17]

The fact that in private he gave constitutionally impeccable advice to Edward that the only way he could stay on the throne was not to marry against the advice of ministers – thus removing the possibility of the Baldwin government's resignation on this issue arising – could be taken as evidence that Churchill was not seeking to intrigue against the government (as the historian Graham Stewart argues). In the feverish atmosphere of the time, however, his political opponents and rivals believed that he was plotting, and he was severely mauled in Parliament when he tried to speak up for the King.[18] Overall, whatever view is taken of his motives, Churchill does not come well out of the abdication crisis, and if events had turned out differently his mistakes and misjudgements might well have produced situations that damaged the institution of monarchy even more – a paradoxical outcome for such a strong monarchist.

George VI naturally viewed Churchill rather coolly and warily at first as a 'last-ditch supporter of King Edward' – the royal family also bridled at his 'pro-Windsor' suggestions later, during the war: that the King and Queen should formally 'receive' the Duchess of Windsor, that she should get an HRH title, and that the Duke should be found a public role after the war as a colonial governor or ambassador somewhere (none of these happened). Furthermore, the King and Queen had been strong supporters of Neville Chamberlain – their appearance with him on the balcony of Buckingham Palace after Munich amounting to an unwise public royal endorsement of an increasingly controversial government policy (appeasement). In 1940, the King had wanted Halifax to succeed Chamberlain and there were initial complaints of offhand, dismissive and cavalier behaviour on the part of the new prime minister (for example, turning up late for short and rushed audiences, delays in informing the King of some matters), which could almost be taken as a sign that Buckingham Palace did not appreciate that there was a war on. There were royal grumbles, too, that the charismatic Churchill seemed to upstage the King and hog the limelight as a national symbol and leader. Before too long, however, George VI and Churchill developed a close relationship of mutual trust and personal friendship ('one of the greatest P.M.–Monarch partnerships in British history,' says Peter Hennessy). They met alone most weeks for a private lunch (to Churchill's relief, there was no repetition of George V's wartime 'pledge') and Churchill entrusted the King with the most secret and delicate information about developments in the war (the King was one of the small circle who knew about 'Enigma' code-breaking and atomic bomb research), Allied plans and strategy, and political and personal issues facing the prime minister. Robert Rhodes James argues that Churchill took the King's comments and advice seriously, but it is clear that when the prime minister wanted to, he ignored his views (he overrode royal opposition in 1940 to the appointment of Beaverbrook as minister for aircraft production and the award of a privy councillorship to Brendan Bracken). With considerable ill-grace Churchill gave way when the King (along with the chiefs of staff) opposed his plan to accompany the D-Day invasion flotilla in 1944 – but he visited the invasion bridgehead six days later anyway and insisted that constitutionally the prime minister had to have full freedom of movement. As Cannadine says, Churchill 'never seems to have changed his mind on a major matter of wartime policy . . . at the behest of his sovereign'. During the First World War, relations between Lloyd George and George V had been terrible; but from 1940 to 1945 prime minister-monarch relations were excellent, and in many ways this was the twentieth-century high point of the system of constitutional monarchy that Churchill understood so well and was so strongly committed to.[19]

George VI told Churchill that he was 'shocked' by the latter's eviction from office by an 'ungrateful' electorate in 1945 (he offered the departing prime minister the Order of the Garter, which he refused – he was later to accept it from Queen Elizabeth II). In an intriguing episode, Churchill briefly considered waiting to meet the new House of Commons before formally resigning (as had been standard practice up to 1868, and as he was constitutionally entitled to do) but changed his mind and went immediately under pressure from the Palace and from senior cabinet colleagues (the King felt strongly that it would be wrong for a 'lame-duck' PM to return to the Potsdam peace conference to represent Britain). To adapt the Churchillism quoted above, a great war had been won, the people had cheered the King, and had then (decisively) turned out the government – and the dutiful constitutional monarch had perhaps registered the consequences of this expression of the 'will of the people' slightly ahead of his understandably stunned prime minister.[20]

The spats and tensions that had marked Churchill's relations with different monarchs earlier in his career were now long in the past, and whether in opposition or government, he remained on excellent terms with George VI for the rest of his reign. After 1952, with the accession of Elizabeth II, the image is almost one of a star-struck prime minister, described as 'besotted' (Pimlott) or 'madly in love' (Colville) with the young Queen. 'Lovely, inspiring,' the old man gushed to Moran, 'All the film people in the world, if they had scoured the globe, could not have found anyone so suited to the part.' He would change into a top hat and frock coat for the weekly audiences at the Palace, which got longer and longer as they chatted about racing, polo, horses and other shared interests. It all called to mind Lord Melbourne and the young Queen Victoria in an earlier age, and he seems to have been the Queen's favourite among her many prime ministers. It was not all sentimentality and benignity, however, for Churchill seems not to have liked or trusted the Duke of Edinburgh and also viewed his uncle, Lord Mountbatten, as a dangerous influence (his role in the end of British rule in India and his open Labour sympathies annoyed Churchill); Churchill, along with older royalty and Palace courtiers, scotched any talk of renaming the House of Windsor the House of Mountbatten. Later Churchill also stood in the way of a Princess Margaret–Peter Townsend marriage (reversing his initial view that 'the course of true love must always be allowed to run smooth' when Clementine Churchill argued that he risked repeating 'the same mistake that he had made at the abdication').[21]

Conclusion

'No institution pays such dividends as the monarchy,' Churchill once said to Moran. It was a 'supreme, invaluable, indispensable instrument'. He was proud to argue (in 1945) that 'We have the oldest, the most famous, the most honoured, the most secure and the most serviceable monarchy in the world'. In the 1930s, he had stressed that the monarchy had 'never been more valid and precious to democracy than it is at the present time'. In those threatening times, he insisted, 'the ancient constitutional Monarchy of this country is the most effectual barrier against one-man power or dictatorship arising whether from the Right or from the Left'. 'Our ancient Monarchy renders inestimable services to our country and to all the British Empire and Commonwealth of Nations,' he declared on the birth of Prince Charles in 1948. This was because of the 'traditions of constitutional government': 'above the ebb and flow of party strife, the rise and fall of ministries and individuals, the changes of public opinion or public fortune, the British Monarchy presides, ancient, calm and supreme within its functions, over all the treasures that have been saved from the past and all the glories we write in the annals of our country.'[22]

Churchill's understanding of the constitutional role of the Crown is not anachronistic. In a system of constitutional monarchy, as he always insisted, ministers responsible to Parliament govern the country and decide the great matters of state and policy. As Philip Ziegler summed up: 'it is hard to think of a single instance in which Churchill changed his views or his course of action on any important question in accordance with his perception of the wishes of the monarch of the time.' 'The constitutional relationships of Crown and People have long been settled and are perfectly understood,' Churchill explained. 'The Crown is a symbol of State; the King, the servant of his people.' Churchill's sense of the Crown's key role in sustaining continuity and legitimacy in the British democratic state also remains valid: this is a crucial function of monarchy, as Vernon Bogdanor argues. What has not stood the test of time so well, however, is Churchill's romantic and idealized vision of the monarchy as a 'glittering' pageant. We can now see that what Bogdanor calls the 'period of magical monarchy', reaching its apotheosis in Churchill's eyes in the early years of Elizabeth II's reign, was (as Pimlott says) 'buttressed in ways that could not be sustained indefinitely'. The final disappearance of Empire; the transformation of media deference into media intrusion; the passing of an age of respect for authority and tradition and deference to hierarchy – these have eroded the old props and demystified the monarchy, with the royal family also making its own contributions to the spectacle of 'royal soap opera'. The 'fairy tale' aspects of Churchill's conception of the monarchy may have gone for good, but the case he made for the important and positive role it plays in a democratic constitutional order remains a strong one.[23]

NINE

Conclusion

'English politicians have been readier to work their system of government than to analyse it in its full complexity,' as the constitutional historian G. H. L. Le May observes. 'Most politicians worry about relatively trivial matters,' it has been argued, 'like questions in the House of Commons or headlines in tomorrow's papers . . . not [about] the authority upon which the whole of government rests.' But Kirk Emmert (author of a study of Churchill's views on empire and imperialism) argues that a key test of a great leader or statesman is whether he has reflected on wider political problems and phenomena – including 'the major institutions' – that he has had to deal with during his political life, the evidence for that reflection seen in speeches, writings and actions.[1]

Winston Churchill meets that test. Churchill was, of course, a professional politician and a statesman, and he was not a political theorist or anything like a 'political scientist', although he obviously had a deep interest in history (and wrote a considerable amount of it). It cannot be claimed that he analysed the British political and constitutional system 'in its full complexity', in an extended or systematic manner. He never published a book like his Conservative colleague Leo Amery's *Thoughts on the Constitution* (1947) or like *Government and Parliament* (1954), written by Labour's Herbert Morrison. Nevertheless, his books like *Thoughts and Adventures* (1932) and *Great Contemporaries* (1937) are of great interest because of the way in which, in the essays they contain, he analyses practical issues and problems of democracy, leadership and politics. Often he is reflecting on his own experiences, and on political events he had participated in and leading statesmen he had known. He writes as a political

230

practitioner not as a political philosopher. But he does express views about the political system, although in an unsystematic way, and draws out lessons and formulates insights – about the premiership, elections or constitutional monarchy, for instance – that cast light on the wider political and constitutional system in Britain. Often starting life as journalistic pieces, his essays do explore deeper political questions in a way that can be provocative but also subtle and acute. His Second World War memoirs contain some significant comments and reflections on cabinet government and the premiership (see chapter 7).[2]

In his public speeches, too, and in cabinet memoranda, Churchill addressed important institutional and constitutional questions – sometimes, to be sure, in a highly polemical and rhetorical fashion when on the public platform or speaking in highly charged House of Commons debates (as during the House of Lords crisis before the First World War), but at other times developing the arguments and following through the analysis in some detail in substantial and incisive cabinet papers (as in his 5,000-word 1925 cabinet paper on Lords reform, for instance). On the other hand, it cannot be denied that on some complex issues he did not produce detailed or rigorous plans able to stand up to criticism (such as his papers on federalism and 'Home Rule All Round' in 1911 or his plan for an 'Economic sub-Parliament' in 1930).

In trying to understand Churchill's thinking about, or commitment to, particular ideas or schemes, one must always be aware of (and therefore cautious about) his character and style as a rhetorical politician. As Charles Masterman once put it: 'In nearly every case an *idea* enters his head from outside. It then rolls round the hollow of his brain, collecting strength like a snowball. Then, after whirling winds of *rhetoric*, he becomes convinced that it is *right*; and denounces everyone who criticizes it . . . [He] can convince himself of almost every truth if it is once allowed thus to start on its wild career through his rhetorical machinery.' Close colleagues noted 'the tendency in him to see first the rhetorical potentialities of any policy'.[3] What is striking, however, is the way in which on issues like Lords reform and Home Rule for Ireland in the Liberal years before 1914, Churchill was at times pretty unrestrained in public, but in private and behind the scenes was often much more moderate, constructive or bipartisan (see chapters 2 and 3).

On the 'peers versus the people' controversy in particular, Churchill sounded much more radical than he really was.

Those who worked with Churchill, such as his private secretary in the 1920s P. J. Grigg, have testified to the torrent of 'ideas, many of them original, some of them startlingly original, which sprang up in that teeming brain'.[4] But on the big constitutional questions, Churchill was usually not taking up original positions, as has been pointed out throughout this book. He admitted as much himself in his February 1910 memorandum on a new second chamber and reform of the House of Lords, for instance. Ideas about federalism, 'Home Rule All Round' and the devolution of power to tackle overload at Westminster had been discussed in British politics for thirty or more years before Churchill arrived on the scene and took them up. In the 1920s and 1930s (as was pointed out in chapter 5), ideas for reform of parliamentary and government machinery were being widely canvassed across the political spectrum and Churchill's own proposal for an 'Economic sub-Parliament' was not particularly novel.

Grigg described how Churchill would always 'indulge in a great deal of personal discussion during which he could talk himself into a knowledge and understanding of any topic or problem which came before him'. But at times, he recalled, there were 'heated and even violent arguments' because Churchill's 'critical faculty stopped short at his own children' and 'the best service those who worked for him could provide was to ensure that he was given time to discover for himself which were the weaklings among the offspring of his own brain'. John Colville, his Second World War and 1950s private secretary in Number 10, commented that Churchill 'always retained unswerving independence of thought'. Of all the men Colville had known and worked with, Churchill, he reckoned, was 'the least liable to be swayed by the views of even his most intimate counsellors', although he could be convinced and was open to argument if his advisers and colleagues were courageous enough to press the point. These views are not incompatible with Charles Masterman's observation from earlier in Churchill's career of him picking up debating points from other people then using them himself in private arguments and public speeches. Masterman believed that he had converted Churchill into an opponent of the Conciliation Committee's women's suffrage bill in 1910, and gave him the arguments to use, but in truth Churchill did not need much pushing to take up that position (see chapter 4).[5]

It cannot be denied that Churchill was a supremely ambitious politician. Political calculations – at tactical and strategic, personal and party levels – were never far from his mind. Proportional representation, as was noted in chapter 4, could never be an abstract and theoretical matter to be considered purely on its merits for a practical politician, and that surely helps to explain to some extent Churchill's shifting views and positions on the electoral reform issue. Inevitably, as a member of a government and bound by the convention of collective responsibility, Churchill had sometimes to defend in public policies that he was uneasy about or had only reluctantly accepted. For instance, on House of Lords reform in 1910, he was very unhappy with the government's policy just to remove the Lords' veto rather than undertaking a major reform and reconstruction of the second chamber. 'We cannot defend intellectually our position,' he told Charles Masterman, 'abusing the government policy up hill and down dale,' and even saying that he would rather resign than accept the policy – but then 'somehow he did manage to find an admirable intellectual defence of it' and went off and started making 'passionate speeches in favour of the veto policy'. A politician's public statements do not necessarily reflect his own private views.[6]

Churchill's 'flair for exploiting each major political issue as it arose and matching his ambition to the hour' should not be underestimated. But that does not mean that he was completely 'opportunistic and unprincipled', as has been claimed, for instance, in relation to his stance over Irish Home Rule. In chapter 3 it was noted that he admitted frankly that in order to 'strengthen myself with my party, I mingled actively in the Irish controversy'. But this widely quoted comment actually only refers to the events of 1914, when his position within the Liberal Party and the cabinet was weak, and he seems to have charged into the Irish situation with his violent speech at Bradford about facing down Ulster's resistance in order to improve his party standing. It is also the case that his attempt to shore up his vote in the Manchester by-election in 1908 lay behind his appealing (unsuccessfully) to the Irish community with what he called a 'new and advanced position' on Home Rule. But to interpret Churchill's stance on Home Rule solely in terms of his struggle to advance his personal ambitions and his political career – as Ian Chambers appears to do – is to go too far. Churchill seems to have been genuinely interested in ideas of devolution, provincial councils and federalism in one form or another not just during the controversy over the Liberals' Home Rule policy, but both before (in 1901-1905) and afterwards (in the 1920s), as chapter 3 shows. And he took many political risks inside the government and with his own party on the Irish issue, particularly by arguing strongly and early for special treatment for or the exclusion of Ulster – hardly something calculated to win him political points on his own side.[7]

Churchill necessarily adapted to changing circumstances. In his essay 'Consistency in Politics' he wrote that 'The only way a man can remain consistent amid changing circumstances is to change with them while preserving the same dominating purpose'.[8] With the Irish question removed from British politics after the early 1920s, the steam largely went out of the devolution issue and it became apparent that there was little support for political nationalism in Scotland and Wales. By the 1950s Churchill had dropped his earlier idea for separate parliaments in Edinburgh and Cardiff. His support for federalism or devolution cannot be explained simply in terms of his changing party identity, however, for his first ideas about this had been expressed in 1901 when he was a Conservative, he then came strongly to support it under Asquith as a Liberal cabinet minister, and he was still flirting with the idea in 1925 and in 1931 after 're-ratting' back to the Conservatives. Similarly, in relation to the House of Lords, it is true that he was arguing as a Conservative in the 1920s for a 'chamber of review' with the power to check the House of Commons with the 'weapon of delay'. But as a Liberal, in his February 1910 cabinet memorandum, he had also talked about the need for a revising chamber able to impose 'the potent safeguard of delay'. In both cases he wanted the Lords to be subordinate to the Commons, and both as a Liberal and a Conservative he supported reform of the composition of the Lords. While as a Conservative he talked of 'strengthening' the second chamber, he was not a reactionary and did not want to put the clock back to before the 1911 Parliament Act. In the 1930s, and later, he was more sympathetic to the case for electoral reform than many other Conservatives (see chapter 4). So, it is not easy to portray Churchill in simple terms as 'radical' on constitutional issues in his Liberal days and 'conservative' when he moved (back) across to the Tories. In the 1920s and 1930s he was actively interested in constitutional reforms of one sort or another. As party leader and in 'elder statesman' vein after 1945, he was still interested in certain issues (Lords reform and PR, for instance), and in private still liked to try out ideas and bat about schemes that he was realistic enough to know stood no chance of being put into practice (such as 'plural voting').[9]

'In politics and indeed all his life,' said John Colville, Churchill 'was as strange a mixture of radical and traditionalist as could anywhere be found.' He had no 'rigid ideology' or 'fixed programme', notes Paul Addison. He moved across the British political spectrum and his ideas evolved as he adapted to circumstances, events and the times. But Martin Gilbert argues that at the level of his 'principal beliefs' he was remarkably 'consistent'. Addison, too, has talked of his 'simple convictions and a vision of Britain acquired early on in life' and of 'values and assumptions he acquired between 1895 and 1900 [which] were to prove fundamental throughout his career'. In the context of this book, the relevant core beliefs relate to Churchill's Whiggish view of the British constitution and his 'Tory Democracy' ideas about 'trusting the people' (see chapter 1). Peter Hennessy has described Churchill as 'the greatest romantic of all about British constitutional practice', and it is true that he had a consistently romantic view of the historical development of British institutions and the constitution – what he called 'the long continuity of our institutions' in his May 1940 'Finest Hour' speech. Churchill, as Gilbert says, 'held the House of Commons and the parliamentary system in the highest esteem' – they were at the centre of his democratic political universe and were also central to his reading of British history and constitutional development. Ferdinand Mount has called 'the continuity myth' a 'smoothed-down version of history' and an over-simplification or a 'useful fiction'. But Churchill saw the stability, strength and legitimacy of the British state and political system as lying in the combination of history and democracy: the historical continuity and adaptability of its major institutions, assimilating and incorporating the political power of the enfranchised masses. He did not see monarchy and elements of aristocracy (the 'leadership of the best') as incompatible with democracy, but rather as essential to its functioning.[10]

Throughout his career, Churchill proposed many constitutional reforms. What would the British constitution look like if all his ideas had been accepted, put into effect and remained workable?

- Ireland might still be part of a federal UK, with devolved assemblies in Dublin and Belfast.
- There would be devolved parliaments in Scotland, Wales and the English regions.
- A specialist economic sub-parliament at Westminster would debate economic and industrial policies.
- There would be a reformed House of Lords or second chamber, part-elected or indirectly elected, and possibly including representatives of the provincial assemblies.
- County councils would have been abolished, their powers taken over by the devolved regional assemblies.
- 'Cabinet government' rather than 'prime-ministerial government' at the centre, with ministerial 'Overlords' co-ordinating groups of departments and the Whitehall committee labyrinth cut back.
- The House of Commons would sit only half the year and function as the 'grand forum' of the 'national debate'.
- Ministers would be able to speak in both the Lords and the Commons.
- General elections would be spread over six weeks with second ballots or staggered voting.
- Proportional representation with multi-member seats (STV) would be used in big towns and cities.
- Compulsory voting, but the voting age increased to twenty-five and extra votes for householders, graduates, etc.
- Women would have been enfranchised more slowly and possibly on a different basis compared with what actually happened.

This checklist gives a misleading impression in some ways, however, for Churchill never advocated all these reforms and changes together at any one time as a single package. The various ideas and proposals emerged at different times and in different circumstances. His approach to constitutional reform was often a piecemeal one, though he sometimes linked particular changes together: Lords reform and federalism in 1925; the economic sub-parliament plan and federalism in 1931; franchise reform, PR and Lords reform in 1934.[11] The interconnections between different reforms, and the implications of change in one area for other parts of the constitution, were often neglected: it is significant that it was only in his 1925 cabinet paper that he tried to tie together second chamber reform and devolution in 'a broad and salutary reconstruction of our constitutional machinery'.

The 'Churchill checklist' shows how little impact he had as a would-be constitutional reformer. More significant constitutional changes occurred under Lloyd George's leadership than under Churchill's (extension of the franchise and votes for women; modernization of Whitehall with the creation of the Cabinet Secretariat, new ministries and the reorganization of the civil service). As a cabinet minister under Asquith and Baldwin, Churchill's big ideas for constitutional reform were usually beaten down by his ministerial colleagues or ran into the sands. Even when Churchill was a tremendously powerful prime minister during the Second World War, he displayed a 'scrupulous regard for the forms of the Constitution' (unlike Lloyd George), and there was no permanent or enduring 'redefinition of the office' as a result of his tenure.[12]

Martin Gilbert has rightly spoken of Churchill's 'genuine belief in the Constitution'. As Robert Rhodes James put it, Churchill 'believed deeply in established, proven institutions, particularly the monarchy, Parliament . . . and the majesty of the British judicial system'. Even when shaken by electoral defeat at Dundee in 1922, Churchill declared his 'regard and admiration' for the British system of government, emphasizing how important it was that 'these great new electorates when they have been enfranchised should have the feeling that the institutions of the country belong to them in the fullest sense, and that they can do what they like and choose by constitutional means and parliamentary processes . . .' The British constitution, he said, 'provides the fullest method and opportunity by which popular wishes, however capricious, however passionate, however precipitate, might be given full effect to'. And he declared that he had been all his life 'a sincere believer in democratic and parliamentary processes by representative government, and in the procedure of the British Constitution'.[13]

The British constitution, Churchill knew, depended upon history, custom, traditions, precedents and conventions. He acknowledged its 'vagueness' and that 'constitutional' or 'fundamental' laws were not set out in any separate legal enactments or specially protected. But all the same, for much of the time he did believe that it was a real entity that should and did set the 'rules of the game', as it were, and constrain politicians. The Lords after 1906 had done more than carry political opposition to the Liberals to a new level, he believed – they had 'broken the constitution'. On the other hand, Churchill also knew that, as a political constitution, it could be decisively shaped by the political needs and imperatives of the moment – what politicians and governments could get away with, subject to the constraints of public opinion. And beyond Westminster was the mass of the electors, who had only to vote 'once or twice with some approach to solidarity to do anything they like with our Parliamentary machinery', as Churchill observed in 1910 (see chapter 2).

Churchill believed basically in the nineteenth-century Liberal model of the constitution, emphasizing parliamentary sovereignty, ministerial responsibility and the rule of law. The division of power and checks and balances in the constitution were other key themes of his, and many of the institutional reforms he favoured would have built in additional checks and constraints on the power of the central executive and limited the power of an electoral majority as expressed through the House of Commons. When in the 1930s he appeared to be 'deeply alienated from the democratic process' (as David Cannadine puts it) and arguing the need to 'retrace our steps', he was still adhering to the Liberal view of the constitution, accepting it as an idealized model, complaining that contemporary practice fell short, and proposing franchise and other changes to try to make political practice better correspond to Liberal democratic-constitutional principles (looking for a more engaged and better-informed electorate, for instance). It might have seemed reactionary, but it can be argued that he actually wanted 'both to maintain and to improve the existing framework of parliamentary democracy', as Martin Gilbert says.[14]

By the end of his political career Churchill had almost become part of the constitution, he had been around for so long and his reputation was so high. Emanuel Shinwell called him (in 1964) 'one of our greatest institutions: the

Throne, the Church, Parliament, the Press and Sir Winston Churchill'.[15] He had been actively involved in most of the big constitutional issues and arguments of the first half of the twentieth century: the reform of the House of Lords, Home Rule for Ireland, the extension of the franchise, votes for women, the abdication crisis. Through two world wars and other periods of great political and social stress and difficulty, he had maintained an unwavering commitment to the institutions and to the values of parliamentary democracy and constitutional government. A mixture of constitutional traditionalist and would-be reformer, he always understood – unlike some politicians and prime ministers, both in his time and later – the importance of the constitution and of constitutional issues.

NOTES

Chapter One

1. Robert Rhodes James, *Winston S. Churchill: His Complete Speeches 1897–1963* (8 vols, London, 1974), vol. IV, p. 3394 (hereafter cited as: Complete Speeches); Joseph S. Meisel, 'Words by the Numbers: a Quantitative Analysis and Comparison of the Oratorical Careers of William Ewart Gladstone and Winston Spencer Churchill', *Historical Research – Oxford*, vol. 73, issue 182 (2000), p. 289.
2. Complete Speeches, vol. VI, p. 6536; Paul Addison, *Churchill on the Home Front 1900–1955* (London, 1992), p. 273.
3. Complete Speeches, vol. VII, p. 7165; Addison, *Churchill on the Home Front*, p. 271.
4. House of Commons debates, 11 February 1935, cols 1649–50.
5. Winston S. Churchill, *My Early Life* (London, 2002; first published 1930), pp. x, 88–90; Complete Speeches, vol. II, pp. 1348, 1453; Clive Ponting, *Churchill* (London, 1994), p. 40; Winston S. Churchill, *A History of the English-Speaking Peoples, vol. IV The Great Democracies* (London, 1958), p. 229.
6. Churchill, *My Early Life*, p. 88; Winston S. Churchill, *Marlborough: His Life and Times* (London, 1933), vol. I, pp. 38, 40; Kirk Emmert, *Winston S. Churchill on Empire* (Durham, North Carolina, 1989), p. 45; Winston S. Churchill, *Great Contemporaries* (London, 1949; first published 1937), pp. 131–2; Complete Speeches, vol. II, p. 1450.
7. Complete Speeches, vol. VII, p. 7566; Randolph S. Churchill, *Winston S. Churchill* Companion Volume 1, Part 2 (London, 1967), p. 751; Anthony Montague Browne, *Long Sunset: Memoirs of Winston Churchill's Last Private Secretary* (London, 1995), p. 164.
8. John Colville, *The Fringes of Power: Downing Street Diaries 1939–1955* (London, 1985), p. 340; Violet Bonham Carter, *Winston Churchill As I Knew Him* (paperback edn, London, 1967), pp. 102, 167, 205; Lucy Masterman, *C. F. G. Masterman: A Biography* (London, 1939), pp. 152, 165; Complete Speeches, vol. II, p. 1424.
9. Winston S. Churchill, *Thoughts and Adventures* (London, 1947; first published 1932), p. 32; Winston S. Churchill, *Lord Randolph Churchill* (London, 1906), vol. I, pp. 293–6.
10. Churchill, *Winston S. Churchill* Companion Volume 1, Part 2, p. 751; Churchill, *Lord Randolph Churchill*, vol. I, p. 293; Maurice Cowling, *Religion and Public Doctrine in Modern England* (Cambridge, 1980), p. 292.
11. *Closing the Ring: Second World War, vol. V* quoted in Colin Coote, *Sir Winston Churchill: A Self-Portrait* (London, 1954),p. 106; Manfred Weidhorn, *A Harmony of Interests: Explorations in the Mind of Sir Winston Churchill* (London, 1992), p. 52; Bonham Carter, *Winston Churchill As I Knew Him*, p. 205.

12. Martin Gilbert, *Churchill's Political Philosophy* (Oxford, 1981), pp. 68, 110; David Thomas, *Churchill: the Member for Woodford* (Ilford, Essex, 1995), p. 40; 'What Good's a Constitution?', *Collier's*, 22 August 1936 (in Kay Halle (ed.), *Winston Churchill on America and Britain* [New York, 1970], pp. 278, 280–82); Complete Speeches, vol. IV, pp. 3850, 4321; vol. V, p. 4550.

13. *Daily Telegraph*, 2 December 1929 (in Winston Churchill (ed.), *The Great Republic: a History of America / Sir Winston Churchill* [New York, 2001], pp. 271–3); Complete Speeches, vol. V, p. 4727.

14. 'What Good's a Constitution?' in *Winston Churchill on America and Britain*, pp. 281, 283; Complete Speeches, vol. III, p. 2224; vol. VII, p. 7594.

15. David Stafford, *Churchill & Secret Service* (London, 1997).

16. Winston S. Churchill, *The Second World War, vol. VI, Triumph and Tragedy* (London, 1954), p. 509; Complete Speeches, vol. II, p. 1530; Churchill, *My Early Life*, p. 364; G. R. Searle, *Country Before Party: Coalition and the Idea of 'National Government' in Modern Britain 1885–1987* (Harlow, Essex, 1995); Robert Leach, *Turncoats: Changing Party Allegiance by British Politicians* (Aldershot, 1995), p. 115.

17. Complete Speeches, vol. II, pp. 1437, 1454, 1487.

18. Chris Wrigley, 'Churchill and the Trade Unions', *Transactions of the Royal Historical Society*, sixth series, vol. XI (2001), pp. 273–293; CHAR 8/36/60–67; Complete Speeches, vol. II, pp. 1822–5; vol. IV, pp. 3766, 3950; Addison, *Churchill on the Home Front*, pp. 268–70.

19. Complete Speeches, vol. II, p. 1451.

20. David Cannadine, *Aspects of Aristocracy* (London, 1995), pp. 158–60; Roland Quinault, 'Churchill and Democracy', *Transactions of the Royal Historical Society*, sixth series, vol. XI (2001), pp. 206–7; Complete Speeches, vol. IV, p. 3821; Winston Churchill, 'Are Parliaments Obsolete?', *Pearson's Magazine*, June 1934; Patrick C. Powers, 'Churchill, Democratic Statesmanship and *Great Contemporaries*', Proceedings of the International Churchill Societies 1992–93 (www.winstonchurchill.org/p92powers.htm).

21. Philip Williamson, *Stanley Baldwin: Conservative leadership and national values* (Cambridge, 1999), pp. 203–5; Ramsay Muir, *How Britain is Governed* (London, 1930), pp. 2–7; David H. Close, 'The Collapse of Resistance to Democracy: Conservatives, Adult Suffrage and Second Chamber Reform 1911–1928', *Historical Journal*, vol. 20, no. 4 (1977), p. 906.

22. Martin Gilbert, *Winston S. Churchill* Companion Volume 5, Part 2 (London, 1981), pp. 859–60; Complete Speeches, vol. V, pp. 4988, 5043; Winston S. Churchill, 'Broadcasting as an Influence in Politics', *Radio Times*, 25 May 1934; 'Cavalcade 1909–1934', *Daily Sketch*, 15 March 1934; 'What's Wrong With Parliament', *Answers*, 5 May 1934; Churchill, *Great Contemporaries*, p. 227; Churchill, *Thoughts and Adventures*, pp. 194–5.

23. Churchill, *My Early Life*, p. 354; Gilbert, *Churchill's Political Philosophy*, p. 25; Martin Gilbert, *Winston S. Churchill* Companion Volume 5, Part 1 (London, 1979), p. 959; Complete Speeches, vol. IV, p. 3386; vol. V, pp. 4554, 4987; Churchill, *Thoughts and Adventures*, pp. 172–3.

24. Complete Speeches, vol. V, pp. 4932, 4988, 5073; CHAR 8/302/124–6; 'How We Can Restore the Lost Glory to Democracy', *Evening Standard*, 24 January 1934; Churchill, *Thoughts and Adventures*, pp. 193–4, 212; Churchill, *Great Contemporaries*, pp. 74–5; 'Penny-in-the-slot Politics', *Answers*, 31 March 1934; 'What's Wrong with Parliament?', *Answers*, 5 May 1934.

25. Complete Speeches, vol. VI, p. 5959; 'System that Guarantees "This Freedom"', *News of the World*, 18 September 1938; *New Statesman and Nation*, 7 January 1939.

26. Complete Speeches, vol. VII, pp. 7565–6, 7572, 7817, 7820; Montague Browne, *Long Sunset*, p. 180; House of Commons debates, 3 November 1953, col. 21.

27.　J. H. Plumb, 'The Historian', in A. J. P. Taylor *et al.*, *Churchill: Four Faces and the Man* (London, 1969), pp. 119–23; Victor Feske, *From Belloc to Churchill: Private Scholars, Public Culture, and the Crisis of British Liberalism 1900–1939* (Chapel Hill, North Carolina, 1996), pp. 186–227; Paul Addison, 'Destiny, history and providence: the religion of Winston Churchill', in Michael Bentley (ed.), *Public and Private Doctrine: Essays in British History presented to Maurice Cowling* (Cambridge, 1993), pp. 242–3.

28.　Complete Speeches, vol. IV, p. 4213; articles by Churchill: 'Are Parliaments Obsolete?', *Pearson's Magazine*, June 1934; 'System that Guarantees "This Freedom"', *News of the World*, 18 September 1938; 'Is Parliament Played Out?', 30 May 1920 (CHAR 8/36/102).

29.　Randolph Churchill (ed.), *Into Battle: Speeches by Rt Hon. Winston S. Churchill* (London, 1941), p. 100; *The Daily Mail*, 13 April 1934; Margaret Thatcher, *Statecraft* (London, 2002), pp. 252–1, 469–71; Winston S. Churchill, *A History of the English-Speaking Peoples, vol. I The Birth of Britain* (London, 1956), pp. 177, 198–202.

30.　Complete Speeches, vol. II, p. 1629; vol. VII, p. 7565; Cowling, *Religion and Public Doctrine in Modern England*, p. 299.

31.　Complete Speeches, vol. VII, p. 7565; vol. VIII, p. 8486; Martin Gilbert, *Winston S. Churchill vol. 8 'Never Despair' 1945–1965* (London, 1988), p. 1327.

32.　Cowling, *Religion and Public Doctrine*, p. 299; Gilbert, *Churchill's Political Philosophy*, p. 100; Feske, *From Belloc to Churchill*, p. 267, fn. 24.

33.　Winston S. Churchill, *A History of the English-Speaking Peoples, vol. III The Age of Revolution* (London, 1957), p. 208; 'What Good's a Constitution?' in *Winston Churchill on America and Britain*, pp. 278–87; *Daily Telegraph*, 2 December 1929 (in Churchill (ed.), *The Great Republic*, p. 270).

34.　'Whither Britain?', *Listener*, 17 January 1934; 'The Constitutions of Great Britain and the United States', *Daily Mail*, 3 June 1935; 'What Good's a Constitution?' in *Winston Churchill on America and Britain*, pp. 283–5.

35.　House of Commons debates, 26 July 1905, cols 363–4; Kenneth W. Thompson, *Winston Churchill's World View: Statesmanship and Power* (Baton Rouge, Louisiana, 1987), pp. 32–4; Hansard Society, *Parliamentary Reform 1933–1960* (London, 1961), p. 159.

36.　Michael Foley, *The politics of the British constitution* (Manchester, 1999), pp. 20, 23–4.

37.　Complete Speeches, vol. II, pp. 1365, 1436; vol. IV, p. 3592; vol. V, p. 4551; vol. VIII, p. 8485; 'Can Labour Govern?', 16 November 1919 (CHAR 8/36/40); 'Freedom and Progress for All', *Listener*, 5 May 1937; Martin Gilbert, *Winston S. Churchill* Companion Volume 5, Part 1 (London, 1979), p. 960.

38.　'Whither Britain?', *Listener*, 17 January 1934.

39.　Churchill, *A History of the English-Speaking Peoples, vol. I*, p. 171; Randolph Churchill, *Winston S. Churchill* Companion Volume 1, Part 2 (London, 1967), pp. 761–2, 765.

40.　Churchill to Bridges, 19.10.1942, PRO PREM 4/63/2; Manfred Weidhorn, *Churchill's Rhetoric and Political Discourse* (London, 1987), p. 48.

41.　Complete Speeches, vol. V. p. 5426; vol. VII, p. 7224; House of Commons debates, 28 October 1943, cols 404–5; David Marquand, *Ramsay MacDonald* (London, 1977), p. 97.

42.　Churchill, *My Early Life*, p. ix; Quinault, 'Churchill and Democracy', p. 220.

Chapter Two

1.　Complete Speeches, vol. II, p. 1367; Winston S. Churchill, *The People's Rights*, first published 1909, new edition with an introduction by Cameron Hazlehurst (London, 1970), pp. 18, 20; Paul Addison, *Churchill on the Home Front* (London, 1992), p. 1.

2.   Randolph Churchill, *Winston S. Churchill* Companion Volume 1, Part 2 (London, 1967), p. 751; Complete Speeches, vol. I, p. 44; House of Commons debates, 26 July 1905, col. 364; Roland Quinault, 'Churchill and Democracy', *Transactions of the Royal Historical Society*, sixth series, vol. XI (2001), p. 203.

3.   Complete Speeches, vol. I, p. 715; vol. II, p. 1521; Randolph Churchill, *Winston S. Churchill vol. II Young Statesman 1901–1914* (London, 1967), pp. 316–18.

4.   Complete Speeches, vol. I, pp. 709–18.

5.   Churchill, *Winston S. Churchill vol. II*, p. 321; Corinne Comstock Weston, 'The Liberal Leadership and the Lords' veto, 1907–10', in Clyve Jones and David Lewis Jones (eds), *Peers, Politics and Power: the House of Lords 1603–1911* (London, 1986), pp. 489–500; Roy Jenkins, *Asquith*, revised edn (London, 1978), p. 173.

6.   Roy Jenkins, *Mr Balfour's Poodle* (London, 1954), p. 33, n.3; Complete Speeches, vol. I, pp. 804–12.

7.   Lucy Masterman, *C. F. G. Masterman: a biography* (London, 1939), p. 114; Complete Speeches, vol. II, pp. 1141–1146.

8.   John Grigg, *Lloyd George: The People's Champion 1902–1911*, Penguin edn (London, 2002), pp. 178–81; Masterman, *C.F.G. Masterman*, p. 176; Roy Jenkins, *Churchill* (London, 2001), pp. 159–61, 165–6.

9.   Churchill, *Winston S. Churchill vol. II*, p. 263; Complete Speeches, vol. II, pp. 1323–4, 1325–7.

10.   Complete Speeches, vol. II, pp.1346–55; Churchill, *Winston S. Churchill vol. II*, p. 326.

11.   Cabinet Paper: Provision for resolving a deadlock between the Houses of Parliament, 9 November 1909 (copy in CHAR 21/17/31).

12.   Martin Gilbert, *In Search of Churchill* (London, 1995), p. 287; Churchill, *Winston S. Churchill vol. II*, p. 3; Weston, 'The Liberal Leadership and the Lords' veto, 1907–10', pp. 508, 514, 516; Masterman, *C. F .G. Masterman*, p. 175.

13.   Complete Speeches, vol. II, pp. 1365, 1369, 1397, 1424, 1436, 1447, 1631.

14.   Complete Speeches, vol. II, pp. 1365, 1370, 1375, 1394, 1441, 1445, 1453.

15.   Churchill, *Winston S. Churchill vol. II*, pp. 330–1; Complete Speeches, vol. II, p. 1846.

16.   Randolph Churchill, *Winston S. Churchill* Companion Volume 2, Part 2 (London, 1969), pp. 965–6.

17.   Churchill, *Winston S. Churchill* Companion Volume 2, Part 2, pp. 968–971 (also at: CHAR 21/17/33).

18.   Grigg, *Lloyd George: The People's Champion*, p. 245.

19.   Addison, *Churchill on the Home Front*, p. 96.

20.   Grigg, *Lloyd George: The People's Champion*, p. 247; Masterman, *C. F. G. Masterman*, p. 158; Weston, 'The Liberal Leadership and the Lords' veto, 1907–10', p. 502; Complete Speeches, vol. II, pp. 1513–16.

21.   Churchill, *Winston S. Churchill vol. II*, pp. 338–46; Complete Speeches, vol. II, pp. 1512–13; Masterman, *C. F. G. Masterman*, p. 175; Weston, 'The Liberal Leadership and the Lords' veto, 1907–10', pp. 503–14.

22.   Churchill, *Winston S. Churchill vol. II*, p. 344; Churchill, *Winston S. Churchill* Companion Volume 2, Part 2, pp. 1031–2; Complete Speeches, vol. II, p. 1847; vol. IV, p. 4300; vol. VII, p. 7551.

23.   Masterman, *C. F. G. Masterman*, pp. 159, 172; Complete Speeches, vol. II, pp. 1522, 1538–41, 1700–1701, 1717.

24.   Complete Speeches, vol. II, p. 1717; Churchill, *Winston S. Churchill* Companion Volume 2, Part 2, pp.1031–2.

25.   CHAR 22/151/103; Complete Speeches, vol. IV, p. 4298.

26. Complete Speeches, vol. IV, pp. 3383, 4299. For the general background see: David H. Close, 'The Collapse of Resistance to Democracy: Conservatives, Adult Suffrage, and Second Chamber Reform, 1911–1928', *The Historical Journal*, vol. 20, no. 4, 1977, pp. 893–918; Philip Williamson, 'The Labour Party and the House of Lords, 1918–1931', *Parliamentary History*, vol. 10. pt. 2, 1991, pp. 317–341; Peter Catterall, 'Failure to Reform the House of Lords 1911–1949', *Parliamentary History* (forthcoming). I am grateful to Dr Catterall for allowing me to see a copy of this paper prior to its publication.

27. Complete Speeches, vol. IV, pp. 3394, 4299–4301.

28. Cabinet Memorandum: 'House of Lords Reform', 17 November 1925, in: Martin Gilbert, *Winston S. Churchill* Companion Volume 5, part 1 (London, 1979), pp. 577–9. (See also: HL (25) 13, CHAR 22/60/17.)

29. Cabinet Memorandum: HLC 21, House of Lords Reform Committee: Memorandum by the Secretary of State for the Colonies, 7 December 1921 (copy in CHAR 22/61/3–7).

30. CP 4052, House of Lords Reform, Memorandum by the Secretary of State for the Colonies, 21 June 1922 (copy in CHAR 22/10B/160).

31. Cabinet Minutes: Cabinet 37 (22), 4 July 1922; Cabinet 38 (22), 7 July 1922, PRO CAB 23/30; CP 4086, House of Lords Reform, 6 July 1922, PRO CAB 24/137.

32. CHAR 22/109/13; HL (25) 20, 10 December 1925, CHAR 22/60/63.

33. CHAR 22/60/45; Cabinet Memorandum: 'House of Lords Reform', 17 November 1925, in: Gilbert, *Winston S. Churchill* Companion Volume 5, part 1, pp. 577–9. (See also: HL (25) 13, CHAR 22/60/17).

34. Addison, *Churchill on the Home Front*, p. 271.

35. HL (25) 20, 10 December 1925, CHAR 22/60/63; CP 27 (26), House of Lords Reform Committee Report, 25 January 1926, CHAR 22/86/31; Complete Speeches, vol. IV, pp. 4302–3.

36. Complete Speeches, vol. V, pp. 4989–90, 5041–2, 5099, 5319–20; Williamson, 'The Labour Party and the House of Lords, 1918–1931', pp. 330, 339–40; P. A. Bromhead, *The House of Lords and Contemporary Poltics 1911–1957* (London, 1958), pp. 151–6; Addison, *Churchill on the Home Front*, p. 272; CHUR 4/73/1; Winston Churchill, 'Are Parliaments Obsolete?', *Pearson's Magazine*, June 1934.

37. Bromhead, *The House of Lords and Contemporary Politics*, pp. 157–176; Complete Speeches, vol. VII, p. 7551.

38. Complete Speeches, vol. VII, pp. 7566–7569.

39. Kenneth Harris, *Attlee* (London, 1982), pp. 351–2; *Parliament Bill 1947: Agreed Statement on Conclusion of Conference of Party Leaders*, Cmd 7380 (1948); Catterall, 'Failure to Reform the House of Lords, 1911–1949'.

40. Tony Benn, *Years of Hope: Diaries, Papers and Letters 1940–1962* (London, 1994), p. 175; House of Commons debates, 12 November 1951, col. 643; Lord Morrison of Lambeth [Herbert Morrison], *Government and Parliament* 3rd edn (London, 1964), pp. 202–3; Lord Moran, *Winston Churchill: the struggle for survival 1940–1965* (London, 1966), p. 399; PRO CAB 130/86, GEN 432; Bromhead, *The House of Lords and Contemporary Politics*, p. 242; House of Commons debates, 8 February 1955, col. 536.

41. John Charmley, *Churchill: The End of Glory* (London, 1993), pp. 282, 486; Lord Normanbrook in Sir John Wheeler-Bennett (ed.), *Action This Day* (London, 1968), p. 45.

42. Lord Moran, *Winston Churchill: the struggle for survival 1940–1965* (London, 1966), pp. 376–7, 399; Anthony Montague Browne, *Long Sunset: memoirs of Winston Churchill's last private secretary* (London, 1996), p. 173.

43. Montague Browne, *Long Sunset*, pp. 172, 182–3; Moran, *Churchill: the struggle for survival*, p. 376; Roy Jenkins, *Churchill* (London, 2001), p. 896.

44. Alistair Horne, *Macmillan 1957–1986* (London, 1988), pp. 82–3, 572–3, 622–4; Anthony Sampson, *Macmillan: a study in ambiguity* (Harmondsworth, 1967), p. 176.

45. Bromhead, *The House of Lords and Contemporary Politics*, pp. 251–4; Benn, *Years of Hope*, pp. 175, 321, 376–7; Tony Benn, *Out of the Wilderness: Diaries 1963–67* (London, 1987), p. 208; Jad Adams, *Tony Benn: a biography* (London, 1992), pp. 109–110, 179, 184, 198; Tony Benn in 'Churchill Remembered', *Transactions of the Royal Historical Society*, sixth series, vol. XI (2001), p. 397.

46. Robert Rhodes James, 'The enigma', in James W. Muller (ed.), *Churchill as peacemaker* (Cambridge, 1997), p. 16; CHAR 21/17/31 (para. 9); Complete Speeches, vol. II, pp. 1524, 1542.

47. Churchill, *Winston S. Churchill* Companion Volume 2, part 2, p. 969; Complete Speeches, vol. II, pp. 1513, 1524, 1542–3, 1552, 1700.

48. Complete Speeches, vol. II, pp. 1525–6, 1628, 1695–6, 1806.

49. CHAR 22/61/5–6; Gilbert, *Winston S. Churchill* Companion Volume 5, part 1, pp. 579–80.

50. Complete Speeches, vol. II, p. 1717.

Chapter Three

1. Winston Churchill, *My Early Life*, first published 1930, (London, 2002), pp. 1–3, 7; R. F. Foster, *Lord Randolph Churchill* (Oxford, 1981), pp. 44, 226–7, 254, 263, 282, 395; Anthony J. Jordan, *Churchill: a founder of modern Ireland* (Westport, Ireland, 1995), pp. 28–9.

2. Randolph Churchill, *Winston S. Churchill* Companion Volume 1, part 2 (London, 1967), p. 751; Churchill, *My Early Life*, p. 34; Winston S. Churchill, *A History of the English-Speaking Peoples vol. IV The Great Democracies* (London, 1958), p. 285; Randolph Churchill, *Winston S. Churchill vol. 1 Young Statesman 1901–1911* (London, 1967), p. 441; Complete Speeches, vol. I, p. 36; Randolph Churchill, *Winston S. Churchill* Companion Volume 1, part 1 (London, 1967), pp. 668–9.

3. Churchill, *Winston S. Churchill vol. 1 Young Statesman*, p. 442; Patricia Jalland, 'United Kingdom devolution 1910–14: political panacea or tactical diversion?', *English Historical Review*, vol. 94 (1979), p. 760; Keith Robbins, '"This Grubby Wreck of Old Glories": the United Kingdom and the End of the British Empire', *Journal of Contemporary History*, vol. 15 (1980), p. 88.

4. Complete Speeches, vol. I, pp. 317, 363, 386–7, 427; Ian Chambers, 'Winston Churchill and Irish Home Rule, 1899–1914', *Parliamentary History*, vol. 19, part 3 (2000), p. 410.

5. Complete Speeches, vol. I, pp. 364–5, 426.

6. Winston S. Churchill, *Lord Randolph Churchill* (London, 1906), vol. II, p. 50; Complete Speeches, vol. I, p. 531.

7. Chambers, 'Winston Churchill and Irish Home Rule, 1899–1914', p. 410; Eunan O'Halpin, *The Decline of the Union: British Government in Ireland 1892–1920* (Dublin, 1987), pp. 44–51; Complete Speeches, vol. II, pp. 386–7; Jalland, 'United Kingdom devolution 1910–14', pp. 758–9, 784; Churchill, *My Early Life*, p. 41.

8. Mary C. Bromage, *Churchill and Ireland* (Notre Dame, Indiana, 1964), p. xi; Paul Addison, 'The search for peace in Ireland', in James W. Muller (ed.), *Churchill as peacemaker* (Cambridge, 1997), p. 187; Andrew Muldoon, 'Making Ireland's Opportunity England's: Winston Churchill

and the Third Irish Home Rule Bill', *Parliamentary History*, vol. 15, part 3 (1996); Patricia Jalland, *The Liberals and Ireland: the Ulster Question in British Politics to 1914* (Brighton, 1980), pp. 60–1; Winston S. Churchill, *Great Contemporaries*, first published 1937 (London, 1949), pp. 112–13; Paul Addison, 'The Political Beliefs of Winston Churchill', *Transactions of the Royal Historical Society*, 5th series, vol. 30 (1980), p. 45.

9.   Henry Pelling, *Winston Churchill* (London, 1974), p. 155; Complete Speeches, vol. I, pp. 980–83; Churchill, *Winston S. Churchill vol. 1 Young Statesman*, pp. 443–51.

10.   Cabinet memorandum by Loreburn, 16 October 1909 (see: CHAR 21/17/29).

11.   Robert Rhodes James, *Churchill: A Study in Failure 1900–1939* (Harmondsworth, 1973), p. 56; Complete Speeches, vol. II, p. 1678; Churchill, *Lord Randolph Churchill*, vol. II, p. 51; Churchill, *Great Contemporaries*, p. 112.

12.   Churchill, *Winston S. Churchill vol. 1 Young Statesman*, pp. 364, 453; Rhodes James, *Churchill: A Study in Failure*, p. 56.

13.   Churchill, *Winston S. Churchill vol. 1 Young Statesman*, pp. 461–7; Roy Jenkins, *Churchill* (London, 2001), pp. 234–6; Muldoon, 'Winston Churchill and the Third Irish Home Rule Bill', pp. 321–23.

14.   Addison, 'The search for peace in Ireland', p. 193 (quoting from Churchill's preface to the 1911 pamphlet *Home Rule in a Nutshell*); Complete Speeches, vol. II, pp. 1638, 1907, 1949–50, 1954–5, 1960.

15.   Complete Speeches, vol. II, pp. 1632, 1681–2, 1900–1901, 1903, 1948, 1951–2, 1955.

16.   Complete Speeches, vol. II, p. 1956; Randolph Churchill, *Winston S. Churchill* Companion Volume 2, part 3 (London, 1969), pp. 1375–7.

17.   Churchill, *Winston S. Churchill* Companion Volume 2, part 3, pp. 1377–8.

18.   Jalland, 'United Kingdom devolution 1910–14', pp. 766–9.

19.   Complete Speeches, vol. II, pp. 1960, 2021–3; Jalland, 'United Kingdom devolution 1910–14', pp. 770–74; John Kendle, *Ireland and the Federal Solution: the debate over the United Kingdom Constitution 1870–1921* (Montreal, 1989), p. 158; *The Daily Chronicle*, 14 September 1912; *People*, 15 September 1912; *Manchester Guardian*, 16 September 1912.

20.   John Grigg, *Lloyd George: The People's Champion 1902–1911*, Penguin edn (London, 2002), pp. 265, 271–2; Randolph Churchill, *Winston S. Churchill* Companion Volume 2, part 2 (London, 1969), pp. 1025, 1031–2; Addison, 'The search for peace in Ireland', p. 194.

21.   Churchill, *Winston S. Churchill vol. 1 Young Statesman*, pp. 469–70; Complete Speeches, vol. II, pp. 1904, 1959, 2020; Kendle, *Ireland and the Federal Solution*, p. 153; Churchill, *Great Contemporaries*, pp. 112–113.

22.   Complete Speeches, vol. II, pp. 1683, 1904–5, 1958, 1959–60; Jordan, *Churchill: a founder of modern Ireland*, p. 44.

23.   Jalland, *The Liberals and Ireland*, pp. 58–9, 63, 67–9, 117–118, 143.

24.   Complete Speeches, vol. II, p. 1960; Jalland, *The Liberals and Ireland*, p. 104; Churchill, *Winston S. Churchill vol. 1 Young Statesman*, pp. 470–71; House of Commons debates, 23 February 1920, col. 1451.

25.   Jalland, *The Liberals and Ireland*, p. 146.

26.   Complete Speeches, vol. III, pp. 2222–33.

27.   Ian S. Wood, *Churchill* (London, 2000), p. 144; Jordan, *Churchill: a founder of modern Ireland*, pp. 51–3.

28.   Violet Bonham Carter, *Winston Churchill As I Knew Him*, paperback edn (London, 1967), p. 316; Kendle, *Ireland and the Federal Solution*, pp. 172–5; Jordan, *Churchill: a founder of modern Ireland*, pp. 55–7; Chambers, 'Winston Churchill and Irish Home Rule, 1899–1914', p. 420.

29.   Kendle, *Ireland and the Federal Solution*, p. 166; Rhodes James, *Churchill: A Study in Failure*, p. 63.

30.   Complete Speeches, vol. II, p. 1679; vol. III, p. 3147; Winston S. Churchill, *Thoughts and Adventures* first published 1932 (London, 1947), p. 165; Addison, 'The search for peace in Ireland', pp. 197–201.

31.   Bromage, *Churchill and Ireland*, pp. 3–4, 65, 73–4, 97, 112, 125; Complete Speeches, vol. V, pp. 5097–5108.

32.   Jordan, *Churchill: a founder of modern Ireland*, pp. 69, 90, 100, 159, 174–5, 193, 195, 197; Complete Speeches, vol. III, pp. 3150–51; John Ramsden, *Man of the Century: Winston Churchill and his legend since 1945* (London, 2002), pp. 248, 259.

33.   Anthony Montague Browne, *Long Sunset: memoirs of Winston Churchill's last private secretary* (London, 1995), p. 203; Wood, *Churchill*, pp. 149, 156; Anthony Seldon, *Churchill's Indian Summer: the Conservative Government 1951–55* (London, 1981), p. 129.

34.   Lord Riddell, *Intimate Diary of the Peace Conference and After 1918–1923* (London, 1933), p. 225; Tony Paterson, *A Seat For Life* (Dundee, 1980), pp. 174–5, 273; Wood, *Churchill*, p. 115; James Mitchell, *Conservatives and the Union* (Edinburgh, 1990), pp. 40–1.

35.   Ronald Butt, *The Power of Parliament* (London, 1969), pp. 106–111; Vernon Bogdanor, *Devolution in the United Kingdom* (Oxford, 1999), pp. 48–50.

36.   Martin Gilbert, *Winston S. Churchill* Companion Volume 5, part 1 (London, 1979), pp. 585–7; Complete Speeches, vol. V, pp. 4989–90; Select Committee on Procedure, HC 161 (1931), pp. 138, 147.

37.   Ramsden, *Man of the Century*, pp. 226–230, 235; Bogdanor, *Devolution in the United Kingdom*, pp. 144, 152, 159; Seldon, *Churchill's Indian Summer*, pp. 127–9; House of Commons debates, 13 November 1951, col. 815; House of Commons debates, 24 July 1952, cols 769–70. The story that Churchill once swatted down a parliamentary question about Welsh devolution with the words 'nothing doing' in Welsh ('dim o gwbl') is, sadly, too good to be true: this was actually a reply to a question about the Civil List (Ramsden, p. 227; House of Commons debates, 12 November 1951, col. 646).

38.   Mitchell, *Conservatives and the Union*, pp. 26, 48; Complete Speeches, vol. VIII, p. 7937; Andrew Marr, *The Battle for Scotland* (London, 1992), pp. 98, 113; Addison, *Churchill on the Home Front*, p. 403; Seldon, *Churchill's Indian Summer*, p. 136.

39.   Complete Speeches, vol. VIII, pp. 7937; Mitchell, *Conservatives and the Union*, p. 50.

40.   Mitchell, *Conservatives and the Union*, pp. 27, 30–31, 37; Complete Speeches, vol. VIII, p. 7938; Lord Home, *The Way the Wind Blows* (London, 1976), p. 108; House of Commons debates, 18 November 1954, cols 569–72.

41.   Churchill, *Winston S. Churchill vol. II*, pp. 241–3.

42.   Addison, *Churchill on the Home Front*, p. 276.

43.   Churchill to Mr Horsfall, 13 February 1908, CHAR 2/33/20–22.

44.   Complete Speeches, vol. II, pp. 1727–8, 2022; Addison, *Churchill on the Home Front*, p. 171; Complete Speeches, vol. I, p. 365; Churchill, *Winston S. Churchill* Companion Volume 2, part 3, pp. 1377–8; *Manchester Guardian*, 16 September 1912; *Municipal Journal*, 20 September 1912.

45.   Gilbert, *Winston S. Churchill* Companion Volume 5, part 1, pp. 585–6.

46.   Martin Gilbert, *Winston S. Churchill* Volume 5 (London, 1976), pp. 240–2, 246, 254–5, 259, 270–73; Gilbert, *Winston S. Churchill* Companion Volume 5, part 1, pp. 1128–9, 1191–2; Clive Ponting, *Churchill* (London, 1994), p. 322.

47.   Complete Speeches, vol. VII, pp. 6850, 7857–8; Seldon, *Churchill's Indian Summer*, pp. 257–8.

48.   Complete Speeches, vol. II, pp. 2167–8.

49.   Alvin Jackson, 'British Ireland: what if Home Rule had been enacted in 1912?', in Niall Fergusson (ed.), *Virtual History* (London, 1997).

50.   Complete Speeches, vol. II, p. 2022.
51.   Complete Speeches, vol. I, p. 364; Jim Bulpitt, *Territory and Power in the United Kingdom* (Manchester, 1983).
52.   CHUR 5/60A/120.

Chapter Four

1.   Complete Speeches, vol. IV, p. 4333; Randolph Churchill, *Winston S. Churchill vol. 1 Young Statesman 1901–1911* (London, 1967), p. 393; Clive Ponting, *Churchill* (London, 1994), p. 134.
2.   *Dundee Advertiser*, 6 January 1910; Complete Speeches, vol. II, p. 1368.
3.   Paul Addison, *Churchill on the Home Front 1900–1955* (London, 1992), p. 48; Randolph Churchill, *Winston S. Churchill* Companion Volume 1, part 2 (London, 1967), p. 765.
4.   Churchill, *Winston S. Churchill* Companion Volume 1, part 2. pp. 751, 767; Robert Roberts, *The Classic Slum* (Harmondsworth, 1973), p. 131.
5.   Geoffrey Best, *Churchill: A Study in Greatness* (London, 2001), p. 39; Addison, *Churchill on the Home Front*, pp. 132–33.
6.   Addison, *Churchill on the Home Front*, p. 48; Tony Paterson, *A Seat For Life* (Dundee, 1980), pp. 67–8; Churchill, *Winston S. Churchill vol. 1 Young Statesman*, pp. 394, 400.
7.   *Dundee Advertiser*, 19 October 1909; Complete Speeches, vol. I, pp. 530–1; vol. II, pp. 1335–7, 1452.
8.   Churchill, *Winston S. Churchill vol. 1 Young Statesman*, pp. 394–8; Addison, *Churchill on the Home Front*, pp. 133–5.
9.   Lucy Masterman, *C. F. G. Masterman: a biography* (London, 1939), p. 166.
10.   Complete Speeches, vol. II, pp. 1582–7.
11.   Addison, *Churchill on the Home Front*, p. 135; Churchill, *Winston S. Churchill vol. 1 Young Statesman*, pp. 398, 401; Troup to Churchill, 17.7.1910 (CHAR 12/2/56–9), 19.8.1910 (CHAR 2/47/72); Trevor Wilson (ed.), *Political Diaries of C.P. Scott 1911–28* (London, 1970), pp. 58–9; Complete Speeches, vol. II, p. 1585; Randolph Churchill, *Winston S. Churchill* Companion Volume 2, part 3 (London, 1969), p. 1456; Lord Riddell, *More Pages from My Diary 1908–1914* (London, 1934), p. 51.
12.   Mary Soames, *Clementine Churchill* (London, 1979), p. 59; Best, *Churchill: A Study in Greatness*, pp. 39–40; Addison, *Churchill on the Home Front*, pp. 135–8.
13.   Churchill, *Winston S. Churchill vol. 1 Young Statesman*, pp. 402–6; Addison, *Churchill on the Home Front*, pp. 160–1; David Morgan, *Suffragists and Liberals* (Oxford, 1975), p. 113; Curzon to Churchill, 20.1.1912, CHAR 2/56/11.
14.   Churchill to Grey, 5.2.1912, CHAR 2/56/28; Addison, *Churchill on the Home Front*, pp. 161–2, 272.
15.   Churchill to Fergusson, 25.4.1927, CHAR 22/183/4; Martin Pugh, *The Making of Modern British Politics 1867–1939* (Oxford, 1982), p. 188; David H. Close, 'The Collapse of Resistance to Democracy: Conservatives, Adult Suffrage, and Second Chamber Reform, 1911–1928', *Historical Journal*, vol. 20, no. 4 (1977), p. 913.
16.   Churchill Cabinet Memorandum: 'The Question of Extending Female Suffrage', Martin Gilbert, *Winston S. Churchill* Companion Volume 5, part 1 (London, 1979), pp. 958–66 (also at CHAR 22/155/119); Close, 'The Collapse of Resistance to Democracy', pp. 914–17; Addison, *Churchill on the Home Front*, pp. 272–3.
17.   Complete Speeches, vol. IV, pp. 4333, 4340; Gilbert, *Winston S. Churchill* Companion Volume 5, part 1, pp. 1009, 1066–67, 1245, 1376–77; 'Why We Lost', *John Bull*, 15 June 1929; Martin Gilbert, *Winston S. Churchill, vol. 8 'Never Despair' 1945–1965* (London, 1988), p. 368.

18. John Grigg, *Lloyd George: From Peace to War 1912–1916*, Penguin edn (London, 2002), p. 71.

19. Winston S. Churchill, *Thoughts and Adventures*, originally published 1932 (London, 1947), pp. 150, 155.

20. Churchill, *Thoughts and Adventures*, pp. 162–3; Roy Jenkins, *Churchill* (London, 2001), p. 389; Winston S. Churchill, *My Early Life*, originally published 1930 (London, 2002), p. 218; *Answers*, 10 February 1934.

21. Churchill, *Thoughts and Adventures*, pp. 150, 151, 154, 155, 159, 160, 161; Winston S. Churchill, *Great Contemporaries*, first published 1937 (London, 1949), pp. 5–6.

22. Martin Gilbert, *Winston S. Churchill* Companion Volume 5, part 1 (London, 1979), p. 559; House of Commons debates, 3 November 1953, col. 22.

23. Winston S. Churchill, 'Election Ahead – and the same old voting system', *Daily Mail*, 29 May 1935; Complete Speeches, vol. V, p. 5041; Winston S. Churchill, 'What's Wrong with Parliament', *Answers*, 5 May 1934; House of Commons debates, 23 June 1948, col. 1386.

24. Complete Speeches, vol. II, pp. 1519, 1624–5; vol. V, pp. 5040–1; Churchill, *My Early Life*, pp. 352–3.

25. Churchill, *Winston S. Churchill* Companion Volume 1, part 2, p. 767; Complete Speeches, vol. II, pp. 1624, 1632, 1696; vol. VII, pp. 7601–3; House of Commons debates, 23 June 1948, cols 1382, 1387; 20 October 1953, cols 1808–9.

26. Winston S. Churchill: 'Are Parliaments Obsolete?', *Pearson's Magazine*, June 1934; 'Whither Britain?', *Listener*, 17 January 1934; 'How We Can Restore the Lost Glory to Democracy', *Evening Standard*, 24 January 1934 ; Complete Speeches, vol. V, pp. 5039–40; Anthony Montague-Browne, *Long Sunset: Memoirs of Winston Churchill's last private secretary* (London, 1995), p. 180.

27. Peter Catterall, 'The Politics of Electoral Reform since 1885', in Peter Catterall, Wolfram Kaiser and Ulrike Walton-Jordan (eds), *Reforming the Constitution: Debates in Twentieth-Century Britain* (London, 2000), p. 141; Complete Speeches, vol. V, p. 5038.

28. Jennifer Hart, *Proportional Representation: Critics of the British Electoral System 1820–1945* (Oxford, 1992); Vernon Bogdanor, *The People and the Party System* (Cambridge, 1981), pp. 120–1; Churchill to G. Fowlds, 28.12.1906, CHAR 10/18; Complete Speeches, vol. I, p. 538; vol. II, pp. 1249–50.

29. Bogdanor, *The People and the Party System*, pp. 126–135.

30. Complete Speeches, vol. IV, pp. 3385, 3422; *Sunday Chronicle*, 2 March 1924; 'The Three Party Confusion', CHAR 8/200/A/90–96.

31. Complete Speeches, vol. V, pp. 4555, 4732; 'Why We Lost', *John Bull*, 15 June 1929.

32. Complete Speeches, vol. V, pp. 5037–41; 'Election Ahead – and the same old voting system', *Daily Mail*, 29 May 1935.

33. 'How We Can Restore the Lost Glory to Democracy', *Evening Standard*, 24 January 1934; 'Election Ahead – and the same old voting system', *Daily Mail*, 29 May 1935; CHAR 2/594/12 and 22.

34. PRO PREM 4/81/5: Churchill to G. W. Rickards, 11.3.1943; James Stuart to Churchill, 6.10.1942; Cmd 6534 (1944).

35. See in general: CHUR 2/64. Memorandum by S. Pierssene on 'The Liberal Vote', 15.3.1950, CHUR 2/64/196–8; Complete Speeches, vol. VII, p. 7594; vol. VIII, pp. 7958–9.

36. Memo by S. Pierssene on 'Relations with the Liberal Party', 31.7.1950, CHUR 2/64/247; Peter Catterall, 'The British Electoral System 1885–1970, *Historical Research,* vol. 73, no. 181 (June 2000), pp. 171–2; House of Commons debates, 27 July 1954, cols 233–34; Churchill to Violet Bonham-Carter, 2.1.1955, CHUR 6/6B/226.

37. Complete Speeches, vol. II, pp. 1699–70; Joseph Schumpeter, *Capitalism, Socialism and Democracy* (London, 1950).

38. Bogdanor, *The People and the Party System*, pp. 11–33.
39. Complete Speeches, vol. II, pp. 1445, 1698, 1716; CHAR 21/17/66–67.
40. Complete Speeches, vol. II, pp. 1626–7, 1650.
41. Churchill to King George V, 23.2.1911 in Randolph Churchill, *Winston S. Churchill* Companion Volume 2, part 2 (London, 1969), p. 1050; Complete Speeches, vol. II, pp. 1698–99.
42. Complete Speeches, vol. II, pp. 1716, 1795–8.
43. Churchill to Curzon, 7.1.1912, CHAR 13/5/5-6; Curzon to Churchill, 20.1.1912, CHAR 2/56/11; Morley to Churchill, 28.3.1911, CHAR 2/51/75; Churchill to Master of Elibank, 18.12.1911, CHAR 2/53/83; Churchill to Grey 20.12.1911 in Churchill, *Winston S. Churchill* Companion Volume 2, part 3, p. 1474; Churchill to Asquith, 21.12.1911, CHAR 13/5/1–4.
44. Bogdanor, *The People and the Party System*, pp. 33, 35; Gilbert, *Winston S. Churchill* Companion Volume 5, part 1, pp. 559, 579; Addison, *Churchill on the Home Front*, pp. 296–7; Complete Speeches, vol. V, pp. 4728, 4731.

Chapter Five

1. John Ramsden, *Man of the Century: Winston Churchill and his legend since 1945* (London, 2002), p. 82; Woodrow Wyatt, *Distinguished For Talent* (London, 1958), p. 196; Complete Speeches, vol. IV, p. 3890; vol. V, pp. 4986, 4988; vol. VI, p. 6282; 'Parliamentary Government and the Economic Problem', in Winston S. Churchill, *Thoughts and Adventures* (London, 1947; originally published in 1932), p. 173.
2. Complete Speeches, vol. II, p. 1689; vol. III, p. 2548; vol. IV, p. 3968; vol. VII, p. 7222; Paul Addison, 'Destiny, history and providence: the religion of Winston Churchill', in Michael Bentley (ed.), *Public and Private Doctrine: Essays in British History presented to Maurice Cowling* (Cambridge, 1993), p. 245.
3. Winston S. Churchill, *My Early Life* (London, 2002; originally published in 1930), p. 359; House of Commons debates, 26 July 1905, cols 363–6; Complete Speeches, vol. III, p. 2520; 'Is Parliament Played Out', 30 May 1920 (CHAR 8/36/103–4); Evidence taken before the Select Committee on Procedure, HC 161 (1931), qs 1542, 1544, 1547–8.
4. Complete Speeches, vol. IV, pp. 3890–1; Winston S. Churchill, 'Is Parliament Merely a Talking Shop?' *Daily Mail*, 17 April 1935; Select Committee on Procedure (1931), q. 1607.
5. Lord Moran, *Winston Churchill: the struggle for survival 1940–1965* (London, 1966), p. 123; Select Committee on Procedure (1931), q. 1584; Christopher Silvester (ed.), *The Pimlico Companion to Parliament: a literary anthology* (London, 1996), pp. 452, 464–6.
6. House of Commons debates, 28 October 1943, cols 403–4; Complete Speeches, vol. VIII, pp. 8108–9; Martin Gilbert, *Winston S. Churchill*, vol. VIII (London, 1988), p. 564.
7. Ramsden, *Man of the Century*, pp. 85–6; Robert Rhodes James, 'Churchill as Parliamentarian', *Parliamentary Affairs*, vol. 18, 1964–5, p. 150; 'Bevan saw him as poet', *Guardian*, 25 January 1965.
8. Robert Rhodes James, *Churchill: A Study in Failure 1900–1939* (Harmondsworth, 1973), pp. 29–40, 410; David Cannadine, *In Churchill's Shadow: Confronting the Past in Modern Britain* (London, 2002), pp. 85–113; Rhodes James, 'Churchill as Parliamentarian', p. 151; Roy Jenkins, *Churchill* (London, 2001), pp. 145, 682; Wyatt, *Distinguished for Talent*, pp. 196–7, 201.
9. Martin Gilbert, *Winston S. Churchill* vol. IV (London, 1975), p. 900; House of Commons debates, 28 October 1943, col. 408; Winston S. Churchill, 'System that Guarantees "This Freedom"', *News of the World* 18 September 1938; 'Is Parliament Merely a Talking Shop?', *Daily Mail*, 17 April 1935; Complete Speeches, vol. IV, pp. 3968–9; vol. VII, p. 7223.

10. Select Committee on Procedure (1931), qs 1526, 1540, 1565; Randolph Churchill, *Winston S. Churchill* vol. II (London, 1967), pp. 39–41; Randolph Churchill, *Winston S. Churchill, Companion Volume* (London, 1969), vol. II, part 1, pp. 126–134; Complete Speeches, vol. I, pp. 487–8.

11. Select Committee on Procedure (1931), qs 1536–8, 1599, 1617, 1642–9; Complete Speeches, vol. VII, pp. 7223–4. For background see: The Hansard Society, *Parliamentary Reform 1933–1960: a survey of suggested reforms* (London, 1961), pp. 55–61; Basil Chubb, *The Control of Public Expenditure* (Oxford, 1952).

12. Complete Speeches, vol. VI, pp. 6311–12; vol. VII, pp. 7222–4; Select Committee on Procedure (1931), qs 1521, 1526, 1549.

13. Churchill, *My Early Life*, p. 359; Select Committee on Procedure (1931), qs 1527–8, 1566, 1627, 1638; S. A. Walkland (ed.), *The House of Commons in the Twentieth Century* (Oxford, 1979), p. 73.

14. Select Committee on Procedure (1931), qs 1637–8.

15. Select Committee on Procedure (1931), qs 1521, 1523, 1530, 1612–13; Complete Speeches, vol. V, pp. 5427–8; vol. VII, p. 7222.

16. Winston S. Churchill, 'The Socialist Government', 1924, (CHAR 8/200A/102–4); Trevor Smith, *The Politics of the Corporate Economy* (Oxford, 1979), pp. 6–49; Complete Speeches, vol. V, pp. 4727–8.

17. Churchill, *Thoughts and Adventures*, pp. 180–82; Select Committee on Procedure (1931), pp. 351–2.

18. Winston S. Churchill, 'What's Wrong with Parliament', *Answers*, 5 May 1934; Select Committee on Procedure (1931), pp. 352–362; 'Parliament and the Economic Problem', *The Economist*, 21 June 1930, p. 1371; Sir Herbert Samuel, 'Defects and Reforms of Parliament', *The Political Quarterly*, vol. 2 (1931), p. 310; Ronald Butt, *The Power of Parliament* (London, 1967), pp. 126–7; Leo Amery, *Thoughts on the Constitution* (London, 1947), p. 67; Emrys Hughes, *Parliament and Mumbo-Jumbo* (London, 1966), p. 152; Clive Ponting, *Churchill* (London, 1994), pp. 351–2.

19. Tony Paterson, *A Seat For Life* (Dundee, 1980); David A. Thomas, *Churchill: the Member for Woodford* (Ilford, Essex, 1995), pp. 28, 33, 41, 97, 113.

20. Martin Gilbert, *Churchill's Political Philosophy* (Oxford, 1981), pp. 103, 106–7; Thomas, *Churchill: the Member for Woodford*, p. 68; Winston S. Churchill, 'Penny-in-the-slot Politics', *Answers*, 31 March 1934; Winston S. Churchill, *Lord Randolph Churchill* (London, 1906), vol. I, p. 69; Winston S. Churchill, 'The Rt Hon Anthony Eden', *Strand Magazine*, August 1939; Complete Speeches, vol. II, pp. 1437, 1487; vol. V, pp. 5357, 5430; vol. VIII, p. 7958.

21. Complete Speeches, vol. VI, p. 6082.

22. Roy Jenkins, *Churchill* (London, 2001), p. 622; Complete Speeches, vol. III, pp. 2517–18, 2546–9, 2552.

23. Sir John Wheeler-Bennett (ed.), *Action This Day* (London, 1968), pp. 152, 229; Jenkins, *Churchill*, pp. 622, 646; Geoffrey Best, *Churchill: A Study in Greatness* (London, 2001), pp. 184–5; Wyatt, *Distinguished For Talent*, p. 201.

24. 1Ramsden, *Man of the Century*, p. 60; J. M. Lee, *The Churchill Coalition 1940–1945* (London, 1980), pp. 21, 40–41; R. M. Punnett, *Front-Bench Opposition* (London, 1973), pp. 409–11; John Campbell, *Nye Bevan* (London, 1997), pp. 92, 98, 10–5, 116, 142–3.

25. Punnett, *Front-Bench Opposition*, pp. 52, 63, 65, 209–10, 222, 357; John Ramsden, *An Appetite for Power: A History of the Conservative Party Since 1830* (London, 1999), pp. 320, 327–8; Complete Speeches, vol. VIII, p. 8074; Moran, *Winston Churchill: the struggle for survival*, p. 327.

26. House of Commons debates, 6 June 1951, col. 1179; Complete Speeches, vol. V, pp. 4987, 5043; vol. VIII, p. 8109; Churchill, *Thoughts and Adventures*, pp .174–5; Stuart Ball, 'Parliament and Politics in Britain, 1900–1951', *Parliamentary History*, vol. 10, part 2 (1991), pp. 247–8.

27. 'Is Parliament Merely a Talking Shop?', *Daily Mail*, 17 April 1935; H. E. Dale, *The Higher Civil Service of Great Britain* (Oxford, 1941), p. 105.

28. *Guardian*, 25 January 1965; Christian Graf von Krockow, *Churchill: man of the century* (London, 2000), pp. 36–7; Complete Speeches, vol. V, p. 4931.

Chapter Six

1 C. I. Hamilton, 'The Decline of Churchill's "Garden Suburb" and Rise of his Private Office: the Prime Minister's Department 1940–45', *Twentieth Century British History*, vol. 12, 2001, pp. 134, 147; John Colville, *The Fringes of Power: Downing Street Diaries 1939–1955* (London, 1985), p. 126.

2 Winston S. Churchill, *Lord Randolph Churchill* (London, 1906), vol. II, pp. 179–82.

3 Winston S. Churchill, *Thoughts and Adventures* (London, 1947; originally published 1932), pp. 34–5; Paul Addison, *Churchill on the Home Front 1900–1955* (London, 1992) pp. 19–20, 23–4, 36.

4 Roy Jenkins, *The Chancellors* (London 1998), p. 309; Martin Gilbert, *Winston S. Churchill Companion Volume IV*, part 2, (London, 1977), pp. 1359–60; P. J. Grigg, *Prejudice and Judgment* (London, 1948), p. 178; Roy Jenkins, *Churchill* (London, 2001), p. 151; Addison, *Churchill on the Home Front*, pp. 72–3, 128.

5 Addison, *Churchill on the Home Front*, p. 92; Winston S. Churchill, *The People's Rights* (London, 1970; originally published 1909), p. 7.

6 Jose Harris, *William Beveridge* (Oxford, 1977), pp. 140, 146, 157, 166; Addison, *Churchill on the Home Front*, p. 73; Anthony Montague Browne, *Long Sunset: memoirs of Winston Churchill's last private secretary* (London, 1995), pp. 175, 258.

7 G. R. Searle, *The Quest for National Efficiency* (Oxford, 1971), pp. 248–50; Addison, *Churchill on the Home Front*, p. 22; Companion Volume II, part 2, pp. 895–8; Clive Ponting, *Churchill* (London, 1994), pp. 82–3.

8 Martin Gilbert, *Winston S. Churchill, vol. IV, 1916–1922* (London, 1975), pp. 893–4; Winston S. Churchill, *The World Crisis, 1916–1918, Part II* (London, 1927), pp. 298–301; Addison, *Churchill on the Home Front*, p. 186; Jenkins, *Churchill*, pp. 332–3.

9 David Stafford, *Churchill & Secret Service* (London, 2000), p. 26; Peter Clarke, 'Churchill's Economic Ideas 1900–1930', in Robert Blake and William Roger Louis (eds), *Churchill* (Oxford, 1994), pp. 81–2; Winston S. Churchill, *Great Contemporaries* (London, 1949; originally published 1937), p. 229; 'How the Chancellor Does his Job', *Sunday Dispatch*, 28 April 1940.

10 Robert Rhodes James, *Churchill: A Study in Failure* (Harmondsworth, 1973), pp. 206–207; Grigg, *Prejudice and Judgment*, pp. 174, 176, 180–82; Jenkins, *Churchill*, pp. 398–401; Addison, *Churchill on the Home Front*, pp. 254–5; Paul Addison, 'Churchill and Social Reform', in Blake and Louis (eds), *Churchill*, pp. 67–8; Peter Hennessy, *Whitehall* (London, 1989), p. 397; Companion Volume V, part 1, p. 600; Complete Speeches, vol. IV, p. 4381.

11 Companion Volume V, part 1, pp. 689–90; Addison, *Churchill on the Home Front*, p. 255.

12 Complete Speeches, vol. III, p. 3217; vol. IV, p. 4350.

13 Complete Speeches: volume III, p. 3217; volume IV, pp. 3542, 4063–4, 4159–60; Kevin Theakston and Geoffrey Fry, 'The Party and the Civil Service' in Anthony Seldon and Stuart Ball (eds) *Conservative Century* (Oxford, 1994), p. 385; 'Can Labour Govern?', 16.11.1919, CHAR 8/36/37–8.

14   Stafford, *Churchill & Secret Service*, pp. 170–73; Martin Gilbert, *In Search of Churchill* (London 1994), pp. 110–19; R. A. C. Parker, *Churchill and Appeasement* (London, 2000) , p. 133.

15   John Colville, *Footprints in Time* (London, 1976), p. 95; Stafford, *Churchill & Secret Service*, p. 181.

16   Sir John Wheeler-Bennett (ed.), *Action This Day* (London, 1968), pp. 48–50, 195; Colville, *Footprints in Time*, pp. 75–6.

17   Companion Volume V, part 3, pp. 1134–5; Andrew Roberts, *Eminent Churchillians* (London, 1994), p. 150; Geoffrey Fry, 'Three Giants of the Inter-War British Higher Civil Service', in Kevin Theakston (ed.) *Bureaucrats and Leadership* (London, 2000), pp. 52–9; J. M. Lee, *The Churchill Coalition 1940–1945* (London, 1980), pp. 37–8.

18   Colville, *Fringes of Power*, p. 125; Colville, *Footprints in Time*, pp. 90–1; Thomas Wilson, *Churchill and the Prof* (London, 1995), p. vi; Lord Moran, *Winston Churchill: the struggle for survival 1940–1965* (London, 1966), p. 321.

19   Hamilton, 'The Prime Minister's Department 1940–45', pp. 134–45; Wilson, *Churchill and the Prof*; John Colville, *The Churchillians* (London, 1981), chapter 3; Lee, *The Churchill Coalition*, pp. 28, 39; Jenkins, *Churchill*, pp. 478–9.

20   Hamilton, 'The Prime Minister's Office 1940–45', pp. 146–62; Colville, *Footprints in Time*, pp. 75–8; Colville, *The Churchillians*, chapter 4; Sir John Martin, *Downing Street: the War Years* (London, 1991); Michael Jackson, *A Scottish Life: Sir John Martin, Churchill and Empire* (London, 1999), chapter 6.

21   Sir Ronald Wingate, *Lord Ismay* (London, 1970), pp. 42–6, 75–8; Colville, *The Churchillians*, pp. 124–8; Kevin Theakston, *Leadership in Whitehall* (London, 1999), pp. 71–5.

22   Churchill to Bridges, 27.8.1942, 19.10.1942 (PRO PREM 4/63/2); J. M. Lee, *Reviewing the Machinery of Government 1942–1952* (Birkbeck College, London, 1977), pp. 8–17; Keith Middlemas, *Power, Competition and the State vol. 1 Britain In Search of Balance 1940–61* (London, 1986), p. 30; Richard Chapman, *Leadership in the British Civil Service* (London, 1984), pp. 96–7; Kevin Theakston, *The Labour Party and Whitehall* (London, 1992), chapter 3.

23   Colville, *Footprints in Time*, pp. 206–7; Martin Gilbert, *Winston S. Churchill vol. 8 'Never Despair' 1945–1965* (London, 1988), pp. 302–303, 324, 402; Addison, *Churchill on the Home Front*, p. 424; Kevin Theakston, *The Civil Service Since 1945* (Oxford, 1995), pp. 77–80.

24   Anthony Seldon, *Churchill's Indian Summer: The Conservative Government 1951–55* (London, 1981), p. 114; Harold Macmillan, *Tides of Fortune 1945–55* (London, 1969), p. 363; Wheeler-Bennett, *Action This Day*, p. 77; Moran, *Winston Churchill: the struggle for survival*, p. 482; Montague Browne, *Long Sunset*, pp. 132, 199.

25   Seldon, *Churchill's Indian Summer*, pp. 28, 32–3; Macmillan, *Tides of Fortune*, p. 138; Colville, *The Churchillians*, pp. 64, 132–33; Montague-Browne, *Long Sunset*, pp. 107–8; Theakston, *Leadership in Whitehall*, pp. 108–109; Colville, *Fringes of Power*, pp. 668–70.

26   Theakston, *The Civil Service Since 1945*, pp. 73–6; Seldon, *Churchill's Indian Summer*, pp. 109–11; Sir Cuthbert Headlam *et al.*, *Some Proposals for Constitutional Reform* (London, 1946); R. A. Butler, 'Reform of the Civil Service', *Public Administration*, vol. 26 (1948), pp. 169–72.

27   Colville, *The Churchillians*, p. 133; Companion Volume II, part 2, pp. 729–30; Complete Speeches, vol. IV, p. 4350.

Chapter Seven

1.   J. Enoch Powell, 'Churchill From the Dimension of Time', Proceedings of the International Churchill Society, October 1988 (www.winstonchurchill.org).

2.   Churchill to Baruch, 24 October 1934, Martin Gilbert, *Winston S. Churchill* Companion Volume V, part 2 (London, 1981), pp. 886–88; G. H. L. Le May, *The Victorian Constitution* (London, 1979), p. 102.

3.   Complete Speeches, vol. II, p. 1688.

4.   Complete Speeches, vol. IV, p. 3382; Churchill to Clementine Churchill, 2 March 1935, Gilbert, Companion Volume V, part 2, p. 1097; Winston S Churchill, 'Premiers on the Sick List', *Answers*, 4 August 1934.

5.   Winston S Churchill, *Great Contemporaries* (London, 1949; originally published 1937), pp. 103, 107, 188; Lord Moran, *Winston Churchill: the struggle for survival 1940–1965* (London, 1966), pp. 605–606.

6.   Gilbert, Companion Volume V, part 2, p. 1097; John Charmley, *Churchill: The End of Glory* (London, 1993), pp. 200, 215; Moran, *Churchill: the struggle for survival*, pp. 326–7, 368; Churchill, *Great Contemporaries*, p. 9; Winston S. Churchill, *The Second World War vol. 1 The Gathering Storm* (London, 1948), p. 187.

7.   Hans Daalder, *Cabinet Reform in Britain 1914–1963* (London, 1964), p. 262; Churchill, 'Premiers on the Sick List'.

8.   Winston S. Churchill, *The Second World War vol. 2 Their Finest Hour* (London, 1949), p. 15; Lord Riddell, *More Pages from my Diary 1908–1914* (London, 1934), p. 109.

9.   Roy Jenkins, *Churchill* (London, 2001), p. 80; Winston S. Churchill, *A History of the English-Speaking Peoples, vol. IV The Great Democracies* (London, 1958), pp. 45, 48–9, 169, 225, 262–3.

10.   Churchill, *Great Contemporaries*, pp. 108, 114–15, 116.

11.   See: Robert Blake, 'How Churchill Became Prime Minister', in Robert Blake and William Roger Louis (eds), *Churchill* (Oxford, 1993), pp. 257–273; 'The Tories versus Churchill during the "Finest Hour"' in Andrew Roberts, *Eminent Churchillians* (London, 1994), pp. 137–210.

12.   Roberts, *Eminent Churchillians*, pp. 203, 207–9; Paul Addison, *The Road to 1945* (London, 1975), pp. 105–106; G. R. Searle, *Country Before Party* (London, 1995), pp. 202–203.

13.   Lord Beaverbrook, *Men and Power 1917–1918* (London, 1956), p. 126; Churchill, *The Second World War vol. 1 The Gathering Storm*, p. 320; Winston S. Churchill, *Thoughts and Adventures* (London, 1947; originally published 1932), pp. 233–4.

14.   Churchill, *The Second World War vol. 1 The Gathering Storm*, pp. 327–8; Winston S. Churchill, *The Second World War vol. IV The Hinge of Fate* (London, 1951), p. 75.

15.   John Grigg, 'Churchill and Lloyd George', in Blake and Louis (eds), *Churchill*, p. 110; Churchill, *The Second World War vol. 1 The Gathering Storm*, p. 328; House of Commons debates, 22 January 1941, cols 257–9.

16.   House of Commons debates, 22 January 1941, cols 263–4; Churchill, *The Second World War vol. 1 The Gathering Storm*, pp. 355–6, 361; Lord Normanbrook and Lord Bridges in Sir John Wheeler-Bennett (ed.), *Action This Day* (London, 1968), pp. 20, 218.

17.   House of Commons debates, 22 January 1941, col. 261; PRO PREM 4/68/3, Churchill to Bridges, 24 May 1940; PRO CAB 21/1622, WP (G) (41) 34, 'Committees: Note by the Prime Minister', 14 March 1941.

18.   David Dutton, *Neville Chamberlain* (London, 2001), p. 120.

19.   Manfred Weidhorn, *A Harmony of Interests: Explorations in the Mind of Sir Winston Churchill* (London, 1992), p. 65; Jenkins, *Churchill*, pp. 51–2n; John Grigg, *Lloyd George: War Leader 1916–1918* (London, 2002), pp. 480–2; Robert Blake, 'How Churchill Became Prime Minister', in Blake and Louis (eds), *Churchill*, p. 271; Michael Carver, 'Churchill and the Defence Chiefs', in Blake and Louis (eds), *Churchill*, p. 356.

20.   Sir Ian Jacob in Wheeler-Bennett (ed.), *Action This Day*, pp. 192–3; John P. Mackintosh, *The*

British Cabinet, 3rd edn (London, 1977), p. 493; P. J. Grigg, *Prejudice and Judgment* (London, 1948), p. 356; Churchill, *The Second World War vol. IV The Hinge of Fate*, pp. 80, 364–5, 498–9.

21.   Mackintosh, *The British Cabinet*, p. 495; Jacob in Wheeler-Bennett (ed.), *Action This Day*, p. 195; John Grigg, 'Churchill and Lloyd George', in Blake and Louis (eds), *Churchill*, p. 110; Geoffrey Best, *Churchill: A Study in Greatness* (London, 2001), pp. 209–212; Daalder, *Cabinet Reform in Britain*, pp. 176–7.

22.   Winston S. Churchill, *The Second World War vol. V Closing the Ring* (London, 1952), pp. 340–1; Lord Normanbrook in Wheeler-Bennett (ed.), *Action This Day*, p. 28; Dennis Kavanagh, *Crisis, Charisma and British Political Leadership: Winston Churchill as the Outsider* (London, 1974), pp. 14–19; Roy Jenkins, *Gallery of 20th Century Portraits* (London, 1988), p. 234; Moran, *Churchill: the struggle for survival*, p. 180.

23.   Wheeler-Bennett (ed.), *Action This Day*, pp. 20–22, 186–7; C.R. Attlee, *As It Happened* (London, 1954), pp. 162–3.

24.   Churchill, *The Second World War vol. IV The Hinge of Fate*, p. 78; Earl of Avon, *The Eden Memoirs: The Reckoning* (London, 1965), p. 497; Wheeler-Bennett (ed.), *Action This Day*, pp. 28, 185–6.

25.   Sir Ian Jacob in Wheeler-Bennett (ed.), *Action This Day*, pp. 191–2; Earl of Avon, *The Eden Memoirs: The Reckoning*, p. 497; Jenkins, *Churchill*, pp. 774–77; Kenneth Harris, *Attlee* (London, 1982), pp. 241–4.

26.   Winston S. Churchill, 'The Rt Hon Anthony Eden', *Strand Magazine*, August 1939; Peter Hennessy, *The Prime Minister: the office and its holders since 1945* (London, 2000), p. 54; Churchill, *The Second World War vol. 1 The Gathering Storm*, pp. 187–8.

27.   John Colville, *The Churchillians* (London, 1981), pp. 162–3, 177; John Colville, *The Fringes of Power: Downing Street Diaries 1939–1955* (London, 1985), p. 128.

28.   Moran, *Churchill: the struggle for survival*, p. 404; John W. Young, *Winston Churchill's Last Campaign: Britain and the Cold War 1951–5* (Oxford, 1996), pp. 222–3.

29.   Moran, *Churchill: the struggle for survival*, pp. 405, 587, 659; Young, *Winston Churchill's Last Campaign*, pp. 42–6; Colville, *The Churchillians*, p. 133; Anthony Montague Browne, *Long Sunset: memoirs of Winston Churchill's last private secretary* (London, 1996), pp. 132, 133–5, 162; Anthony Seldon, *Churchill's Indian Summer: the Conservative Government 1951–55* (London, 1981), pp. 381, 410–11; *The Economist*, 9 April 1955, p. 100.

30.   Seldon, *Churchill's Indian Summer*, pp. 85, 406–7; Young, *Winston Churchill's Last Campaign*, pp. 45, 159–60, 164, 270–89; Lord Kilmuir (David Maxwell-Fyfe), *Political Adventure* (London, 1964), p. 193; Alistair Horne, *Macmillan 1894–1956* (London, 1988), p. 348.

31.   Churchill to Bridges, 19.10.42, PRO PREM 4/63/2; Daalder, *Cabinet Reform in Britain*, pp. 280–95; PRO PREM 4/6/9, MG (43)2 and MG (45) 5.

32.   See: Daalder, *Cabinet Reform in Britain*, pp. 108–120; Seldon, *Churchill's Indian Summer*, pp. 102–106; Peter Hennessy and David Welsh, 'Lords of all they Surveyed? Churchill's Ministerial "Overlords" 1951–1953', *Parliamentary Affairs*, vol. 51, no. 1, 1998, pp. 62–70.

33.   *The Economist*, 29 November 1952, p. 605; John Colville, *The Fringes of Power: Downing Street Diaries 1939–1955* (London, 1985), p. 633.

34.   House of Commons debates, 3 November 1953, col. 20; Lord Butler, *The Art of the Possible* (London, 1971), p. 160; Moran, *Churchill: the struggle for survival*, p. 517; Peter Hennessy, *Muddling Through: Power, Politics and the Quality of Government in Postwar Britain* (London, 1996), p. 189.

35.   Seldon, *Churchill's Indian Summer*, p. 80; Daalder, *Cabinet Reform in Britain*, pp. 110, 112, 115; House of Commons debates 21 November 1951, col. 432; Complete Speeches, vol. VIII, pp. 8372–3.

36. *The Economist*, 10 May 1952, pp. 353-4.

37. PRO PREM 11/174, Churchill to Brook, 16 November 1951, 23 November 1951; PRO PREM 11/3223, memos to PM, 21 April 1953, 27 January 1954; Hennessy, *The Prime Minister*, pp. 186–8.

38. Hennessy and Welsh, 'Lords of all they Surveyed?', p. 65; House of Commons debates, 3 November 1953, col. 20.

39. *The Economist*, 29 November 1952, p. 605; 12 September 1953, pp. 679–80; Hennessy and Welsh, 'Lords of all they Surveyed?', p. 66; Harold Macmillan, *The Middle Way* (London, 1938), p. 292; PRO PREM 4/6/9, MG (45) 5, p. 2; House of Commons debates, 13 May 1952, cols 1111–12.

40. Montague Browne, *Long Sunset*, p. 162; Moran, *Churchill: the struggle for survival*, p. 527.

41. Moran, *Churchill: the struggle for survival*, p. 354; Lord Woolton, *Memoirs* (London, 1959), p. 377.

42. Horne, *Macmillan 1894–1956*, p. 334; Woolton, *Memoirs*, p. 377; Hennessy, *The Prime Minister*, pp. 196–7.

43. Moran, *Churchill: the struggle for survival*, p. 404; Peter Hennessy, *Cabinet* (Oxford, 1986), pp.134–141; Seldon, *Churchill's Indian Summer*, p. 85.

44. Richard Rose, *The Prime Minister in a Shrinking World* (Cambridge, 2001).

45. Seldon, *Churchill's Indian Summer*, pp. 60–61; Michael Cockerell, *Live From Number 10* (London, 1988), p. 15; Colin Seymour-Ure, 'Prime Minister and the Public: Managing Media Relations', in Donald Shell and Richard Hodder-Williams (eds), *Churchill to Major: the British Prime Ministership since 1945* (London, 1995).

46. See: R. L. Borthwick, 'Prime Minister and Parliament', in Shell and Hodder-Williams (eds), *Churchill to Major*; Patrick Dunleavy and G. W. Jones, 'The Decline of Prime Ministerial Accountability to the House of Commons, 1868–1990', in R. A. W. Rhodes and Patrick Dunleavy (eds), *Prime Minister, Cabinet and Core Executive* (Basingstoke, 1995).

47. Hennessy, *Cabinet*, pp. 100–101.

48. Kavanagh, *Crisis, Charisma and British Political Leadership: Winston Churchill as the Outsider*, pp. 22, 30.

49. Hennessy, *Cabinet*, pp. 49–50; Moran, *Churchill: the struggle for survival*, p .527.

Chapter Eight

1. R. W. Thompson, *Churchill and Morton* (London, 1976), p. 118.

2. Acknowledgement should be made to the two outstanding essays on this subject: Philip Ziegler, 'Churchill and the Monarchy', in Robert Blake and William Roger Louis (eds), *Churchill* (Oxford, 1994); and David Cannadine, 'Thrones: Churchill and Monarchy in Britain and Beyond', in his book *In Churchill's Shadow* (London, 2002). An earlier and shorter version of the Cannadine essay appeared in *Transactions of the Royal Historical Society*, sixth series, vol. 11, 2001, pp. 249–72.

3. Lord Moran, *Winston Churchill: the struggle for survival, 1940–1965* (London, 1966), p. 192; Sir John Wheeler-Bennett (ed.), *Action This Day* (London, 1968), pp. 75–6; John Colville, *The Fringes of Power: Downing Street Diaries 1939–1945* (London, 1985), p. 128; Complete Speeches, vol. VII, p. 7164; vol. VIII, p. 8337; Winston S. Churchill, *Great Contemporaries* (London, 1949; originally published 1937), p. 160; Ben Pimlott, *The Queen: a biography of Elizabeth II* (London, 1997), p. 194.

4. Randolph Churchill, *Winston S. Churchill*, vol. I (London, 1966), p. 336; Martin Gilbert,

Winston S. Churchill, vol. VIII (London, 1988), pp. 367, 570; WSC broadcast on Radio Luxembourg, May 1937, CHAR 9/125/65–9; Complete Speeches, vol. VI, pp. 5847–9.

5. Moran, *Churchill: the struggle for survival*, pp. 374, 402–3; Pimlott, *The Queen*, p. 189; Anthony Montague Brown, *Long Sunset: memoirs of Winston Churchill's last private secretary* (London, 1996), p. 173.

6. Complete Speeches, vol. II, p. 1370; vol. VII, p. 7164; vol. VIII, pp. 8486–7, 8567; Pimlott, *The Queen*, pp. 194–5, 207.

7. Robert Blake, *Disraeli* (London, 1966), pp. 490–1; Pimlott, *The Queen*, pp. 81, 173; Robert Rhodes James, *A Spirit Undaunted: the Political Role of George VI* (London, 1999), pp. 179, 210; Martin Gilbert, *Winston S. Churchill*, vol. VII (London, 1986), p. 251.

8. Philip Ziegler, *King Edward VIII* (London, 1990), p. 244; Winston S. Churchill, 'Cavalcade 1909–1934', *Daily Sketch* 15 March 1934; Moran, *Churchill: the struggle for survival*, p. 399; Cannadine, *In Churchill's Shadow*, p. 48; Winston S. Churchill, 'Will the Kings Come Back?', *Answers*, 19 May 1934; Winston S. Churchill, 'Mr H. G. Wells and the British Empire', November 1927, CHAR 8/215/9.

9. Kenneth Rose, *King George V* (London, 1983), pp. 160–1; Frank Prochaska, *The Republic of Britain* (London, 2000), p. 202; Churchill, 'Will the Kings Come Back?'; WSC broadcast on Radio Luxembourg, May 1937; Gilbert, *Winston S. Churchill*, vol. VIII, p. 367; Winston S. Churchill, 'Monarchy versus Autocracy', 1 February, 1920, CHAR 8/36/80–2.

10. Churchill, 'Will the Kings Come Back?'; Complete Speeches, vol. II, p. 1370 (see also pp. 1421–2); House of Commons Debates, 10 December 1936, col. 2190; Randolph Churchill, *Winston S. Churchill*, vol. II (London, 1967), p. 327; Gilbert, *Winston S. Churchill*, vol. VIII, p. 366.

11. Martin Gilbert, *Winston S. Churchill*, vol. V (London, 1976), p. 1037; Complete Speeches, vol. II, pp. 1421–2; Winston S. Churchill, *A History of the English-Speaking Peoples, vol. IV, The Great Democracies* (London, 1958). pp. 45, 225, 299; Churchill, *Great Contemporaries*, pp. 249–50, 256–7.

12. Complete Speeches, vol. VII, pp. 7164–5; vol. VIII, pp. 8336–7.

13. Churchill, 'Monarchy versus Autocracy'; Churchill, 'Mr H. G. Wells and the British Empire'; WSC broadcast on Radio Luxembourg, May 1937.

14. Cannadine, *In Churchill's Shadow*, pp. 54–8, 60, 82; Ziegler, 'Churchill and the Monarchy', pp. 188–191; note by Robert Rhodes James in Complete Speeches, vol. II, p. 1512; Rhodes James, *A Spirit Undaunted*, p. 200; David Cannadine, *The Pleasures of the Past* (Penguin, Harmondsworth, 1997), pp. 37–8; Rose, *King George V*, pp. 151, 200–1, 260, 337.

15. Churchill, 'Mr H. G. Wells and the British Empire'; Roy Jenkins, *Churchill* (London, 2001), p. 498; Moran, *Churchill: the struggle for survival*, p. 192; Rose, *King George V*, pp. 390–92.

16. Ziegler, 'Churchill and the Monarchy', p. 194; Rhodes James, *A Spirit Undaunted*, p. 219; Ziegler, *King Edward VIII*, pp. 391–2, 421, 425–6, 434–5, 548–51; Jenkins, *Churchill*, p. 504.

17. It is worth noting that in September 1937 (nine months after the abdication), Churchill's book *Great Contemporaries* was published, in which he argued that in the choice of a prime minister the monarch's 'prerogative is absolute'. Discussing the choice by George V of Baldwin over Curzon in 1923, he noted (p. 221) that 'it is not for any Party to offer a Prime Minister to a Sovereign. Once a Minister has the commission to form a Government, he is free to do so if he can. Nevertheless, it is perhaps more in harmony with the spirit of the Constitution that the King should allow the dominant party to choose its own leader, before committing himself to any particular man'. He went on to argue that 'It is inherent in the British political system that the Crown should not be drawn into a potentially controversial decision, except when, owing to a deadlock or an emergency,

there is no escape. A needless shock would be sustained by the Crown if, for instance, the new Prime Minister was not accepted as the leader of the party possessing the majority in the House of Commons'. Was this an indirect admission that Churchill ultimately recognized the dangers of such a (potentially lethal) 'shock' to the position of the Crown in the event of a putative breakaway 'King's Faction' prime minister failing to command majority party support in the Commons? (Later – upholding the sovereign's constitutional right to choose the prime minister – Churchill did not give any formal advice to the Queen about who should be his successor when he retired in 1955, though Eden had been the heir apparent for many years. But in January 1957, on Eden's resignation, he did go to the Palace to recommend the appointment of Macmillan.)

18. Jenkins, *Churchill*, p. 500; Ziegler, 'Churchill and the Monarchy', p. 192; Robert Rhodes James, *Churchill: A Study in Failure 1900–1939* (Penguin, London, 1981), pp. 349–51; Graham Stewart, *Burying Caesar: Churchill, Chamberlain and the Battle for the Tory Party* (paperback edn, London, 2000), pp. 266–7, 492–3 fn. 108.

19. Rhodes James, *A Spirit Undaunted, passim*; Sarah Bradford, *King George VI* (London, 1989), pp. 312–14, 339–40, 358–60; Peter Hennessy, *Never Again: Britain 1945–1951* (London, 1992), p. 23; Cannadine, *In Churchill's Shadow*, p. 69.

20. Rhodes James, *A Spirit Undaunted*, pp. 271–4.

21. Pimlott, *The Queen*, pp. 181, 183–6, 193–4, 218; Ziegler, 'Churchill and the Monarchy', pp. 197–8; Moran, *Churchill: the struggle for survival*, p. 403 (see also pp. 399–400, 607).

22. Moran, *Churchill: the struggle for survival*, p. 372; Churchill, 'Mr H. G. Wells and the British Empire'; Complete Speeches, vol. VI, p. 5849; vol. VII, pp. 7165, 7743.

23. Ziegler, 'Churchill and the Constitution', p. 198; Churchill, 'Mr H. G. Wells and the British Empire'; Vernon Bogdanor, *The Monarchy and the Constitution* (Oxford, 1995), p. 305; Pimlott, *The Queen*, p. 195.

Chapter Nine

1. G. H. L. Le May, *The Victorian Constitution* (London, 1979), p. 2; Richard Rose quoted in Philip Norton, *The Constitution in Flux* (Oxford, 1982), pp. 22–3; Kirk Emmert, *Winston S. Churchill on Empire* (Durham, North Carolina, 1989), p. xvi.

2. James W. Muller, '"A kind of dignity and even nobility": Winston Churchill's *Thoughts and Adventures*', *Political Science Reviewer*, vol. 16 (1986), pp. 282–3; Patrick C. Powers, 'Churchill, Democratic Statesmanship and *Great Contemporaries*', Proceedings of the International Churchill Societies, 1992–3 (www.winstonchurchill.org/p92powers.htm). Martin Gilbert agrees that the basis of Churchill's political philosophy was not theoretical. (Martin Gilbert, *Churchill's Political Philosophy* [Oxford, 1981], p. 2.)

3. Robert Rhodes James, *Churchill: A Study in Failure 1900–1939* (Harmondsworth, 1973), pp. 33–34; Lucy Masterman, *C. F. G. Masterman: A Biography* (London, 1939), p. 128.

4. P. J. Grigg, *Prejudice and Judgment* (London, 1948), p. 175.

5. Grigg, *Prejudice and Judgment*, pp. 175–6; John Colville, *The Fringes of Power: Downing Street Diaries 1939–1955* (London, 1985), p. 125; Masterman, *C . F. G. Masterman*, pp. 166, 177.

6. Masterman, *C. F. G. Masterman*, pp. 159, 173; Ian Chambers, 'Winston Churchill and Irish Home Rule 1899–1914', *Parliamentary History*, vol. 19, part. 3 (2000), p. 413.

7. Piers Brendon, *Winston Churchill: A Brief Life* (London, 1984), p. 51; Chambers, 'Winston Churchill and Irish Home Rule', p. 407.

8. Winston S. Churchill, *Thoughts and Adventures* (London, 1947; originally published 1932), p. 22.

9. Anthony Montague Browne, *Long Sunset: Memoirs of Winston Churchill's last private secretary* (London, 1995), p. 180.

10. Colville, *Fringes of Power*, p. 128; Paul Addison, *Churchill on the Home Front 1900–1955* (London, 1993), pp. 438–9; Martin Gilbert, 'In Search of Churchill's Character', in Harry V. Jaffa (ed.), *Statesmanship: Essays in Honor of Sir Winston Spencer Churchill* (Durham, North Carolina, 1981), pp. 13–14; Paul Addison, 'The Political Beliefs of Winston Churchill', *Transactions of the Royal Historical Society*, 5th series, vol. 30 (1980), p. 35; Peter Hennessy, *The Hidden Wiring: Unearthing the British Constitution* (London, 1995), pp. 142, 205; Ferdinand Mount, *The British Constitution Now* (London, 1993), pp. 15–17.

11. Martin Gilbert, *Winston S. Churchill* Companion Volume 5, part 1 (London, 1979), p. 587; Complete Speeches, vol. V, pp. 4989–90; 'How Can We Restore the Lost Glory to Democracy?', *Evening Standard*, 24 January 1934.

12. John Grigg, 'Churchill and Lloyd George', in Robert Blake and William Roger Louis (eds), *Churchill* (Oxford, 1993), p. 111; Dennis Kavanagh, *Crisis, Charisma and British Political Leadership: Winston Churchill as the Outsider*, Sage Professional Paper in Political Sociology (London, 1974), p. 22.

13. Gilbert, *Churchill's Political Philosophy*, p. 104; Robert Rhodes James, 'The enigma', in James W. Muller (ed.), *Churchill as Peacemaker* (Cambridge, 1997), p. 16; Tony Paterson, *A Seat for Life* (Dundee, 1980), p. 283.

14. A. H. Birch, *Representative and Responsible Government* (London, 1977), pp. 65–66, 79; House of Commons debates, 26 July 1905, cols 363–4; Complete Speeches, vol. VII, p. 7565; David Cannadine, *Aspects of Aristocracy* (London, 1995), p. 158; Gilbert, *Churchill's Political Philosophy*, p. 68.

15. John Ramsden, *Man of the Century: Winston Churchill and his legend since 1945* (London, 2002), p. 86.

INDEX